Minstrel of the Appalachians

*M*instrel of the *A*ppalachians

The Story of Bascom Lamar Lunsford

Loyal Jones

Music transcribed by
John M. Forbes

THE UNIVERSITY PRESS OF KENTUCKY

Publication of this volume was made possible in part by a grant from the National Endowment for the Humanities.

Reprinted 2002 by The University Press of Kentucky
Scholarly publisher for the Commonwealth,
serving Bellarmine University, Berea College, Centre
College of Kentucky, Eastern Kentucky University,
The Filson Historical Society, Georgetown College,
Kentucky Historical Society, Kentucky State University,
Morehead State University, Murray State University,
Northern Kentucky University, Transylvania University,
University of Kentucky, University of Louisville,
and Western Kentucky University.

Editorial and Sales Offices: The University Press of Kentucky
663 South Limestone Street, Lexington, Kentucky 40508-4008
www.kentuckypress.com

Frontispiece: Bascom Lamar Lunsford in his sixties.
Courtesy of Jo Lunsford Herron

Cataloging-in-Publication Data available
from the Library of Congress

ISBN 978-0-8131-9027-3 (pbk: acid-free paper)

This book is printed on acid-free recycled paper meeting
the requirements of the American National Standard
for Permanence in Paper for Printed Library Materials.

Manufactured in the United States of America.

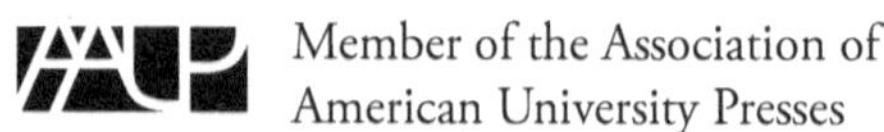

Member of the Association of
American University Presses

For the young Appalachians
Who have never known a minstrel
And who look beyond their mountains
For story and song.

May they come to know
That their kin
Hold enough magic
To charm a jaded world.

Contents

Foreword ix

Introduction xiii

1. Mountain Bred 1

2. Personal and Vocational Ventures 11

3. The Real Calling 27

4. Fulfillment 51

5. Mostly Personal 89

6. Bouquets and Arrows 117

Bibliography 145

Appendices 149

A Lunsford Sampler 191

Foreword

From about 1880, articles, books, short stories, and novels have been written about Appalachia by journalists, local color writers, and missionaries from the outside. These papers have been too general, or too colored, or too specialized to reveal the delicate, complex folkways and lifestyles of the "natives." At worst they have established no more about the mountain people than cliches, stereotypes, and surface observations. By the 1920s some rather acceptable but sweeping studies had come forward, but, in the main, cliches were burned in to the bone. So late as the 1970s I read in *The New York Times* a review of an Appalachian book by a well-known critic, who, though he had chosen the volume to review for his paper, couldn't bear to end the evaluation without adding, ". . . Civilization went round the Appalachian barrier and its miserable people." With myriads of such remarks so often repeated it would seem that the sturdy people of the Southern Highlands have been rubberstamped to death.

Can the wrongs be righted? Can the bell be untolled? Will the ages mellow and color the scene? No. Only when the people take the offensive and write of themselves. Now is the time for a good new beginning. The Mountains have been discovered again. This time however there is a difference. Natives of the region have been going everywhere to earn degrees in education and in the professions for many decades, seeing their hills from afar and coming to know themselves, knowing their own identity. Upon returning they are at ease with their nurture and culture. Their spirited writings in the forms of articles, stories, studies are beginning to cast a true light on life in the hills. To them Appalachia is the best place in the world to be from—and to come back to.

The present book is a good example of the new approach to life in the mountains. It is written by a native of the area where the subject of the book, Bascom Lamar Lunsford, grew up and flourished for 91 years. Although the author, Loyal Jones, covers a good scope of time and space, he is not a generalizer. He focuses on Western Carolina from before the Civil War to the present. Bascom's father, a teacher at Mars Hill, provides Bascom and the other family members with a good basic education. Not satisfied with the baccalaureate and a teaching career, Bascom goes on to graduate studies in law, and finally is admitted to the bar of his state. Bascom marries a girl from nearby South Turkey Creek, and when a portion of property comes to her, they move to the country. Their six children grow up and go off to schools and colleges. Their country place becomes a center for music groups, dance parties, and later it is sought out by traveling troubadours and folk dance leaders.

Early in his life Bascom was given a fiddle by his father. Even earlier, he and his brother had contrived a cigar-box variety of the rowdy American instrument, the banjo; and they played together for fun and later for dances and parties. The banjo became Bascom's favorite for singing, recording, and continual public appearances. This kind of story of self-sufficiency has often been told in the hills. In this instance it is a beautiful if sacrificial one. Bascom was torn between his two passions—and livelihoods—law and music. As he became the "Squire of South Turkey Creek," his law practice suffered. Especially after a newsbee buzzed in his ear. (He thought of a regional festival.) He had generated enough interest about Buncombe County to make something greater of his leadership and talents. But a large regional get-together had not often been staged in America, or kept going if one had been. With the Asheville Chamber of Commerce as sponsor, he was persuaded.

The memorable event came on the scene then, casually, in the summer of 1928, "about sundown" on Pack Square. It was crowded with Bascom's musical friends, neighbors, groups of dancers from neighboring counties and beyond. The area was rich in folklore, old-time customs, arts and crafts. They had a marvelous time. The tone of all such festivals thereafter was set by a friendly and casual atmosphere of fun and entertainment. Invited performers had a place and a time to shine on the platform, Bascom varying the procession to the stage from lively dance groups, individual singers, tale-tellers, spiritual and religious groups to buck and clog dance specialties.

Let us keep in mind and reflect on the deep and long background that had made this festival a natural and spontaneous development. It had evolved out of and was supported and fed by the local village and rural community social gatherings that had performed their traditions and oral literature in America for 200 years, and in the Old World for 2,000 years and had been changed and adapted by the mind and imagination to suit the changes of time and place. Bascom, a natural and symbolic leader, felt the moment and called individuals and small groups out in celebration and made folklore public and spectacular. One of his words of wisdom was that he wanted to keep folklore performance "respectable."

With his attitude and charm and humor, Bascom had little opposition. Northern Calvinism had softened by the 20th century, and the more graceful way of life of the Southern states had mellowed mountain austerity. Bascom's Mountain Dance and Folk Festival was held year after year and is still flourishing. People came from afar to perform and to observe. The importance of this mountain phenomenon—and the beauty of it—now becomes evident. Leaders in school, college, church, recreation and drama came from the crossroads and the largest cities to Asheville to learn from Lunsford. An example among many in the text may be mentioned. Sarah Gertrude Knott, a drama teacher who had been with Dr. Frederick Koch in his folk theater of the University of North Carolina, was directing a drama program in St. Louis in 1933. She was unable to make the journey to the sixth festival in Asheville. Observing the affable master of the fiddle and banjo with his sure touch in handling some of the finest folk performers ever assembled, she returned to St. Louis with a vision. In the very next year (1934) she founded the National Folk Festival Association. It is still going as the National Council for the Traditional Arts.

Bascom's rich and varied career is detailed in the text and the reader will want to follow it to the end. How he continued his vocation as an attorney but had to relinquish it as his music avocation grew more demanding and absorbing of his time and spirit. How his children grew up and helped to entertain at home and to tour the region with their father. Bascom was called upon from other regions to come and "open" festivals. He founded several in his home state and others over the nation. Once he was invited to the White House to perform for the visiting king and queen of England. He went abroad to Venice, Italy, and to England to perform before international audiences.

Loyal Jones saw this festival movement rise in his home region, was taken by it, became part of it. After receiving his degree at Berea College he went to the University of North Carolina for a master's degree. Working for the Council of the Southern Mountains in private and governmental programs, he succeeded Perley Ayer as executive director of the Council. Now he is director of the Berea College Appalachian Center where, among other programs, he runs an annual folk festival. Always interested in the folk arts he became knowledgeable of Bascom's festival and its inner spirit—including problems and conflicts. In the text he sets forth these recurring difficulties. There was the old debate about the traditional versus the new and the innovative. Since Bascom had composed several songs and had performed them for years, some by constant request, such as his world famous "Old Mountain Dew," he was tolerant toward adapted folk materials, though he sometimes turned from the stage those who wanted to sing their own songs. There were quibbles about the Devil's instrument, the fiddle, and the snappy plucking of the banjo. The clog step in square dancing had evolved in the region but was almost unknown elsewhere. Bascom let it evolve, but it too got some discussion because dancing became a contest—with prizes. The people had their way here. It stirred the blood of the audience and they cheered it on. These and many more aspects of the festival and its "star" performers are presented with relish and humor in the book.

This is a well-researched and presented study of one remarkable person but also of mountain people in general. It is told by a sympathetic writer, who depicts a way of life as it was—and is. No cliches of the hillfolk, no apologies for their frisking and frolicking, buck-winging and clogging on the platform. No excuses for their sad songs of love and death in the hills. This book is about a man, a people and a movement. It portrays vividly the vitality of our traditional literature and culture. We hope Loyal Jones and others will continue in-depth studies of life in our southern mountains.

Leonard Roberts, Director
Appalachian Studies Center
Pikeville College
Pikeville, Kentucky
1982

Introduction

I first met Bascom Lunsford in 1956 at the North Carolina State Fair in Raleigh, but I did not have a reason to communicate with him again until I became director of the Berea College Appalachian Center in 1970. Then I wrote to invite Mr. Lunsford to come and perform a concert at the college. Within days I received a telephone call: "This is Bascom Lamar Lunsford. Why, I can't come up there. I'm eighty-nine years old. You come to see me." And so I did. In his apartment in West Asheville I spent an afternoon interviewing and visiting with him and his second wife, Freda.

That visit had a profound effect on me. Lunsford had not forgotten much that was important to him, and his life unfolded in almost nonstop talk for four hours. I recorded it, and it was a marvelous story. My intention was to gather material for the Mountain Collection at Berea College and to write an article, which I did (*JEMF Quarterly*, spring, 1973), and then move on to something else. But Bascom would not let go of me, even though he died in September of 1973.

After seeing my article, Bascom's daughters Kern and Jo called to ask if I would write a biography of their father. I told them that I just didn't have the time. At a meeting of the Appalachian Consortium Press at Mars Hill College soon thereafter, the director asked me to look at a small manuscript on Lunsford written by Dr. Angus McLeod, retired English professor at Mars Hill College, and to see if I might work with Dr. McLeod in expanding the manuscript into a suitable account of Lunsford's life and work. I reluctantly agreed, and although this collaboration never came about, I made good use of McLeod's forty-some page manuscript. My book, slowed by my full-time job, evolved over about twelve years, changing as I gathered materials, conducted interviews, and gained insight into Lunsford's unusual career and the implications of his contributions. The book was first published by the Appalachian Consortium Press in 1984.

Archie Green, my favorite folklorist, read early versions and gave advice, suggesting that I make clear my politics of culture. This brought me up short. The politics of culture was a vague concept to me. However, Archie got me to thinking in a new way about Bascom's work and about Appalachian traditional lore—and Appalachians themselves—in relation to mainstream culture. Archie thought my cultural politics ought to be clear throughout the book, but I had trouble because I saw it as Bascom's book, and whenever I intruded with my opinions, I didn't feel right. So, my politics of culture are here in this introduction.

I see all life as being a tension between the old and the new, between traditional and progressive ways. My mother, contemplating religion and values, would have said "Old ways are best," but she readily changed from canning to freezing foods when she was able to get a freezer. We are all pulled by the past and the promise of the future, some more one way than the other. The liberal/conservative schism in this country is a problem for many of us. Some liberals are hellbent on changing everything, and some conservatives are just as determined on keeping things as they are (as if they could). On the extreme ends of the political continuum are those we generally call radicals or reactionaries. Some of the latter want to preserve a past that never was, and some of the former want to destroy traditions of the past in order to build a more just society. This battle challenges those of us who want to preserve and extend the enriching and strengthening traditions and values of the past while wiping out harmful prejudices, stereotypes, and exploitive practices. I want both to preserve and change elements of our culture.

I believe that cultural tradition—the religion, values, and folkways handed down from the generations before us—is vital to who we are. In a sense, culture is just as real to us as the physical world in which we exist. Robert Penn Warren put it this way when asked about his childhood culture, "It is the capital we draw off of all of our lives." We draw from it, but we do not all live in the same culture we lived in as children; therefore, if we are to benefit from our traditional culture, we must carry it into new times and places, in the sense that the great preacher Howard Thurmond commented, "You can't be at home everywhere until you are at home somewhere." I believe we are secure and have integrity (have our elements integrated) only if we are able to maintain this sense of identity. As Appalachian people we do not become strong by throwing off our culture and assuming a new identity but by knowing who we are and going on from there. And, of course, we can go where anyone else has gone.

Appalachia has been presented as a place of poverty, ignorance, and superstition by scholars, novelists, journalists, and screenwriters. Generations of Appalachians have grown up feeling a sense of shame because of the prevailing stereotypes about the region. Some have lived uneasy lives, and some have fled and denigrated their place of birth. Others, thanks to the work of Bascom Lunsford and numerous scholars and writers in recent years, have helped us to gain a sense of identity and pride that is a source of strength. Not much is more important personally than knowing who we are and being at ease with that knowledge.

Bascom Lunsford found a way to strengthen the old folk traditions and use them to instill regional pride in mountain culture at a time when most messages people got about Appalachia were negative. I believe that Bascom's work was of profound importance. He helped to create a climate in which folk traditions and mountain people, regaining a sense of pride and worth, could flourish. There is still a need for this work in a new time, because the old stereotypes about Appalachia, often easier to deal with than meticulous research, never really die.

I do not believe that we can "preserve" folklore by just collecting it for an archive or sponsoring a festival, but I do believe that those of us who have access to grants, media, and people and institutions of influence, can, like Bascom, create an atmosphere in which practitioners will feel good about performing their traditions. Thus we extend the notion that it is all right for regional people to participate openly in their own culture. The National Endowments for the Arts and Humanities have done much to encourage this kind of work. Traditions persevere when persons of influence practice them and indicate that they are important and worth preserving. We who respect the integrity of group traditions must resist local, regional, or national movements that denigrate or deny regional and ethnic differences, and we must resist any movement that implies that any one group is of greater or lesser intrinsic worth than another. Appalachian people have unique qualities, and in recognizing and applauding them, we must respect and applaud the unique qualities of other groups.

That is my politics of culture, much of it learned from the subject of this book.

Those looking for more information on the politics of culture as related to Appalachia can consult the following books: Joe Wilson and Lee Udall, *Folk Festivals: A Handbook for Organization and Management* (1982); David Whisnant, *All That Is Native and Fine: The Politics of Culture in an American Region* (1983); Henry Shapiro, *Appalachia on Our Minds: The Southern Mountains and Mountaineers in the America Consciousness, 1870–1920* (1978); W.K. McNeil, *Appalachian Images in Folk and Popular Culture* (1989); Daniel Patterson, *Sounds of the South: A Report and Selected Papers . . .* (1991); Jane S. Becker, *Selling Tradition: Appalachia and the Construction of an American Folk, 1930–1940* (1998); Rodger Cunningham, *Apples on the Flood: The Southern Mountain Experience* (1987); Charles Joyner, *Shared Traditions: Southern History and Folk Culture* (1999); Neil Rosenberg, *Transforming Tradition: Folk Music Revivals Examined (1993)*; and Benjamin Filene, *Romancing the Folk: Public Memory and American Roots Music* (2000).

Many people contributed to this book. Bascom's children, Kern, Lamar, Jo, Nelle, Merton, and Lynn submitted to interviews, wrote letters, telephoned, copied materials, loaned precious papers and photographs, and invited me into the Lunsford family. Lamar and Kern are gone now, but most of the others have kept in touch. They appreciate their father's contributions and are more interested in scholarship than in keeping family secrets.

Others providing invaluable help were the late George Stephens, a longtime friend of Mr. Lunsford's; the late scholar and poet Jim Wayne Miller, a native of North Turkey Creek, who shared reminiscences and interviewed family and former neighbors for me; Archie Green; the late Cratis Williams, scholar and ballad singer; David Whisnant and Deborah Kodish, who studied Lunsford before me; Joe Hickerson, of the Archive of American Folk Culture; Marilyn Graff, of the Indiana University Archives of Traditional Music; the late Artus and Mabel Moser, and their daughter, Joan Moser, who shared their perspectives, recordings and notated tunes; and Norm Cohen, then editor of the *JEMF Quarterly*, who prepared the Lunsford commercial discography included in this work.

I am grateful to Bob Lindsey, of the Asheville Chamber of Commerce, for his fine photographs of the Mountain Dance and Folk Festival. I am indebted to the staff at Mars Hill College Library—William Tydeman, Mildred Thomas, Polly Cheek, George White, and Richard Dillingham—for making the Lunsford Collection available to me and arranging copies of materials and photographs. I'm especially grateful to Richard Dillingham and Sterling Lawrence for providing such good copies of original photographs for this new edition, and to Harry Rice at the Berea College Southern Appalachian Archives for photographs there, since the plates to the original edition had been lost.

Leonard Roberts, author of many books related to folklore, was an old and valued friend, who agree to write the foreword to this book. As it happened, this was one of the last pieces he wrote, for he was tragically killed in a highway accident in 1983. I am proud to have this foreword written by one of the pioneer scholars of Appalachian folklore, and I dedicate the book to his memory.

I owe a special thanks to John Forbes, a colleague at Berea College, now at Baker University, who provided the musical notations for the songs and tunes included in this book.

I also thank Genevieve Reynolds for finding all the stuff I lost, bringing order out of bedlam, and typing the original manuscript. She was indispensable.

Finally, thanks to my wife Nancy, who went with me on trips to South Turkey Creek, to Mars Hill, and thereabouts and who in may ways supported this work.

I had a grand time with Bascom Lunsford, his family, and the many people who knew him. I hope much of this experience comes alive for the reader.

Berea, Kentucky
2002

CHAPTER 1

Mountain Bred

To use a mountain saying, Bascom Lamar Lunsford would cross hell on a rotten rail to get a folk song. But folk songs were only a part of his calling and of the magic that he sought and used for a larger purpose. Across that precarious rail, Lunsford viewed Appalachian culture and identity that were being uprooted by the irrevocable push of progress.

The people of the Southern Appalachian Mountains are among the most old-fashioned and thus traditional in the country. The great treasure of ballads, songs and tales that the settlers brought from the British Isles and the continent of Europe was kept alive by their offspring to a degree not found elsewhere in the country. By the time Lunsford reached adulthood, however, this devotion to traditional ways had begun to weaken, especially among the progressive folk who were intrigued by new ways, and Lunsford made it his job to rekindle new interest and respect for the old traditions. Long before this mission was revealed to him, though, he had been determined to learn all he could about the folk arts and ways of his people. Thus Lunsford became a walking library of Appalachian arts. As a performer, he reflected the breadth of Appalachian folk traditions.

He was a remarkable performer, recording more than 300 songs, tunes and tales from memory for posterity. But more importantly to him, he sought to present what he considered to be the best of mountain performers to a public that was growing away from the old folk traditions. The vehicle he chose was the song and dance festival, the first of which he began in 1928 and out of which other festivals grew. His Mountain Dance and Folk Festival, still going strong in Asheville, North Carolina, is perhaps his greatest monument.

He was an engaging and energetic man, and he achieved most of what he wanted to in his busy 91 years. And in doing so, he became a legend.

Lunsford was born in the heart of his beloved mountains, at Mars Hill, Madison County, North Carolina, on March 21, 1882. He was later to call Madison County "the last stand of the natural people." It was, and remains, a rural county with numerous interrelated families who sang the old ballads, told folk tales, played the fiddle and banjo, danced and held on to other traditional ways of working, worshipping and coping with the problems of living. But just south of Madison, in Buncombe County, was Asheville, which had already developed as a shipping and trade center,whose civic leaders hawked the virtues of its healthy climate. The first railroad was completed to Asheville the year before Bascom was born. Asheville had real streets and brick buildings, several hotels, a public library and was in the process of laying water and sewer lines.[1] As people came out of the solitude of the rural counties surrounding Asheville to trade, they came into contact with different kinds of people from the Lowland South or the North who spoke optimistically of the future and invested accordingly, and who described progress almost in religious tones and dreamed of wealth as a sure reward for the faith they held in the future. Eventually many country people moved to Asheville, like the Joyners in Thomas Wolfe's fiction,[2] to get ahead in the world. Others, like the homebound Joyners, stayed in Madison County or Yancey County, troubled and offended by the changes they observed in their former kin and neighbors.

Bascom later was to set down an anecdote that richly illustrated the differences between the Asheville folk and the country folk:

> One night I visited Mike Teague, and he said he had some people visit him from Asheville. They liked this good country-fried chicken. They never could get any just like that in Asheville. And this wonderful milk and butter we have, they said that was fine. They said, "We'll never forget the good times and the good food we've had while we were here. When you come to Asheville this fall to sell your tobacco, you just come and make our house your home for what time you are there. We want you to do that." Well, he said, when fall came he got his tobacco all handed out and nicely graded and put down in hogsheads, hitched up his mules, rolled the hogsheads onto the wagon, got his better clothes on, so he could feel like he's somebody, after he got his work done. So he went over to the old Banner Warehouse and got his tobacco on the floor, and put his mules in the livery stable, and went up to the corner of what was then North Main and South Main, now Biltmore Avenue and Broadway. He looked around, and after a while he saw his friend. He walked by him and spoke to him, and he went on in a hurry. "Well," he said, "I guess he's thinking about something else. I'll wait until he comes back." After a while he saw him come along. He said "Say, I came over here and got my tobacco in the warehouse. Now I'm kind of looking for a place to stay." His friend said, "Well, right over here at the Old Buck Hotel is about as good a place as you can get. If I were you, I'd stay right over there." So that was Mike Teague's story of how he got along in making return visits in Asheville.[3]

Rapid change is not a phenomenon of just the 20th century. The history of people is a story of conflict, disruption, migration and resulting change. One needs only to read the Old Testament for evidence of this. Yet, in every age, people are apprehensive of change, and leaders arise to deal with the problem of continuity of meaning, values and integrity amidst change. The boy born in Madison County that March day in 1882 was to become such a person.

Lunsford's mother and father were descendants of pioneer settlers. His mother, Louarta Leah Buckner, was the granddaughter of Thomas Shepherd Deaver, born in 1803 in the upper Pigeon River Valley in Haywood County. Deaver came to what is now Madison County and settled near the Forks of Ivy, where he became known as Squire Deaver because of his extensive holdings. One of the founders of Mars Hill College in 1856, he was named in the original charter and was a member of the Board of Trustees from 1859 to 1891. This is of interest because Bascom's father, James Bassett Lunsford, was teaching at

Mars Hill College when Bascom was born. The new child was named for Bascombe Carter, the son of Edward Carter who gave land for Mars Hill College, and Lucius Quintas Cinncinnatus Lamar, a southerner who became a U.S. congressman and senator, Secretary of the Interior and Associate Justice of the U.S. Supreme Court.

Bascom's paternal grandfather was Alan Lunsford who married Mary Bassett, daughter of an artist and Revolutionary War veteran. They came from Virginia to Burke County, North Carolina, and thence to East Tennessee.[4]

Bascom's father, James Bassett Lunsford, was born in East Tennessee in 1840. When he was 12, his family moved to North Carolina for two years and then migrated to Texas. At the beginning of the Civil War, he went to Dallas and enlisted in J.P. Douglas' battery of artillery which was attached to the 4th Texas Brigade. According to the book, *Texans Who Wore the Gray*,[5] "In the capacity of a private soldier, he served the Confederacy every day of the war, participating in every battle and skirmish in which his company was engaged, with the exception of the engagement across Duck River, on Nov. 9, 1864. Indeed, the battery was in some of the bloodiest battles of the war, including Chickgamauga, Missionary Ridge and the Battle for Atlanta, as well as numerous small battles and skirmishes. Lunsford was slightly wounded at Elkhorn and had a horse shot from under him in the battle of Richmond, Kentucky."[6] In the citation on Lunsford in *Texans Who Wore the Gray*, the writer described him this way:

> Mr. Lunsford spent his youth on the farm in daily toil and had only meagre school privileges, his last attendance being at the school at Bunker Hill, near the present site of Overton, during the session of 1858-59....While Mr. Lunsford's educational advantages were limited, he had what has been called the "divine hunger for knowledge," and all through his strenuous military service he kept some text books with him and was everlasting 'pegging away' at them during his intervals of leisure.[7]

It was J.B. Lunsford who wrote the history of Douglas' Battery for *Texans Who Wore the Gray*.

After the war, when James Bassett Lunsford's brothers asked him if he would return to Western North Carolina to care for their mother and sisters, he did return to Madison County. Soon he became interested in Louarta Buckner, the granddaughter of Thomas Shepherd Deaver, the staunchest of the Unionists in that county. Deaver liked to tell how wartime Governor of North Carolina, Zebulon B. Vance, before he changed his allegiance to the side of the Confederacy, had sent a message which read, "Squire, stand by the Union." Since Louarta's father, Hiram Buckner, had died during the war, she was under the protection of the Deavers. When the Confederate veteran announced his intention of marrying Louarta, it no doubt caused some consternation in the Deaver set.

Madison County had been badly split during the Civil War, with battles raging throughout the county and several atrocities being recorded. Deep feelings smoldered on after the war. In fact, the war went on in the county for several years after Appomattox in clashes between the Ku Klux Klan and the Union League. Someone with Klan sympathies wrote a song, "Ain't no Ku Klux out Tonight," which derided Squire Deaver and his son Reuben Manning. It was a song that Bascom Lunsford was to sing occasionally.

NO KU KLUX OUT TONIGHT

2. He run so fast, he run so free,
   He run Old Baldy against a tree.

   (Chorus)

3. Old Rube Manning jumped in a tub.
   Said, "Yonder comes the Ku Klux Club."

   (Chorus)

4. Old Rube Manning, you may come out.
   There ain't no Ku Klux here about.

   (Chorus)

5. Yes, Old Rube Manning, he got mighty bold.
   He run Line Massey in a groundhog hole.

   (Chorus)

6. There was Miles and he swore with a flirt,
He'd get Merlan a flashy shirt.

(Chorus)

7. There was Wes and he swore by all
He'd get old Cindy a coal black shawl.

(Chorus)

8. Old Rube Manning he got drunk.
He fell in the fire and kicked out a chunk.

(Chorus)

9. Old Rube Manning heard the rebel yell.
He turned around and run like hell.

(Chorus)

As Manly Wade Wellman has stated in *The Kingdom of Madison*,[8] this last verse is a malicious libel: the Deavers never ran away from anything. But Squire Deaver's mill was burned out in the conflict, and the Unionists at Mars Hill were apparently outnumbered. Later the president of Mars Hill College,an outspoken Unionist, had to resign because most of the trustees had Southern sympathies.[9]

Such a background indicates the conditions that James Bassett Lunsford found when he came to be a member of the Deaver Family. However, he gained consent to marry Louarta Buckner and made the concession of becoming a Baptist (he was a Methodist), if not a Republican. Later he became a staunch supporter of Baptist causes and a writer of local Baptist history.

Lunsford first established a subscription school at the Forks of Ivy. He taught at Mars Hill College during the school year of 1871-72, then moved to the Leicester community in Buncombe County where he purchased a farm on the Rabbitham side of Hanlon Mountain. However, he was teaching again at Mars Hill in 1882 when Bascom was born.

James Bassett Lunsford, although mostly self-educated, was an erudite man with meticulous grammar, as evident in his letters and his contribution to *Texans Who Wore the Gray* and his *History of the New Found Baptist Association*.[10] Perhaps because he had worked so hard for it, he prized education. He was a devoted teacher, and both he and his wife were determined that their children would have educational opportunities. The citation in *Texans Who Wore the Gray* stated, "Instead of making the accumulation of property their ideal of life, this devoted couple gave themselves up to the moral and educational culture of their children."

The Lunsfords encouraged their children to memorize poetry and other materials, and they made a time for recitation in the home. Bascom remembered that the house would be called to order, "and all would come in and take part. If we had visitors, they could take part just the same. It went on that way possibly as long as we stayed together as one family."[11]

Bascom's brothers and sisters all got a good education and did well in their professions. The oldest son, Gudger, began as a teacher but became superintendent of public instruction for East Feliciana Parish in Louisiana. The next son, Blackwell, who played the fiddle with Bascom, became a teacher and principal in Selma, Louisiana. Florida Belle became a nurse but also studied art and piano and wrote poetry. (Her piano teacher wrote: "She was my first what might be called 'Professional' piano pupil, and a most interesting and happy one....She always expressed such deep and true interest.') Zilpah taught school for a few years and then also took nurse's training. She later studied painting and was much interested in botanical gardens. Jennie taught school until 1915, when she became an occupational therapist in Washington, D.C. Between the years 1903 and 1907 she kept a detailed diary which gives a flavor of the times. Before going to Washington to work for the government, Azalea taught school near Rutherford College. She also studied voice and sang in church choirs.

It might appear to some that the Lunsford family was unusual for the mountains for they were well-educated professional people, but there have always been persons in all parts of the Appalachians who have taken advantage of whatever opportunities were open to them and have aspired and achieved by general American standards. They defy the stereotypes imposed on mountain people. The fact that James Bassett Lunsford was born in Tennessee, moved to North Carolina and on to Texas as a boy, and saw much of the South during the Civil War argues against the usual notion of Appalachian isolation. Certainly he was not alone in these experiences. Yet the Lunsfords were uncommon in many ways. They had a sense of who they were and what they were about.

Bascom Lamar Lunsford and his work cannot be understood apart from his background. He endured a great many hardships, but his family and his training as a child helped him not only to endure but to use his early experiences to further his purposes.

Among the items in the Lunsford Collection at Mars Hill College is an unpublished manuscript of more than 100 pages entitled "Reminiscences." In this manuscript Mr. Lunsford pictures rural life in the mountains as it was when he was a boy. He recalls his home life, typical of many at the time. He tells of the chores he performed at home and in the fields of the neighbors, the planting, cultivating, and harvesting of crops with crude implements, many of them homemade. He describes such customs as cornshucking, soapmaking, beanstringing, molasses-making, quiltings, dancing, and other pastimes. He also recounts anecdotes of feasting, church-going, and political activities.

His memory was remarkable almost from his beginning. He recounted,

> You won't believe this. Just do the best you can about it. We moved away from Mars Hill when I was about eighteen months old. I was riding in front of a fellow on a

horse from there to near Asheville. My father had a school over there then. I was riding on the saddle horn. He was holding me kind of in his lap, and the horse started to drink crossing Big Ivy, and it looked like he was moving up the river. I can remember that to this day. Some man told me that I had a very good memory. Well, I do have a memory.[12]

Bascom became interested in music at an early age. He learned many songs from his mother. He said of her,

> She had a big deep voice and sang many of the old ballads. She was reared on Ivy Creek between Buncombe and Madison Counties, and her people sang and played the old-time music, and she held many of them in her memory.

Bascom's father was not a musician, but he described him as one of the best judges of fiddle music in the mountains. Bascom related a trip with his father to see his mother's uncle, Os Deaver, a noted fiddler. The trip made a great impression on little Bascom.

> I vividly recall, when a lad of seven years, riding behind my father on our faithful family horse, Charlie, the distance of forty miles from our home on Hanlon Mountain in Buncombe County to visit my great-uncle, Osborne Deaver, who lived at the Forks of Ivy in Madison County, near Mars Hill College, the place of my birth. I had looked forward to this trip for many days, because Uncle Osborne was a great fiddler of the old school. I had often heard my mother, his niece, sing and hum many of the songs she learned in her youth, some of which she stated were Uncle's fiddle tunes....So one can imagine my deep interest when at my journey's end I was able to see my aged uncle take his precious violin from the black wooden case which he always kept under his bedside, draw the bow across the catgut and glide sweetly into some of the old favorites I could recognize.[13]

The old fiddler no doubt influenced Bascom, for he was a man of some consequence in the area. A prominent Republican, he held positions in Republican administrations in Washington following the Civil War up until Cleveland was elected in 1884, when he came home to run a farm and country store. Through the decade following his return to Madison County, he kept a diary in which he recorded important events of the day, such as altercations growing out of various hostilities, the weather, daily happenings on the farm and what he sold in his store.

Bascom and Blackwell's first attempt at making music was with fiddles constructed from cigar boxes. Their mother helped them to twist and resin thread for the strings and to attach horsehair to bent sticks for the bows. She hummed tunes she had learned from Uncle Os, and they learned to play together. Bascom remembered, "Our neighbors heard the sounds and remarked that they believed the Lunsford boys had got some pet crows up there, for they were hearing them holler a great deal."[14]

Seeing the boys' interest in music, J.B. Lunsford bought a violin from Sam Boyd for $3.00. Boyd came by later to teach them how to play. Blackwell then traded his watch for another fiddle so that they could play together. They learned fast, and soon they were playing for the neighbors. Lunsford recalled:

> People who lived close by would come to our house,especially in the wintertime, and we'd put on another backlog, build a big fire and start the evening entertainment....My brother and I would act out the dialogue called "Arkansas Traveler."[15]

When Bascom was about 10, the brothers were invited to play at an end-of-school entertainment by the schoolteacher, Edgar Triplett, who was to become Bascom's brother-in-law. Here Bascom saw the remains of candles that had been used in a magic lantern show, and he remembered thinking how nice it would be to entertain large groups of people. He commented that his desire was bolstered when, after their part of the program, someone said, "Boys, you've got it cut and dried." This performance was the first of many they gave at school entertainment programs.[16]

When Bascom was in his early teens, Blackwell bought a banjo, and Bascom promptly adopted it as his basic instrument. He commented:

> The banjo brings out the balladry in my system, so at an early age I was a full-fledged ballad singer of the southern Appalachian type. Whereupon, I began the erection of a muscial layer-cake, with work and school as a filling, and such social ingredients as bean stringins, butter stirrin's, apple peelin's, tobacco curin's, candy breakin's, corn shuckin's, log rollin's, quiltin's, house raisin's, serenades, square dances, shoe-arounds, shindigs, frolics, weddings and school entertainments....These contacts brought about the exchange of song ballets between the young people with whom I mingled....The mountain counties of Buncombe, Madison, Haywood and Henderson in North Carolina embrace the extent of my range in that early period. Some of the songs I sang then were "Cindy", "Darby's Ram," "Little Willie," "Old Gray Mare" and "Jenny Jenkins." Of course, a few others of the type of "Kitty Wells," "Rosewood Casket" and "Old Black Joe" I would use, but could never get the response to those that my nature seemed to crave.[17]

At Snow Hill, one of the schools Bascom attended on South Turkey Creek, he met Tom Boyd, son of Sam Boyd who sold them their first fiddle. He was a good banjo picker who impressed Lunsford. He was a grown man who attended Snow Hill along with the children. Boyd sometimes played music for square dance sets during the lunch hour, and from him Bascom learned banjo styles and the songs "Free Little Bird" and "Going Down Town."

Bascom first saw Nellie Triplett, whom he later married, at Snow Hill. She and her brother, the teacher, were bringing two joints of stovepipe into the schoolhouse. He thought she was the prettiest girl he had ever seen.[18]

Fletch Rymer was another banjo picker who influenced Lunsford, who described the settings for Rymer's music-making:

> He'd pick around at parties where we'd get together after a corn shucking, or at the tobacco barn, where they'd sit up and cure the bright-leaf tobacco....Boys in the community would gather up, and sometimes girls, and they'd roast apples and potatoes, or chickens....Fletch Rymer would pick the banjo and sing.[19]

Bascom learned "That Blue-Eyed Girl," "Swannanoa Tunnel" and "Dry Bones" from Rymer.

Bascom later attended Camp Academy at Leicester, where its founder, A.C. Reynolds taught. When Mr. Reynolds went to Rutherford College in 1901, 19-year-old Bascom went with him as a student. At Rutherford, he quickly made friends with others who were interested in music. He remembered that, after his first year in college as he waited for "Old 35" to Asheville, W.B. Love, Fred Moody, and Letch Reynolds sat up with him at the railway station, playing and singing the night hours away. It was from Fred Moody that he learned "I Wish I Was a Mole in the Ground," always one of his favorite songs. Lunsford also remembered that when he arrived in Asheville that morning in 1902, he caught the streetcar as far as it went, then walked the remaining 15 miles home. On the way he stopped at the home of Nick Rogers, who had two musical daughters. They fed him good sausage for breakfast, and they played and sang for a while.[20]

As one can see, Bascom Lunsford came from strong and capable people who represented many conflicting emotions and values, but who agreed on the value of education, of religion, and on the worth of the traditional arts. He grew up at a time when people were in the habit of making their own entertainment out of their own wits and memories and when people lived close to the soil and seasons. He absorbed all that he was a part of, and because he had a remarkable memory, he held on to what he learned. All of this was later to be a rich resource.

Lunsford began his involvement with folk traditions naturally, like most folk practitioners. He learned to play the banjo and fiddle and began acquiring a repertory of songs and tunes. Like others, however, he soon became captive of that which he had captured. He began to speak of his activities in religious terms. The Baptists among whom he lived talked of "the call" to preach. They had little regard for the preachers who were "educated" into the ministry, but expected their ministers to receive a dramatic and identifiable calling from the Lord. Lunsford referred to "his calling" and talked of being "proud as a preacher" of his work and of "spreading the gospel of folk music." The calling would come later, but the seeds of his faith were sown early.

NOTES

1. Forster A. Sondley, *Asheville and Buncombe County* (Asheville, The Citizen Co.), 1922, pp. 170-89.

2. Thomas Wolfe, *The Hills Beyond* (New York: Harper and Row), pp. 222-239.

3. Bascom Lamar Lunsford, *Reminiscences*, unpublished paper in the Lunsford Collection in the Mars Hill College Library.

4. John Angus McLeod, *Minstrel of the Appalachians*,unpublished biography of Lunsford in the Mars Hill College Library, 1973.

5. Sid S. Johnson (ed.), *Texans Who Wore the Gray* (no publisher noted), 1907, p. 209.

6. *Ibid.*, pp. 395-405.

7. *Ibid.*, p. 209.

8. Manly Wade Wellman, *The Kingdom of Madison* (Chapel Hill: University of North Carolina Press), 1973, p. 98.

9. John Angus McLeod, *From These Stones* (Mars Hill, North Carolina: Mars Hill College), 1955, pp. 20; 68-69, 270.

10. This undated history of the Newfound Association was written for the use of the church but was later mimeographed, apparently by Bascom Lunsford.

11. Anne Winsmore Beard, *The Personal Folk Song Collection of Bascom Lamar Lunsford*, unpublished master's thesis (Oxford, Ohio: Miami University), 1959, p. 3.

12. Author interview with Bascom Lamar Lunsford in West Asheville, N.C., 7-27-71.

13. Beard, *op. cit.*, p. 4.

14. *Ibid.*, p. 4.

15. *Ibid.*, p. 5.

16. *Ibid.*, pp. 5-6.

17. *Ibid.*, p. 7.

18. McLeod, *Minstrel of the Appalachians*, p. 13.

19. Beard, *op. cit.*, p. 8.

20. *Ibid.*, pp. 8-9.

CHAPTER 2

Personal and Vocational Ventures

Bascom Lunsford was a restless spirit, with more interests than time. He worked hard to be practical, though, at least for a while. He started out to be a schoolteacher, but then he became a nursery salesman, bee and honey promoter, went back to college, served as a supervisor of boys at a school for the deaf, breezed through law school, practiced law, became county solicitor, college teacher, a newspaper editor, war bond salesman, Justice Department agent, newspaper publisher, church field secretary, New Deal programs worker, reading clerk of the North Carolina House of Representatives, and also a performing artist, collector and festival promoter. These diverse jobs may appear to be unrelated, evidence of an erratic life. Nevertheless, there was a unifying thread through all of them, a consuming interest in the folk traditions of North Carolina and the Appalachian Mountains. Lunsford had to make a living, and to do so he selected the most interesting job at hand. Then he used that job to further his knowledge of people and their traditions and to become deeply involved in the folk arts. Without each of these experiences, he would not quite have been the man he became.

Bascom's two brothers, Gudger and Blackwell, and his sister Jennie, were already employed as teachers in 1902 so it was natural for the school authorities at Cross Rock, in the Sandymush section of Madison County, to come to the Lunsford home looking for another teacher. Bascom was offered a job the summer following his year at Rutherford College, and he accepted it. He took an examination at the county court house and received a second grade certificate. Cross Rock was a subscription school, which meant that the parents paid a set amount for each child in school, ensuring Bascom a salary of $23.45 a month.

"I boarded at Jim Payne's. His children and their families have been friends of mine ever since. That was about a mile straight down from Doggett's Gap, a mountain pass about 2,500 feet in elevation. [Years later he was to learn or make up a song about the Gap (a parody on "Cumberland Gap") which became one of his favorites.] While I was there I'd go up to the home of Old Uncle Jesse Grant, there at a big willow tree, and listen to Lola, his young daughter and a schoolmate of mine, play the old-time organ. I learned "Down at Johnson's there in 1902."

He boarded at Payne's during the week but usually went home on weekends and attended parties with picking, singing and dancing. He remembers one particular party while he was teaching in Madison County. He and Bill Payne, Jim's

Bascom Lamar Lunsford at about twenty years of age
(courtesy of Lunsford Collection, Mars Hill College)

son, walked over to Little Pine Creek to visit Bill's cousin Frank Payne and to borrow his horse for Bascom to ride to Marshall to pick up his first paycheck. While he was gone, Bill organized a party. Bascom gave a full description:

> He had done himself proud in preparing for a gathering of young people at the double-cabin mountain home of Dolf Payne, a kinsman in the Pawpaw section. The Brown girls and the Farmer girls were to be there. Uncle Dolf with his long beard and black cap came in early, riding a small rat-tail mule. His saddlebags indicated he would be in a good humor. It proved to be an all-night session with candy breakin', fiddling, ballad singing and dancing.
>
> The candy breakin' came first. They took stick candy of different stripes, broke it into four or five pieces, put it in a covered basket and stirred it up. The boy and the girl he had chosen to draw candy with would walk up. They'd put their hands under this covering and draw out a piece of candy. Then they would compare them and the judges would say whether they were alike or not. If they were not alike, they'd have to go to the back of the line and try again. If they were alike, the girl would have the wonderful opportunity of kissing the boy and the boy had the wonderful opportunity of kissing the girl. That went on for some time.

Then next followed the singing games, of which there were many. One of them was "Jolly is the Miller." It was here that I first learned the game, "Doctor Jones."

Doctor Jones is a great man, great man, great man.
Doctor Jones is a great man. He saved a many poor soul.
Ladies and gentlemen, sail around, sail around, sail around.
Ladies and gentlemen, sail around, and kiss just who you please.

This game may have contributed somewhat to the lateness of the session. Anyway, Bill and I took Sunday breakfast at the Farmers.[1]

When school was out in 1903, Bascom met Hebe Davis from Haywood County, who worked for the East Tennessee Nursery Company of Clinton, Tennessee. Davis persuaded Bascom to take a job as a salesman with the company. At first both traveled together on horseback, carrying a book illustrating the fruits, flowers and shrubs the company had to sell as well as personal belongings in saddlebags. Davis was also a singer, and from him Bascom learned "Going Back to Georgia", a variant of "The Wagoner Lad." Soon Bascom was on his own as a nursery salesman, except for a brief period when Blackwell accompanied him. He commented:

A change of vocation after the close of my school to that of canvassing in various mountain counties representing a nursery company brought me in close contact with rural folk, and extended my territory again. I was able to cover to a great extent the counties in western North Carolina, and dip into the adjoining states of Tennessee, Georgia and South Carolina. Songs from the valleys of Cheoah and Stecoah in Graham County, where Miss Lela Ammons and others sang, were added to my collection, such as "Old Stepstone" and "Old Garden Gate." From the valleys of the beautiful Hiawassee in north Georgia, and Clay and Cherokee counties in North Carolina, and from the communities of Gum Log, Hightower, Shooting Creek, Tusquittee and Bear Meat, I acquired other songs. I especially recall Miss Ada Greene singing "Row Us Over the Tide," "Lula Wall" and "The Dying Girl's Message."[2]

His practice was to give a fruit tree to his host as payment for food and lodging for himself and his horse, but he was more generous with those hosts where he enjoyed himself the most, picking and singing into the night. His boss finally wrote him in some exasperation, "You and your horse ate up five hundred dollars worth of fruit trees in Henderson County." This was not the last time that his zeal for mountain music interfered with his current vocation.

The following description of his visit to the home of Sam Sumner on a cold rainy day gives a flavor of his encounters with mountain singers:

I called on rainy evening at the home of Sam Sumner, near Cleveland's Bald, near Bat Cave, North Carolina. The man of the house was not home, but they said they would allow me to stay all night. It was a large old pine frame house, large apple trees around, barns and so on. It was a drizzly, dreary afternoon. They'd built a big fire in the living room which they used for a kitchen also. They said that Mr. Sumner would be in in a little bit. So, sitting there by the fire, I looked out the window and saw Mr.Sumner coming up through the orchard, a little pathway, and he had something in a sack on his shoulder. He came on through the big house. I heard some lumbering about in there, and then he came on in and they told him that they had some company. They introduced me and we talked a little bit. I told him that I was selling fruit trees. He said "All right. Glad to have you. Make yourself at home." He turned around to the ladies and said, "Build a fire in yonder."

So they went out and came back in, and very modestly and very humbly said that there was a fire in the other room, and that we could go in there.

We went into the other room, and there was a roaring new-made fire in a big cold dark room. We sat there a few minutes, and he asked, "What might be your name again?" I said, "My name's Lunsford," and he said, "You've been through this country before?" I said, "Some, not much."

He went back to a big chest, took a key and unlocked that chest and took that same sack out, I suppose, and he shook it down and poured a little out of a jug into a glass, and he offered me a little of it. Of course it was a cold rainy day, and I took a little, and then he took some himself. He looked down into the fire again.

He said, "Do you play?" I said I did. He wanted me to play the song "Jesse James." I played it and he sang it. Although there are many texts to the song, the text old Sam Sumner gave me is comparable to any of them.[3]

In later years he talked often of his work with the nursery company, for it was a valuable and important experience:

These trips of mine were made on horseback, sometimes with horse and buggy. It would be hard to conceive now how one could ride mountain trails such as the old route from Andrews to Aquone in the valley of the matchless Nanthahala—"sun straightup"—and across the Wayah Bald down Cartoogachaye without being moved with patriotic pride at the beauty of the highlands.

A singing at Sam Higdon's on Ellijay, near the home of Jim Corbin, the noted banjo player, or a square dance at Bascom Picklesimer's on Tesantee, and like events tended to keep me satisfied in the field as a nursery salesman.

I recall one occasion in Rabun County, Georgia, I spent the night at the home of Ed Lovell. A fellow sojourner by the name of Brown entertained us during the evening by singing "Lord Lovell." Probably the name of our host brought the old song to mind.[4]

He often visited the home of Sheriff Ammons of Graham County, North Carolina, and collected several songs from Lelia Ammons, the sheriff's daughter. One was "Old Stepstone," which was to become another favorite. When he visited the Ammons home, the family and relatives would gather around the piano in the parlor and sing. (Years later, in 1934, while on the way to give a program at the University of California at Los Angeles, Bascom visited Lelia in Tennessee to get the name of her daughter who lived in Los Angeles. During this program at the University, he introduced the daughter and her son and explained their connection with his folksong collection.)

His affection for the mountain people he visited while selling trees colored his feelings for the songs he learned from them. His respect for the people had always been strong, and he had always enjoyed the easy sessions of picking and singing. But during this period he began to think beyond his easy acquaintance with his people and to try to understand something of their history and culture. His travels with the nursery took him through most of Western North Carolina, Northwestern South Carolina, parts of North Georgia, and into the Cumberland Mountains of Tennessee, and he thus learned that the traditions of his native Madison and Buncombe Counties extended over a wide territory. Yet he noted the variations which might have escaped a casual observer. The mountain music and dances led him into a lifelong study of the profound meaning behind the cultural traditions of Appalachian people.

The following passages from Lunsford's tapes and notebooks show the variety of his experiences as a salesman and how it related to his interest in folklore:

> I attended dances on Mills River near the Pink Beds where Rack Kimsey and Bob Reed did the calling. The Posey girls and Ella Warlick, splendid square dancers, were there, and the Posey boys sang and played this little couplet:
>
> "Shout, little Lula, shout your best,
> Your old grandma's gone to rest."
>
> I heard some words to "Italy" on Sugarloaf Mountain; Hebe Davis first sang "Goin' Back to Georgia," Anderson Williams sang his "Mr. Garfield" and Miss Queen Justus taught me "Bonnie Blue Eyes." "The Weeping Willow Tree" was added to my collection here, along with many others.
>
> A "change of venue" with a program similar to that pursued along the Blue Ridge and the Great Smokies, brought me to the beautiful Brushy Mountain section of North Carolina, my first acquaintances being made around Little Mountain, Union Grove, New Hope and Olin townships in the county of Iredell. Dodge Weatherman and Charlie Weatherman were young men then, and their father, Rev. John G. Weatherman, a Baptist preacher and one of the best old-time singers, was alive and in his vigor. I made my home with them for quite a while, and attended every sort of gathering from protracted meetings, funerals, weddings and baptizings to country picnics and parties. Preacher Weatherman was a kindred spirit and often requested me to aid him in what way I could at weddings, funerals, and gatherings when he needed a handy man to serve in a kind of "pinch-hitter" capacity....
>
> Dodge and Charlie were good singers and from them and their circle of friends I secured quite a number of songs which I prize highly. "Ella's Grave" and "Who Will Be a Witness" were among them. I shall never forget the night the boys and I returned from a seining trip in Rock Creek near the old mill close to Chipley Ford, where we caught a twenty-two pound carp. It was brought home in the early morning, and after the family was well awake and all enjoying the story of the catch, Charlie picked up the old banjo and sang the old song still extant in Iredell:
>
> Sal likes sheep and Sal likes mutton.
> Sal's got a toenail as round as a button.
> Ho, Ho, Old Jimmie Sutton,
> Eat all the sheep, but I'll eat the mutton.
>
> This was really "border territory," and I could notice the difference in the rendering of these songs. Marvin Bowman, a young guitarist who came to that section from Mitchell County, often visited at the home of the Stacks in Olin. I called there often for mail and to share in an occasional evening of fun. From him I learned "The Bully of the Town" and "Carve That Possum." Miss Birdie Stack sang "Homesick Boy" (or "Roanoke River") to my liking, and often enough for me to remember without having to copy it.
>
> As to the noticeable difference in intonation of the mountain singers and those of the "flatwoods," I recall an incident in point. I had walked one evening through the old-fashioned covered bridge near the home of Nels Summers some distance from Olin, and, finding his family had quite a number of stringed instruments, I asked for a night's lodging with a view to making a sale, of course. Summers was a "good liver"—had "plenty about his house." He had an elegant home and it was well-furnished, so the mountain boy was put to it in using his best behavior. The family, in

point of numbers, measured up to a typical mountaineer home. Especially do I remembered "Crack" and "Hum," two girls who sang songs of the popular variety. However, in modern-day parlance, my songs "seemed to go over." Next morning, Summers bought some cherry trees, and when I asked for my bill for lodging, he said, "All I want is for you to get the banjo and play "Mole in the Ground" one more time."

Extending this sort of canvas further into the settlements along Hunting Creek, the Yadkin and Little Yadkin rivers, Roarin' River and Reddy's River in the counties of Wilkes, Alexander and Caldwell enabled me to get first-hand information as to the genuine worth of a carefree and hospitable people. It was in "Little Alec" in the Vashti section where the people of the countryside were filled with superstitious consternation when, during a terrible storm, about an acre of earth and rock on Sugarloaf Mountain sank some several feet. Some thought it an ill omen, while others considered it more lightly, and even sang, "If I was a mole in the ground, I'd root old Sugarloaf down."

It was here one summer evening where I had stopped at a farmhouse in the mountains to spend the night and had begun to arrange the strings on a homemade banjo preparatory for an evening of song that a storm-cloud began to gather. Thunderheads arose over the mountains and a rumbling in the distance could be heard. The good housewife remarked, "Well, you aint't a-goin' to try to pick the banjer and hit a-comin' up a storm, air ye?" I often wondered whether my reputation for banjo-picking had preceded me to this home, and I was puzzled some on the use of the word "try" as to whether she thought that was all I could do, or whether, if I persisted in my merrymaking with a tack-headed banjo in the face of a thunderstorm, I would get struck by lightning. At any rate, the statement took the song out of me completely, so "nary a note" did I strike during my visit there.

Near this place is where I caught some idea of life from the standpoint of the feudist. I happened up one day when Bill Baumgarner and his brother-in-law, Mark James, had seemingly ended a difficulty between them. I arrived in time to see Baumgarner leave the scene after firing a shotgun at James, who was walking between the plough handles. Dr. Hollar from Taylorsville had James placed on a mattress under a shade tree, and I assisted him in picking 64 shot from the body of James. He recovered, and I afterwards called at his home occasionally. He claimed to be a kin to the noted desperado, Jesse James, with some degree of pride.

It was customary for the agents to be called to the nursery early in autumn to prepare for delivery, and to get an object lesson in the growing and handling of nursery products. For many weeks I was able to avail myself of the riches in the song-life of those in Powell's Valley and along the Clinch River in East Tennessee, my interest in those things far exceeding my taste for tree-digging and standard fumigation. Miss Neva Black, a Miss Powell, a boy called "Greasy Foot" and I rounded up "John Hardy," a companion song of "John Henry." This was my first time to hear it, but by no means the last.[5]

His nursery work ended in 1904, and Lunsford returned to his family home on Hanlon Mountain in Buncombe County. Soon, however, he was in the honey business with George Elmore, who traveled through Western North Carolina, gathering honey from beeyards which he had established on mountain farms. Lunsford described Elmore and their work together:

Mr. Elmore was a well-educated man, a native of East Tennessee, and something of a naturalist with a deep interest in folks. We traveled and worked together, and often after a day's journey through the mountains, the evening hours would find us seated at the cabin door of some mountaineer with the family gathered 'round, listening to the banjo or fiddle. The higher into the mountains, the better the pasturage for bees. Naturally most of the yards were located high up where the linden and poplar blooms insure a good crop. This also insured to me a good harvest in balladry. The very names of some of the localities are indicative of rustic life: Friesland, Spring Creek, Sandymush, Peep Eye, Sandy Bottoms, Brush Creek, Bear Creek and Trail Branch. Most of these places have been the scenes in time of the most joyous social gatherings, where the rural fiddler, clogger or singer would be the center of attraction. I kept this contract as a sort of summer vacation for five years.[6]

The little girl Bascom had observed carrying stovepipe at the Snow Hill School, Sara Nellie Triplett, had grown into a pretty young woman, and they had been "talking" for several years. Nellie had become a close friend of the Lunsford family and was especially close to Bascom's sister, Jennie, who often mentioned her in the diary she kept between 1903 and 1907. They had been thinking of marriage, but his prospects and income were both slim. Then in 1906, his fortunes looked up a bit when he and Elmore visited the Jim King farm on Big Sandymush Creek in Madison County.

Nellie Triplett Lunsford in 1904
(courtesy of Lunsford Collection, Mars Hill College)

We had 15 or 20 large hives there and I remember there was a big one up in the corner of the fence. So we got our veils and our smokers ready, the pans to dig the honey out and boxes to carry the frames in. We went over to the big hive in the corner, and Mr. Elmore said if that hive didn't have anything in it, why we'd go back, because it was always good. It was a beautiful honey flow that year. The wonderful locust trees were in bloom and had been for some time. So we went up to this hive....Elmore prized up the lid and looked in there. There were ten frames full of honey, which would weigh altogether about 45 pounds; as full a tap of honey as I've ever seen. That was on the 28th day of May, 1906. Nellie and I had been thinking of getting married at the first opportunity. Looking down at that honey, I decided it was all like that in that yard, and in all the other yards in Buncombe and Madison Counties. We went ahead and worked that yard, and as we went out I said to myself, "I'm going to get married." So we were married on the second day of June, 1906, in Asheville, N.C.[7]

Nellie Triplett came from a practical and prosperous family. Nellie's mother died when her daughter was very young. Her father, Thomas S. Triplett, later married Sophia Roberson, who never bore children of her own. Bascom's daughter Nelle, named for her mother, gives this memory of her grandparents:

Grandpa and Grandma had everything they needed or that they possibly would ever need for years to come. They spent their lives from the day they were married maintaining the farm and home on South Turkey Creek and rearing the two children (Nellie and Edgar), with such tangible results as a cement spring house, a wash house, a smoke house, etc. Grandpa attended to every practical detail. The home and the buildings had been designed and built by him. He had made by hand as many things as he possibly could from wood, leather, or iron. Door latches and hinges, wooden pegs for hangers, chairs, tables, and all such painstaking articles were still in use for years after he died. There was an apple house at the end of the huge orchard. I believe the first floor was built into a hill so the apples would not freeze. Grandpa saw to the needs of the farm and household. The best stove wood for the kitchen was always available in quantity in the wood shed. Back logs of green hickory were musts for the living and sitting room fires.

Grandma worked just as diligently as grandpa. Her thriftiness and preparation for some possible lean years resulted in canned goods which probaby never were eaten. Her supply of linens grew. She made quantities of quilts which were kept in a quilt press.[8]

Thomas Triplett, Nellie's father, was a stern man with a black spade of a beard. He disapproved of Bascom Lunsford's footloose ways and feared that Bascom would never get ahead in the world. To him, getting ahead meant working long hours in the fields, being frugal, and acquiring property that one could improve. He was a substantial man in the community, a lifelong member in and supporter of the Western Chapel Methodist Church on South Turkey Creek.

A good "honey flow" was not exactly what Thomas Triplett would have called substantial prospects. No doubt Triplett noted that Bascom had had a year at Rutherford College, had been a school teacher, fruit-tree salesman, in addition to his current occupation in the honey business and was not reassured. But he was a kind and fair-minded person, and there is no evidence that he strongly objected to seeing his only daughter marry a man of dubious prospects. Nellie and Bascom were married on June 2, 1906, and set up housekeeping in the old Lunsford home on Hanlon Mountain.

In the meantime, his father, J.B. Lunsford had obtained a teaching job at Connelly Springs, near Rutherford College. He had moved with his four daughters (Mrs. Lunsford had died in 1902) to Connelly Springs, so that the girls could continue their education at Rutherford College. Times were hard in 1906, for the young couple and for the J.B. Lunsford family as well. Bascom's letter to his father on August 18, 1906, stated he was sending them $5.00, amended in a P.S. to $6.50. The larger amount was sent after Bascom had received a letter apparently indicating money was needed to help the family and keep his sisters in college.

Lunsford informed his father that he had just received a payment from George Elmore of $6.00, making a total of $76.40 that the honey business had brought him. He indicated his disappointment with his current pursuit, but wrote that "it certainly beats no job." He also expressed gratitude for a mare that Elmore had left with them and which Nellie had ridden to visit a neighbor to get some beans. He reported that they were involved in drying peaches from the trees on the place, and he mentioned that the neighbors were all very "cleaver" (generous) and that they had, in the current custom, given the newlyweds foodstuff. Even though their circumstance may sound grim to today's readers, they were probably better off than most other newly-married couples of their time.

Bascom and Nellie soon joined the family at Connelly Springs where he attended Rutherford College for three more years. After graduating in 1909, he began teaching again at Greenlee in McDowell County, but he was asked to move to nearby Nebo when a vacancy occurred in the middle of the school year. A favorite story was of an event at the end of the school term at Nebo. Only two students were graduating, but the parents wanted appropriate graduating exercises. Lunsford was hard-pressed to find suitable musicians. Then he remembered Uncle Billy Hill who carried the mail on horseback between Connelly Springs and Rutherford College and who was a fine old-time fiddler. Lunsford invited him to play, realizing that some respectable people in the community thought that fiddle playing, dancing and such were sinful. He got Uncle Billy into a long-tailed coat, high collar and tie and put him on stage. He reported that the shock of the sight put a quietus on the audience, but when Uncle Billy hit his stride, they clapped and shouted for more. Uncle Billy was a hit.[9]

After commencement exercises in 1910,Lunsford accepted a job as supervisor of boys at the North Carolina School for the Deaf in Morganton. He began then to study law in his spare time. He left little to indicate his motivation, but it could have come about from his interest in politics, although this interest was not manifested until later. It could have been also that he felt the need to establish

Lunsford at Rutherford College
(courtesy of Lunsford Collection, Mars Hill College)

himself in a more substantial profession than the ones that he had been pursuing. After a year and a half of reading law, he enrolled formally as a second-year student at Trinity College which was later to become Duke University. One of his teachers was Samuel Fox Mordecai, a distinguished teacher and also dean of the college. He studied two years at Trinity, passed the bar examination, and was granted a license to practice in August of 1913.

His first job in the legal profession was as a soliciter of Burke County, a position that was apparently vacant at the time he was admitted to the bar, since he was appointed by the county commissioners.[10]

While Bascom was studying, teaching and supervising the boys at the School for the Deaf, he and Nellie were making a family. Sara Kern was the first-born, in 1908. Blackwell Lamar, named after Bascom's brother and himself, their only son, was born in 1911, and Ellen Chapman followed in 1913. During those years, Lunsford put a primary interest on earning a living, although he shifted from one job to another, and he always had his ear cocked for a ballad. However, his musical involvement was apparently limited mainly to easy picking and singing sessions and other get-togethers.

He was still serving as Burke County solicitor when he was invited in 1914 to teach English and history at Rutherford College. This gave him an opportunity to spend more time on his folkloric interests. A handbill from the time announced that Bascom Lamar Lusford would give his "noted lecture" on "North Carolina Folklore, Poetry and Songs." It is interesting that he used the word "folklore" in relation to his lecture and musical program.

The blurb on the handbill, written apparently by President M.T. Hinshaw, was perhaps extravagant, but it promised an interesting program:

> This treat is a medley of the richest and best of North Carolina Literature and song. No one who loves his state should miss it. Those who have scruples against a hearty laugh should stay away.
>
> Prof. Lunsford has been an instructor in Rutherford College for a number of years and now holds the chair of English in this institution. He is a young man who has given the greater part of his life to the study of literature and elocution and is known to be one of the most eloquent educators in the state.
>
> His program will be interspersed with instrumental music. Stringed instruments are used with a most happy effect in various impersonations.

Even though he had performed on many occasions as a boy and a young man, this occasion seems to have been the first in which he gave a formal lecture-concert, his "Noted lecture" term notwithstanding. Photographs taken for the program show Bascom dressed in white tie and tails. It is important to point out that other folk performers, such as Kentucky preacher-balladeer Buell Kazee, imitated the dress of classical concert performers when they first gave programs of folk music. It was a natural for Bascom to feel he should dress in this manner, especially because of the college setting.

COMING!

IN INTEREST OF

RUTHERFORD COLLEGE

Professor Bascom Lamar Lunsford

Gives his noted Lecture

"North Carolina Folklore, Poetry and Song"

This treat is a medley of the richest and best of North Carolina Literature and song. No one who loves his state should miss it. Those who have scruples against a hearty laugh should stay away.

Prof. Lunsford has been an instructor in Rutherford College for a number of years and now holds the chair of English in this institution. He is a young man who has given the greater part of his life to the study of literature and elocution and is known to be one of the most eloquent educators in the state.

8 p. m.

His program will be interspersed with instrumental music. Stringed instruments are used with a most happy effect in various impersonations.

ADMISSION 25 Cts., Students 15 Cts.

M. T. Hinshaw,

President RUTHERFORD COLLEGE.

Handbill (courtesy of Lunsford Collection, Mars Hill College)

He later described this performance:

> My work had given me more confidence in myself. Whether this was well-founded or not, I don't know. So I had arranged a discourse of more than an hour's length on no less a subject than "North Carolina Folklore, Poetry and Song," and while I had slipped away a time or two to deliver it at schools where the teacher was kind enough to take the risk, I really gave it its initial test at Rutherford College. To my surprise and to the startling of the students and the "natives," it went over. The parts of it pertinent to ballads and folksongs, the part I was on nettles about, such as singing with a banjo accompaniment "Swannanoa Tunnel" and "Free a little Bird," was the high spot in the program. When my good friend, Professor Creal, a teacher of Greek, and I took a vacation floating down Catawba River on a raft of our own construction, I asked his opinion of my lecture. His reply was, "Well, you are in fine shape now to go and take training."...While I never did go and take training, I have never abandoned the habit of going out many times during the year to talk or lecture or entertain or what you will at schools, clubs, and colleges.[11]

Lunsford taught for two years at Rutherford College and then tried auctioneering. Someone commented that he could sell a tin dipper to a spring lizard. For a year he was editor and publisher of the *Old Fort Sentinel* in McDowell County. By that time the United States was into the Great War. Lunsford was classified as unsuitable for the draft, but he sought a means of serving his country nevertheless. At first he sold war bonds in Asheville and then managed to get an appointment, probably through Congressman Zebulan Weaver, as a special agent with the Justice Department. The original appointment was for three months, although he served for the better part of the year. He was sent to New York and spent most of his time chasing draft dodgers. In 1919, he was sent to Nashville to investigate some aspect of the DuPont Powder Company, his last assignment.[12]

One positive result of Lunsford's work as a "G-Man," according to John Angus McLeod,[13] was that Lunsford spent some time in Washington and met Maude Karpeles, secretary and partner to Cecil J. Sharp, the English musicologist who collected songs in the Southern Mountains in the years 1916-1918,[14] and that she introduced Lunsford to scholarly folklorists and collectors, perhaps the first he had ever met. Before the 1920's, Lunsford had been on his own as a collector and interpreter relying mostly on his instincts. He was soon to meet and work with persons more in touch with the youthful field of academic folklore.

After his work with the Department of Justice was finished, Lunsford returned to Marion, North Carolina, and started another newspaper, the *McDowell Sentinel.* He was assisted by W.M Shuford and by Miss Beatrice Cobb, an experienced newspaper woman. The printing was done on the presses of the *Hickory Record*.

Being a newspaperman, public performer and lecturer, a lawyer with natural political instincts, he was approached by local politicians to help various races. Lunsford was a strong Democrat, taking after his father, the old Confederate, rather than after his Republican-Unionist relatives on his mother's side of the family. So, it was the Democrats who sought his aid against well-entrenched Republicans. Bascom was asked to help reorganize the party after its chairman resigned and to elect a Democratic sheriff and other officials. Lunsford's success in bringing in a complete slate of Democrats brought his name to the attention of party leaders in Raleigh.[15]

In addition to involvement in politics as well as his two vocations in the law and news, Lunsford was a churchman. He had joined the Methodist Church shortly after his marriage to Nellie, a Methodist, and his enrollment at Rutherford College, which was supported by the Methodists. He had earlier been baptized into the Newfound Baptist Church, where his father and mother were members. In 1919, he was made secretary of the local Epworth League, the Methodist youth organization, and this led to his being appointed field secretary for all of Western North Carolina. His travels for the Church gave him an opportunity, once again, to visit in the homes of persons with whom he could exchange songs and stories. He was later to have trouble with local Methodist ministers who disagreed with his activities in promoting dancing and secular songs in the communities that their churches served. Apparently this issue did not arise while he worked for the Epworth League, since he was not as yet active in organizing folk activities.

Lunsford had made a place for himself at Marion, but it was a long way from the real mountains of Madison and Buncombe Counties. He was always restless for the highlands and spent much time in Asheville. A permanent move back was made possible in 1925, when Nellie's father divided his farm on South Turkey Creek in Buncombe County between Nellie and her brother, Edgar Triplett. Bascom and Nellie moved their family into a small house on the 84 acres that became her portion.

Actually, the house was an old store building that Lunsford remodeled, using slabs (the outside planks with bark on one side that were usually discarded by sawmills or sold for firewood) to make an attractive rustic siding for the old building. When he was finished it had a kitchen, living room, bedroom and a sleeping porch downstairs and three small bedrooms upstairs.[16] It was a modest house for a family that had grown to include six daughters and a son: Sara Kern, Blackwell Lamar, Ellen Chapman, Lynn Huntington, Nellie Triplett, Merton and Josefa Belle. It would be 10 years before he and Nellie could afford to build a more suitable dwelling.

Both spiritually and physically, Lunsford was back home. He no doubt had good intentions of establishing a respectable law practice in his new office in the Technical Building in Asheville, but a letterhead from the time indicates that he was more interested in his avocation of folklore than he was in his vocation of the law. Under his name and address was a list of titles, "lecturer, musician, radio artist, folklorist, writer, record artist" and a column of testimonials. He also probably intended to farm Nellie's 84 acres, but the call of music was stronger than his resolve to earn a good living for the family.

NOTES

1. Anne Winsmore Beard, *The Personal Folk Song Collection of Bascom Lamar Lunsford*, unpublished master's thesis (Oxford, Ohio: Miami University), 1959, pp. 10-11.
2. *Ibid.*, p. 13.
3. *Ibid.*, pp. 13-15.
4. *Ibid.*, p. 13.
5. *Ibid.*, pp. 15-18.
6. *Ibid.*, p. 18.
7. *Ibid.*, p. 19.
8. Letter from Nelle Lunsford Greenawald, 6-2-74.
9. John Angus McLeod, *Minstrel of the Appalachians*, unpublished biography of Lunsford in the Mars Hill College Library, 1973, p. 15.
10. *Ibid.*, p. 10.
11. Beard, *op cit.*, p. 20.
12. *Ibid.*, p. 21: McLeod, *op. cit.*, pp. 16-17.
14. See Sharp and Karpeles, *English Folk Songs from the Southern Mountains*, 2 vols. (London: Oxford University Press), 1932, reprinted 1952, 1960.
15. McLeod, *op. cit.*, p. 19.
16. Telephone conversation with Nelle Lunsford Greenawald, 7-8-81.

CHAPTER 3

The Real Calling

The decade of the 1920s finished the shaping of Lunsford into a collector, performer and promoter of the folk arts, and it brought the call to service.

He never knew for sure just what had started him on his unusual primary career as a singer, instrumentalist, dancer, folklorist and festival promoter. He thought it might have been his mother, "a blue-eyed girl who sang as spontaneously as the mountain daisies bloom." His father undoubtedly had an influence, for he was lover of fiddle music and would occasionally hum tunes and even break into song, and he had certainly encouraged his children's early musical interest. Uncle Os Deaver was also a great influence; the trips to the old fiddler's home made a strong impression on little Bascom. He commented once that it was Uncle Os who had inspired him to play the fiddle.

But just growing up in Madison and Buncombe Counties of Western North Carolina in the last years of the 19th century would have influenced anyone with a yen for traditional music and related lore, for the woods were full of fine musicians, singers and common folk whose heads held ballads, songs, hymns, tales, rhymes, riddles and square dance figures. The common people around the turn of the century performed freely, as pointed out by Cecil Sharp, in contrast to later years when socially aspiring people began to take on what they thought to be more sophisticated ways.

Once he was tuned into music and dance, and once he got the bug for performing, Bascom found many opportunities for learning new materials and techniques. His reminiscences are full of specific instances when he was able to enrich his repertory while he was going to school, doing routine chores, or pursuing one or the other of his various careers. He expected to find precious material wherever he went. "One man can walk through a garden and not see anything but bushes and weeds," he commented, "while another man can walk through the same garden early in the morning when the dew is still on the roses and see it all—see the whole world."

At first, he was mainly interested in learning to play and sing as many songs as possible for his own satisfaction or for family entertainment. After he and Blackwell began playing for school programs, it was important for them to improve their repertory and to give some thought to the presentation of the material. Even as a young man, he appeared to have a feel for the worth of the traditional material he learned and the value also of performing it in ways traditional to the area where he found it. Later on he reported that he sometimes tinkered with verses to make them suit his taste better, but he made it clear that he mainly stuck faithfully to the versions he had learned.

Yet showmanship became important to him from the time he surveyed the waxen remains of the stereoptican show in the school where he and Blackwell performed, and his ambition to entertain sprang up there full blown. He learned the traditional styles on fiddle and banjo and faithfully practiced them. Likewise, he learned the ballads and folk songs and made them part of himself. He had grown up with many of the ballads and songs and certainly with the hymns. Since he was as much a part of the culture as was the material he gathered, they were in harmony. His love for the culture and the music was so great that he always respected the integrity of the songs which he collected.

He made numerous references to the dances and parties that he attended as a boy and as a young man. The Appalachian style of square dancing was a natural skill for him, learned as a part of the process of growing up in Madison and Buncombe counties. It is obvious that Bascom was a very bright young man, entertaining, witty and popular, and as such he was invited to most of the parties and dances. He was never one to sit out the dances or decline to play or sing. Harold H. Martin described an older Bascom Lunsford as a man who "walks all reared back, as the saying is ....When he stands, he stands all reared back, like a man of substance...with dignity....he would not only sing loudly and willingly,...he would do so while...at the same time doing a nimble buck-and-wing. He is a ballad-singing man, and a dancing man who will dance all night to the strains of mountain music, prancing with surprising agility...and calling the sets himself in a voice vibrantly joyful, like that of a coon dog on a breast-high scent."[1]

But he felt the need to go beyond just what most people knew, and he began to seek out musicians who had unusual talent or repertories. Fortunately, his memory for his early contacts was nearly flawless, and he could talk about almost all of the outstanding musicians whom he sought out. He could also remember a great deal about the lives of these persons, where they lived, including the county, township, river, creek or branch, what the circumstances were on the day he visited them, and what songs he learned from them. This quality put Lunsford head and shoulders above most collectors. Coming from the Appalachian region, he related personally with other natives of the region, and he had a genuine interest in all aspects of their lives. He respected them for possessing important cultural traditions, and above all he wanted to make sure that their names were kept alive in connection with the music they had freely given him. This is in contrast to collectors who reported only that they obtained song from a fiddler, an old woman, a sailor, etc.

Lunsford often voiced his admiration for mountain people.

> Here in the Appalachian region the people are sturdy and they are fine, and they have held on to their traditions. Knowing the proper approach has helped me a whole lot, knowing how the other man thinks and what to depend on. A man's home is his

castle. When you go to see a man about playing, you take your hat off. You don't just go in and say, "Josie, get your banjo, I want to hear you play." You can't do that. You go in and ask where the man of the house is. Then you tell him, "I'll tell you why I come. I hear that you make music and sing ballads, and I wonder if you'd sing for me." Just because they are limited in some ways doesn't mean that their morals are low. Their morals are high. You go in there and treat them like ladies and gentlemen.[2]

Because he treated them well, mountain musicians treated Lunsford well, and he remembered them to the end of his long life. He was profoundly grateful for the gifts they had given him, and those which he would give to new generations, usually linked to their sources by name and place and situation. "I never claimed that I discovered a song. The songs were there to be found. My only contribution is in preserving them, intact, as I found them. It would truly be sad if they were lost."

By the time Lunsford had completed his nursery and beekeeping work, he had committed to memory and rough notes a great repertory of songs, ballads, hymns and square dance figures. He began to see that there was something in these traditions beyond just an extensive collection which he could perform. He commented, "I began at this time to realize something of the literary value of these songs, but I only wanted to learn more songs to sing myself. I tried to remember only such songs as I could use for entertainment purposes. I neglected to acquire the older ballads which were more difficult to render. I realize how much good material I must have let slip away from me then. A song collector can realize how often and how thoroughly disappointed I am to find the trail a cold one now, and a former singer merely a memory in the community."[3]

Up to World War I, he had been pretty much on his own as a collector, with no contact, except through the printed word, with scholars in the field of folklore. He soon became personally acquainted with some of the best experts in the field.

About 1922, Frank C. Brown of Duke University approached Lunsford, as he did many other singers in the state, to record songs. He got several songs from Lunsford, although some are attributed to those who had originally given the songs to him. This is another indication that Lunsford did not allow his healthy ego to get in the way of giving proper credit to his sources. Brown's recordings were done on wax cylinders.[4] Lunsford gives no indication that Brown was a major influence on him at this time, although he spoke of his later association with Brown in the North Carolina Folklore Society.

The person who did have a definite influence on him as a collector was Robert Winslow Gordon who came to Western North Carolina in 1925 to collect folk songs. He asked Lunsford to sing for him and to guide him through the mountains and into the homes of persons who could sing and play the old songs. Gordon, educated at Harvard, had taught English at both Harvard and the University of California. He was, as near as the country afforded, a professional folklorist, a member of numerous folklore and related organizations, a frequent contributor of articles to various publications, and he conducted the department "Old Songs that Men Have Sung" for *Adventure* magazine for a number of years in the 1920s. Gordon was to establish the Archive of American Folk Song at the Library of Congress in 1928.

Lunsford took Gordon to the homes of persons he had met on his various trips. They spent the night at the home of Willard Randall in Rock Hill, South Carolina, and Lunsford wrote that "morning came and found us still up and Randall still going strong." At the recently finished new home of Anderson Williams of Fletcher, North Carolina, they sat on the floor of the empty building to hear Williams play the banjo and sing "Mr. Garfield."

Lunsford developed another technique for gathering songs. He would arrange entertainment at a school house, charge admission, and then give a prize for the best ballad or song contributed by students. He took Gordon to such a program in Jackson County, North Carolina, where he offered a five-dollar gold piece for the best ballad. He remembered that "just preceding the program I secured 'The Merry Golden Tree' from Miss Ada Moss of the Canada section of that county. Had this been submitted it would have taken the prize over 'Flo Ella' submitted by Miss Mary Powell."[5]

Gordon was impressed with the contacts that Lunsford had cultivated and by his methods of collecting songs. He encourged Lunsford in his work and im-

Lunsford rendering "Dogett's Gap," accompanied by Mr. and Mrs. Lyda Brooks and Gaither Robinson on the occasion of the filming of a Movietone News feature in 1927 (courtesy of Lunsford Collection, Mars Hill College)

pressed upon him the need to be as thorough and systematic as he could in collecting and preserving the songs. This encouragement and advice from Gordon fanned Lunsford's enthusiasm. His belief in the value of music was reinforced, but beyond that he gained new insights that moved him into true scholarship in the field of folk traditions. He continued to grow as a performer and promoter, but he also began building a treasury of material that would eventually contain some 3,000 songs and related material, including ruled tablet sheets with songs scrawled in pencil by school children, notebooks he maintained, bits of pieces of lore that he clipped from newspapers and magazines and letters and song sheets that were sent to him by friends and fans. This was in addition to his "memory collection" of over 300 songs, fiddle and banjo tunes, dance calls, singing games and stories. He prided himself in having a good memory and was proud of knowing more songs than anyone of his acquaintance. He enjoyed memory work and could recite a wide range of poetry at will, and thus it is obvious that he had consciously and steadily built his memory collection over a lifetime.

In the January, 1926, issue of *Adventure*, Gordon praised Lunsford and announced that he had consented to become the magazine's official collector in Western North Carolina. In the same issue he also printed Lunsford's version of "Cindy." Perhaps this notice in *Adventure* encouraged the editor of *Southern Life*, devoted to country clubs and outdoor life, to ask Lunsford to contribute articles.[6]

In addition to his collecting for *Adventure* and contributing to *Southern Life*, for several years during the 1920s Lunsford conducted a column in *The Asheville Citizen*. The late Scott Wiseman, of the popular radio team of Lulu Belle and Scotty, indicated the influence of that column:

> Mr. Lunsford certainly had an influence on my career in country music, beginning with the days when I used to read his column in *The Asheville Citizen*, "Songs and stories of the Appalachians." During the '20s, when I was still in high school, I read his column regularly. Although I knew the tunes to most of the songs, many of the verses were unknown to me until I clipped them from Bascom's writings and later memorized them. Some of these songs, such as "Pretty Little Pink," "On Top of Old Smoky" and others, I gave to Bradley Kincaid when he came to the Carolina Mountains looking for songs.[7]

Lunsford was invited in 1924 to go to Atlanta to record for Okeh records, a division of the General Phonograph Company of New York. It is unclear how Lunsford came to the attention of Okeh. Most likely, Polk C. Brockman, an Atlanta furniture store proprietor who was also a scout for Okeh, heard of him and invited him down, but it is possible that Ralph Peer, recording director of Okeh had encountered Bascom, or heard of him on one of his frequent field trips.[8] At any rate, Lunsford recorded two numbers for Brockman in Okeh's Atlanta studio on March 15, 1924. The two numbers were "Jesse James," which he had learned from Sam Sumner at Bat Cave, on that long-ago winter evening when he was selling fruit trees, and "I Wish I Was a Mole in the

Lunsford with Lulu Belle and Scotty Wiseman
(courtesy of Lunsford Collection, Mars Hill College)

Ground," which he had learned from Fred Moody, a fellow student at Rutherford College. He said that he was paid nothing for the recording, and he had to spend $50.00 of his own money for travel to Atlanta.[9]

In the late summer of 1925, Brockman set up a studio in Asheville to record local artists, including Lunsford. However, Lunsford had a larger role than just that of a recording artist. *The Asheville Citizen* of August 30, 1925, published a long article under this headline, *"MOUNTAIN FOLK SONGS RECORDED BY B.L. LUNSFORD OF ASHEVILLE WRITES SONG ABOUT W.J. BRYAN."*

> One of the unique enterprises which has been attracted to Western North Carolina and to Asheville is the recording by the General Phonograph Corporation of New York City of mountain folk songs. To make these recordings this company has improvised a laboratory on the roof of the George Vanderbilt Hotel where a number of artists have been pursuing this work for the past several days.
>
> This company has been attracted to this rich field of folklore largely through the efforts and influence of Bascom Lamar Lunsford, an attorney and folklorist of Asheville, who has recorded for this company in the past in Atlanta and New York*, and who has taken an interest in folklore and songs of the southern Appalachian mountains. He is said to have one of the largest collections of folk songs in the South. He, with his brother Professor Blackwell Lunsford of this county, who plays the violin, is said to be an excellent interpreter of the spirit of these songs, has been busy for several days during the past week at the laboratory making other recordings for the company.

*There is no record that Lunsford recorded in New York.

R.S. Peer, of New York City, director of record production for the General Phonograph Corporation, has paid Mr. Lunsford a very high compliment in choosing him from a great number of artists interested in this class of music, to arrange words and music for a recording which would reflect sentiment from the standpoint of a fundamentalist relative to the Dayton trial and death of William Jennings Bryan. He expresses himself as being highly pleased with the production of Mr. Lunsford and will put it on the market soon as a special number ....

Another number recorded by the artist is entitled, "The Fate of Santa Barbara," and is done at the request of P.C. Brockman of Atlanta, Georgia, connected with the company and who inducted Mr. Lunsford into this work several years ago and who desired the artist to find music suitably sad for the words lately written about the catastrophe of the Santa Barbara earthquake.

Among other numbers of the artist is: "Mountain Dew," music and words composed by him so as to reflect the exact sentiment of a young boy who having been caught in the law for the first time and facing a liquor charge, openly tells the court how strong the temptation is when people prominent in society request that he get them a little of the "mountain dew". . . .

Mr. Lunsford, as an entertainer, has appeared before many audiences in this part of the country within the last few years, having appeared before practically all the civic organizations and literary clubs of Asheville from time to time. It is interesting to hear him relate the origin of many ballads of the mountain section. He hopes to make records of these as the work progresses. He has had many requests for the recording of "Kidder Cole," a song learned in Jackson County and which is of very romantic origin and will be recorded at an early date. The many friends of the artist have congratulated him on his splendid success in the work and hope he will find it pleasant as well as profitable.

There is some confusion in regard to the authorship of "Bryan's Last Battle" and "The Fate of Santa Barbara." The above newspaper article implies that Lunsford was commissioned to write the former and was instructed to find a suitable tune for the latter, to words already written, presumably by Brockman. About the earthquake song, Lunsford commented on his Columbia University recordings of 1935, "Mr. Brockman....came to Asheville, and he asked me to arrange the words and get a tune for a song entitled "The Fate of Santa Barbara." I did, and this is the result." He commented further in regard to the song about Bryan:

This came as a result of the trial at Dayton, Tennessee, which is known as the Scopes Trial. This text, together with the text of the Fate of Santa Barbara, was brought to me by Mr. Brockman of Atlanta to have put on phonographic recordings, which I edited some and put on phonographic recordings at the time, and I have heard frequently coming back to me in a way. I give them here as a collection of those things founded on known happenings.

But on the Library of Congress recordings in 1949, he said:

The title of this song is "Bryan's last Battle." The footnote to this is Mr. Brockman, who worked for the Okeh Phonograph Company, asked me to put a song on record telling something of the Dayton Trial, and he gave me some data, and I composed the following in 1925 and sang it to an old religious tune.....

It appears that Lunsford did the words for "Bryan's Last Battle" and recorded it to a hymn tune and that Brockman gave him suggested words to "The Fate of

Santa Barbara," which he may have reworked and then recorded to the tune of "The Little Rosewood Casket."

Of these two numbers, only "The Fate of Santa Barbara" was released, with "Sherman Valley" on the reverse side. Lunsford had recorded traditional numbers as well as the above-mentioned composed songs. Unfortunately, something went wrong with the recording machine and only two numbers were suitable for release.[10] Apparently Brockman never attempted to set up another recording session. Of the two songs composed for Brockman, it seems that "Bryan's Last Battle" would have had the greater appeal, both because of the national attention directed towards the Scopes trial and Bryan's popularity in many sections of the country. Thus it is strange that the song was forgotten by Brockman and Okeh.

In 1928, Lunsford went to Ashland, Kentucky, to record 12 numbers for the Brunswick-Balke-Collender Company, in 1930 (see Appendix I for a discography). For Columbia Phonographic Company, he recorded two items in Atlanta, "Speaking the Truth," an orally transmitted version of William P. Brannan's "Where the Lion Roareth and the Whangdoodle Mourneth,"[11] and "A Stump Speech in the Tenth District," a preposterous election bid, centering on Lunsford's own congressional district. In the latter, Gid Tanner's and Clayton McMichen's famous "Skillet Lickers," who happened to be in the studio, did an instrumental introduction and concluding piece.[12]

Lunsford's recordings were never a commercial success. Perhaps he did not have popular appeal, but he appeared unwilling to sacrifice his basic commitment to traditional music and styles in order to become popular. When record companies sought him out, he would record, but either because he never really had the opportunity or did not choose to, he did not go down the road that many other musicians were to travel, from traditional to topical, popular and sometimes short-lived songs. When fame came, it found him on his own ground.

He was well aware of the recording business, and was willing to help others. He recommended singers to Okeh's Brockman, and he wrote a letter of introduction to Ralph Peer at Victor Records for Jimmie Rodgers, before Rodgers went to Bristol, Tennessee/Virginia for his famous 1927 recording session there.[13]

This is as good a place as any to comment on Lunsford's best-known composition and other numbers that have been attributed to him. He never took his compositions too seriously. However, his "Mountain Dew" is a song probably known by more people than most compositions of more earnest songwriters. In fact, the song has been so thoroughly accepted in the folk tradition, it is considered to be a folk song by most of those who hear or sing it. He composed it in 1920 when he was frequently in the courts defending someone who had been accused of moonshining.

Lunsford's recording of "Mountain Dew" was released by Brunswick in 1928, but it was made famous by such entertainers as Lulu Belle and Scotty Wiseman,

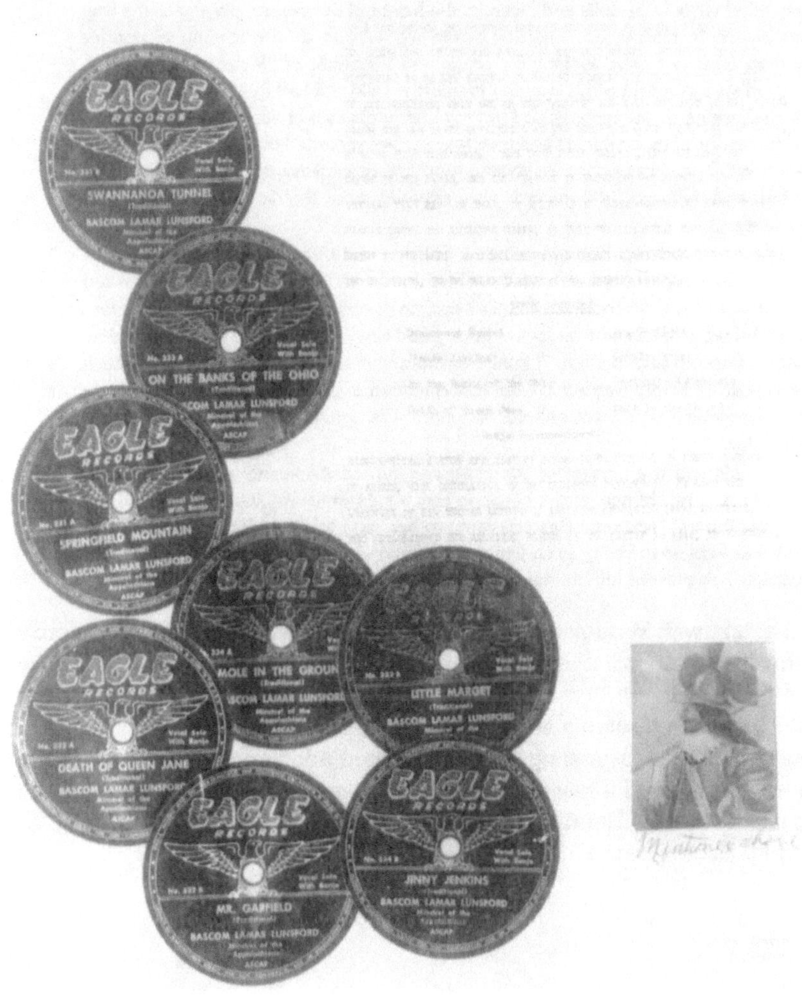

Labels for Lunsford's Eagle recordings that later were released on Folkways. The accompanying text describes the session recorded by Ralph Auf der Heide. (Courtesy of Lunsford Collection, Mars Hill College)

Grandpa Jones and Roy Acuff. Scott Wiseman described how his and his wife's names became attached to the song, along with Lunsford's:

> Bascom visited us at our log-cabin vacation cottage several times.....I remember that I had heard him sing "Mountain Dew" a few times....The refrain of the song stuck in my mind while Lulu Belle and I were at the height of our career, playing all the way from Boston to Hollywood. The day before we were to do a recording session for Vocalion label, we were looking for songs and I thought of "Mountain Dew." Mr. Lunsford's version told of his first day in court....I did not feel that it had the kind of universal appeal to sell records, so I put together a new set of verses based largely on my knowledge of moonshiners and their ways....We recorded the song, and although Station WLS would not allow us to sing it on the air because of their taboos against alcohol and tobacco, the record was released and the song started to gain popularity....
>
> A year or two later, Bascom came to Chicago and visited us at the Barn Dance shows....He was delighted with what we had done with "Mountain Dew" and invited us to come to his hotel room to reminisce and go over some old songs. John Lair was there, and we spent several hours just talking and singing old songs. When it was time to leave, Bascom said to John, "I think I've thought of a way to pay my train fare back to Asheville. If Scotty wants it, I'll sell him my interest in "Mountain Dew." I wrote a simple agreement on a piece of hotel stationery. We signed it, and I gave him a check for $25.00.
>
> I copyrighted my version of the song and turned it over to a publisher. They secured other recordings, and it began to pay a substantial royalty through BMI and other publishers. Next time Bascom came to see us, I told him I had made sure his name was kept on the song as co-writer and would see that he received his part of the royalties. This pleased him tremendously, and we were good friends until his death.[14]

The meeting with Wiseman and Lair described above was during Lunsford's trip to the National Folk Festival (Chicago, 1937). The story illustrates how Lunsford lived near the bone as he did his work. Lair still chuckles over the scene of Lunsford's trading a song for a ticket home.

"Mountain Dew" was a song that encouraged additional verses. Other performers who have used it have supplied new ones. The following version gives the original words by Lunsford. Included also are the words and music as published by Scott Wiseman.

> To show how a song that passes through many hands is subject to change, yet can hold its identity, I give the now familiar song "Old Mountain Dew", which originally when I wrote it in 1920 was the story of a young man the first time he was charged in court on a liquor count. It is his plea to the court. [Lunsford's note]

On my first day in court I wish to report,
Now witness my story so true.
When the state closed its case a young man raised his face,
And began all these facts to review.
Yes, they call it that Old Mountain Dew
Said those who refuse it are few.
While I know I've done wrong, the temptation is strong
When they call for that Old Mountain Dew.

The deacon drove by in his auto so shy
Said his family was down with the flu.
Said he thought that I ought to just get him a quart
Of that good Old Mountain Dew.
Yes, he called it that Old Mountain Dew,
Said those who refuse it are few
So I thought that I ought to just get him a quart
Of that good Old Mountain Dew.

The doctor he phoned just to see me alone
One night about half a-past two.
Said he'd close up his mug if I'd fill up his jug
With good Old Mountain Dew.
Yes, he called it that Old Mountain Dew,
Said those who refuse it are few,
So I closed up his mug when I filled up his jug
With good Old Mountain Dew.

The conductor said with a nod of his head,
"My wife she never knew
That I take my fun when out on my run,
So bring me a quart or two
Of that good Old Mountain Dew,"
For those who refuse it are few
But his wife said to me, you can bring me three
Before his train is due.

My attorney began to turn the lid on the can.
I knew then my case was lost.
Said his honor to me,
I'll set you free if you will pay the cost
For they call it that Old Mountain Dew
And those who refuse it are few.
But you acted the man when you took that stand
To swear what is so true.

MOUNTAIN DEW

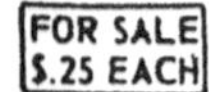

Words and music by SCOTT WISEMAN
and BASCOMB LAMAR LUNSFORD

2. Now the preacher drove by with his head h'isted high,
Said his wife had been down with the flu,
And he thought that I ought just to sell him a quart
Of that good old MOUNTAIN DEW.

3. Mister Roosevelt told them just how he felt
When he knew that the dry law was through.
"If your liquor's too red, it will swell up your head,
Better stick to your MOUNTAIN DEW."

4. Now if you are the sort who can relish a snort,
Here's a piece of advice that is true.
Get it straight from the hills where the moonshiner's stills
Make a drink called that MOUNTAIN DEW.

5. Now there's old Uncle Mort, he is sawed off and short,
He's just five feet and one inch or two,
But he thinks he's a giant when he gets him a pint
Of that good old MOUNTAIN DEW.

A word is in order about the Irish relative of "Old Mountain Dew." Some have suggested that Lunsford may have created his song from knowledge of an earlier Irish song. There is indeed an Irish song that uses the same term for moonshine:

Where the grasses grow and the waters flow
In a free and easy way,
Just give me enough of the rare old stuff
That flows by Galway Bay.
Come gowagers all from Donegal,
From Sligo and Ceitrim too.
Take off your coat and grease your throat
With the rare old mountain dew.[15]

Celtic authority Grady McWhiney, professor of history at Texas Christian University, believes that "mountain dew" as well as "moonshine" are terms of Irish origin. The Irish song has been documented as early as 1916.[16] Except for the term 'mountain dew' and the general idea, the words of the two songs are not similar and neither are the tunes. It is possible that Lunsford heard the Irish song before composing his. It is more likely, however, that he was familiar with the Irish term for liquor and used it in his song. Perhaps others can speculate further.

He composed another song dealing with moonshining, "Nol Pros Nellie." "This is a parody," he explained, "of the beautiful old folk song "Nellie Gray" that we all love so well. I apologize for having made the parody. I'm rather opposed to parodies, using the well-loved themes." "Nol-Pros" is a legal term meaning that the charges in a court case are not going to be pressed. In Lunsford's song, Nellie is a moonshiner who has fled the law. Unable to locate her, the authorities will just have "to file a nol pros." He recorded "Nol Pros Nellie" for Brunswick Records in 1928.[17]

Anne Beard, in her thesis on Lunsford, lists four other songs as Lunsford compositions: "Doggett's Gap," "Bill Ormand," "Booth" and "I'm Going Away." However, in the Columbia University recordings Lunsford does not claim authorship for any of the four, although his comments leave open the possibility that he may have written or supplied verses to some of them. Anne Beard had access to Lunsford's notebooks, lost in the mails between her and Lunsford, to his great dismay, and it could be that she based her claim on evidence that is no longer available.

Of "Doggett's Gap" he said, "The tune is part of the well-known tune of "Cumberland Gap" which dates back, of course. I got a text of this song about 1926." Here he seems to refer to "Doggett's Gap," but he could mean that he got a text of "Cumberland Gap" in 1926. He describes Doggett's Gap as being 10 miles from his home, and elsewhere he said it was directly above Cross Rock School, his first teaching assignment.

He said "Booth" was from an old fiddle tune. "I heard my father hum it and sing a few stanzas when I was a boy about 6 or 10 years old." He sang two versions of it in the Columbia recordings, describing the second as a more modern text. "This is the fiddle tune of Booth, and the words Mr. [W.J.] Morgan gave me, of Transylvania. He gave me many ballads." This statement implies that it was just another song in the oral tradition. "Booth" was one of four songs he sang about the assassination of presidents.

"Bill Ormand," Lunsford explained, "is based on a tragedy that occurred in the Piedmont section of North Carolina in about 1924 or 1925." He recorded this song in 1925 for R.W. Gordon, to the tune of "Jack O' Diamonds." He does not however, explain how he came to be singing it so soon after the tragedy occurred.

Of "I'm Going Away," he said only, "This is the only set of words I've ever heard to "Cacklin' Hen" [the fiddle tune]." Although the Columbia recording is so distorted that the words are hard to distinguish, it appears to be a humorous song with unconnected verses:

I'm a goin' away never for to stay,
If I don't go away the devil'll be to pay.
Cacklin' hen laid in a loft
Soon's she'd laid couldn't get her off.

It is interesting that these four songs which Beard attributed to Lunsford are not found in several standard collections of American songs. This may indicate that Lunsford did indeed have a hand in their composition.

In 1928, an opportunity came along that brought Bascom's former efforts into focus. He was asked to present a program of folk dances and music as a part of the Rhododendron Festival which was to be organized by the Asheville Chamber of Commerce to call attention to "The Land of the Sky." The Chamber had been searching for a tourist-oriented idea to promote Asheville since the early 20s. The festival was scheduled for June to coincide with the celebrated flowering of the rhododendron on surrounding ridges. A great publicity campaign was announced in the April 9 issue of *The Asheville Citizen*. The president and other prominent persons were to be invited. Many clubs and organizations were in support of the effort. Railroads were inveigled to set special rates for travelers, and businesses called attention to the festival in their advertisements. Fifteen states were to send young women to represent them at balls and on floats and to vie for Rhododendron Queen. On May 27, the *Citizen* announced a full schedule including the crowning of the Rhododendron King and Queen, parades, pageants, water sports, a baby parade, a dog parade and folk songs and dances.[18] David Whisnant wrote in a critical analysis of the festival:

> For all of its spectacular success as a promotional scheme, the Rhododendron Festival must at least be seen as a product of the peculiar social and economic pathology of the late 1920s,imported like a gaudy souvenir shawl and thrown around a mountain version of Miami madness. Asheville was on the make and speculative subdivisions were springing up almost daily. Fantasies of instant wealth were the dominant preoccupation; pretension was the dominant style.[19]

"Miami madness" that Whisnant referred to was the boom and bust of Florida land and tourism promotion earlier in the 20s. The Asheville Chamber of Commerce was to hire Fred L. Weede, late of the Miami Chamber, to do for Asheville what he had attempted in Florida.[20]

Thomas Wolfe, novelist from Asheville,, described his town's growth from frontier village to tourist town in his *Look Homeward, Angel:*

> The town of Altamont [Asheville] had been settled soon after the Revolutionary War. It had been a convenient stopping-off place for cattle-drovers and farmers in their swing eastward from Tennessee to South Carolina. And, for several decades before the Civil War, it had enjoyed the summer patronage of fashionable people from Charleston and the plantations of the hot South. When Oliver first came to it, it had begun to get some reputation not only as a summer resort, but as a sanitarium for tuberculars. Several rich men from the North had established hunting lodges in the hills, and one of them [George Vanderbilt] had bought huge areas of mountain land and, with an army of imported architects, carpenters and masons, was planning the greatest country estate in America....
>
> But most of the population was still native, recruited from the hill and country people in the surrounding districts. They were Scotch-Irish mountaineers, rugged, provincial, intelligent, industrious.[21]

In 1900, the year Thomas Wolfe was born and about the time Bascom was completing his academy work and getting ready to attend Rutherford College, Asheville was a town of 15,000. By the time Wolfe was working on his first novel and Bascom had returned to Asheville, the town had grown into a city of 50,000. In his last novel, Wolfe described the latter times:

> The sleepy little mountain village in which he had grown up—for it had hardly been more than that then—was now changed almost beyond recognition. The very streets that he had known so well, and had remembered through the years in their early aspect of early afternoon emptiness and drowsy lethargy, were now foaming with life, crowded with expensive traffic, filled with new faces he had never seen before. Occasionally he saw somebody that he knew, and in the strangeness of it all they seemed to him like lights shining in the darkness of a lonely coast.
>
> But what he noticed chiefly—and once he observed it he began watching for it, and it was always there—was the look on people's faces. It puzzled him, frightened him, and when he tried to find a word to describe it, the only thing he could think of was—madness. The nervous, excited glitter in the eyes seemed to belong to nothing else but madness. The faces of natives and strangers alike appeared animated by some secret and unholy glee. And their bodies, as they darted, dodged and thrust their way along, seemed to have a kind of leaping energy as if some powerful drug was driving them on. They gave him the impression of an entire population that was drunk—drunk with an intoxication that never made them weary, dead or sodden, and which never wore off, but which incited them constantly to new efforts of leaping and thrusting exhuberance....
>
> The real estate men were everywhere....One could see them on the porches of houses, unfolding blueprints and prospectuses as they shouted enticements and promises of sudden wealth into the ears of deaf old women. Everyone was fair game to them.[22]

Wolfe wrote that the great enemy of the true American dream was "single selfishness and compulsive greed."[23] He was deeply troubled by what he saw happening to his town. There is no comparable record of Lunsford's feelings about the real estate boom and the boosting of the Land of the Sky as a tourist paradise. There are many clues about his feeling that the traditional culture must be preserved as people entered a new era of progress, and he was quick to use the vehicles of boosterism to further this cause of preservation. It is doubtful that he, a practical man if there ever was one, hesitated long when he was asked to assemble musicians and dancers for the Tuesday evening program of the Rhododendron Festival. Yet, he must have known the problems he faced in linking himself with a rather crass plan to create the semblance of substance mostly out of fantasy. Perhaps the craziness of the times made it all the more important for him to call attention to the genuineness of the rural folk culture when the future and fortunes of many people were based on paper and promises. Wolfe's character, George Webber, returns home to a boom town and meets a friend-turned salesman who describes what it was like:

> "Lord Lord." he said. "They've all gone clean out of heads here. . .Never saw anything like it in my life....Why they're all crazy as a loon." He exclaimed...."They're getting prices for property here that you couldn't get in New York."
>
> "Are they getting it?"
>
> "Well," he said with a falsetto laugh, "They get the first five hundred dollars....You pay the next five hundred thousand on time."
>
> "God!" he said. "I don't know....All you want, I reckon ....Forever!....It doesn't matter....You sell it next day for a million."
>
> "On time?"
>
> "That's it." he cried, laughing. "You make a half million just like that."
>
> "On time?"
>
> "You've got it!" said Sam.[24]

Actually the fires of real estate speculation had already consumed all of the easily-promised paper credit before the Rhododendron Festival came to fruition. Bascom himself had been badly burned by the real estate craziness. He commented that he had done well in his law practice in the middle twenties, earning several hundred dollar fees, but he acknowledged "the grave mistake of speculating in real estate." The slump in land values wiped him out.[25] The festival, and other schemes laid by the Chamber of Commerce, was an attempt to bring new fuel and to blow new life once again among the darkening embers. The boom was based on the hope that Asheville could be ballyhooed into the greatest tourist and summer-home center in eastern America. The area, including the magnificent Great Smokies to the west and the Blue Ridge with its towering Blacks and Craggies to the northeast, had long been touted as a healthful place for those with respiratory diseases and a low tolerance for hot weather. The task now was to re-double efforts to sell the Land of the Sky as a playground for the well-to-do and those who hoped, as most did in the twenties, to do better than they were doing. The festival plan was to get great numbers of tourists, as well as more people like the Vanderbilts and the Groveses (who had invested magnanimously), to come to the area early in the season when the mountains were at their freshest beauty. Despite the withering of the first rank growth toward prosperity, the boosters still preached an early age of prosperity and progress.

The progress they envisioned, however, had to be based on their natural assets, primarily of climate and scenery, but they knew that tourists did not travel great distances to see people and products just like those they saw all year. They knew too that the tourists would have read the local color novels and descriptive books that presented the Southern mountaineers as a quaint people, somehow set apart from their fellow Americans, engaged in tasks and pastimes that conjured pictures of antiquity. Those in the Chamber instinctively knew that the folk culture could be sold, and they dispatched employees to round up handicrafts, and they visited Bascom Lamar Lunsford, whose interest in folklore was well-known, to put together a song and dance show. Bascom must have listened guardedly, his mind at work on possibilities and pitfalls, but he agreed to the proposition, knowing it was a chance for him to show off some of the people he knew and admired to a ready-made audience, and of course, a chance to show what he could do.

The Asheville Citizen referred to Lunsford's part of the festival as "folk songs and dances" and as a "mountain folk song and dance festival." It was put together by a committee, including Bascom, but it seems clear that it was his show.[26] *The Asheville Citizen* of Tuesday, June 6, announced "Two Big Events to Feature Tonight Dance Festival on Pack Square, Flower Pageant at Stadium," and went on to describe the events:

> The mountain folk song and dance festival on Pack Square at 6:30 o'clock this evening and the Rhododendron Pageant at Memorial Stadium at 8:00 o'clock this evening will be major features of the Rhododendron Festival today.
>
> Five dancing clubs from Western North Carolina will compete on the platform on the Square. There will be $100.00 in prizes awarded the dancing club winners and $100.00 for the winners in string bands. Old fashioned songs and dances of the mountains will be given in the program which is being directed by Bascom Lamar Lunsford.[27]

The *Citizen* announced the next morning that five thousand people had attended the program on Pack Square, crowded around the dance platform, clustered on the monument to Zebulon Vance, North Carolina governor, senator and Confederate general, hung from office windows on the square, shouting appreciation for the music the *Citizen* called a "throwback from the modern jazz mad world." The newspaper went on to say that the scene suggested "a permanent thing, something that might be continued from year to year as a festival of Western North Carolina—on the order of the great festivals of older nations which have been handed down from generation to generation."[28]

Perhaps this idea of the festival as a permanent thing took root in Bascom's head and set his resolve toward building a permanent festival, or it could be that

Bascom had planted the notion in the writer's head. Although it appears that the Chamber of Commerce took the initiative in the folk dance and song part of the wider festival, it is clear that Bascom liked what happened and saw the value of it, perhaps especially in contrast to much of the rest of the festival which had to do with kings and queens and castles—make-believe pageantry in the cause of commercial interests.

Lunsford organized a dance and music program for the 1929 Rhododendron Festival, again on Pack Square in June. However, in 1930 the Mountain Dance and Folk Festival, as Lunsford now called it, was separated from the Rhododendron Festival and was moved to a later date. The *Citizen* of July 27, 1930, announced:

> *MOUNTAIN SONGS, DANCES WILL DRAW VISITORS HERE*
>
> The 1930 presentation of mountain songs and dances will be staged July 29 and 30....at McCormic Field in Asheville....More than 200 mountain dancers and musicians from Western North Carolina will take part....Bascom Lamar Lunsford, widely known collector of mountain ballads and mountain dance customs, has charge of the organization of the mountain folk dances this year.

Boom and bust had come to Asheville, even earlier than it had to the rest of the country. Speculators in the mountain city, including Bascom, had lost their shirts, and the dreams of prosperity were dimmed by the crash of 1929. The Chamber of Commerce kept the Rhododendron Festival going through the 1930s, but events were dropped from year to year and the festival was discontinued during World War II. Efforts to revive it in 1946 were unsuccessful. Lunsford's Mountain Dance and Folk Festival, on the other hand, grew and gained strength. Perhaps the bursting bubble of 1929 emphasized in the minds of many people the difference between that which is long-standing and genuine in tradition and that which is manufactured and imposed as a substitute for tradition.

Although Lunsford was never led too far away from his "calling," he was diverted from his pursuits from time to time, for example, into politics. His work with the Democratic Party organization in McDowell County to get a sheriff and other officials elected made his name known to Democratic leaders in Western North Carolina and in Raleigh. In 1920, '22, '24, he managed the successful campaigns of Zebulon Weaver for re-election to the U.S. House of Representatives. Weaver served the Tenth District (which Bascom later celebrated in his humorous mock speech, "A Stump Speech in the Tenth District") from 1917 to 1929, the Eleventh from 1931 to 1933 and the Twelfth District from 1943 to 1947. he was a strong supporter of Western North Carolina interests, including the Great Smoky Mountains National Park, the Blue Ridge Parkway and the Tennessee Valley Authority.[29]

In 1924, Bascom managed the unsuccessful primary campaign of Josiah W. Bailey for the governorship. Bailey had studied law at Trinity and under Samuel Fox Mordecai, with whom Bascom also had studied. Bailey had been a kingpin in the U.S. Senator Furnifold McClendel Simmons' political machine that had controlled the Democratic Party in North Carolina since 1912, but he broke with Simmons in 1921 over the senator's absolute control of the party. In 1928, he and Simmons were bitter antagonists in the candidacy of Al Smith for President. Simmons, a strict prohibitionist, refused to support Smith because of his call for the repeal of the Eighteenth Amendment. Bailey supported Smith, but the Republicans carried North Carolina for the first time since the election of Ulysses S. Grant in 1872. In 1920, he beat Simmons in the primary by accusing him of abandoning the party. He was elected to the Senate by the largest majority ever recorded in a Senate race in North Carolina. Although he supported Franklin Roosevelt for president, he was one of the major antagonists of New Deal Programs. He was also opposed to anti-lynch laws, hour and wage legislation and was a staunch isolationist until 1941.[30]

Perhaps Lunsford's own politics are evident in the interests of the men whom he promoted for office. He would have liked Weaver's efforts on behalf of Western North Carolina. Bailey's conservatism on social issues was more extreme than Lunsford's but it is likely that they shared many attitudes and values.

From 1931 to 1934, Lunsford served as reading clerk of the House of Representatives in Raleigh. "In bed one night," he said, "I lay on one side and nominated myself for the office of reading clerk of the state legislature. I turned over on the other side and accepted the nomination." There was more to it than that, but however it came about, he was nominated by the Democratic caucus held in Raleigh and was elected by the legislature. He soon became a focus of controversy. His opponents said he did not read distinctly, which cut to the quick since Lunsford prided himself as a public speaker.

Sam J. Ervin Jr. from Morganton, Democratic Floor Leader in the House in 1931 and later N.C. Supreme Court Justice and U.S. Senator, relates both the humor and the hurt of this incident in Lunsford's life:

> On the evening before the formal opening of the General Assembly of 1931, the Democrats of the House met in caucus in the House chamber and nominated their candidates for major House offices.
>
> After two residents of Wake County had been nominated for the post, I placed the name of a third candidate in nomination for the office of reading clerk. He was Bascom Lamar Lunsford, of Buncombe County, who in after years rightly received nationwide acclaim as one of America's foremost collectors and preservers of folk ballads and folk music.
>
> "Fellow Democrats," I said, "we have thus far exercised political wisdom in selecting our candidates... In naming our candidate for reading clerk, we must not forget the Democrats residing in the west. Like the Democrats of other areas, they are troubled by the world, the flesh, and the devil. Unlike the Democrats of many other areas, however, they are compelled to wage unceasing warfare with other foes, the Republican neighbors."
>
> Pointing to the portrait of Zeb Vance, North Carolina's most beloved son of all time, which was hanging on the wall of the House chamber, I closed with these words: "I place in nomination as our candidate for reading clerk a Democrat who resides in Zeb Vance's country of Buncombe, Bascom Lamar Lunsford."

Lunsford won the nomination. Next day he was elected reading clerk.

Lunsford was handicapped in the performance of his duties as reading clerk by a slight inablity to pronounce correctly words unfamiliar to him. For example, he always pronounced *chiropractor* "ki-row-prax-ker."

Some of the House members, who were outstanding linguists and who esteemed the capacity to pronounce words with precision an indispensable qualification for reading clerk, became inordinately dissatisfied with Lunsford's deficiency and began to proclaim that the House had a reading clerk who could not read.

A delegation of them visited me. They said I was responsible for Lunsford being reading clerk, and they importuned me to persuade him to resign and accept another position with the House. They promised that he would be given a larger salary in the other position if he would do so.

When I communicated their wishes to him, Lunsford declared, "I was elected reading clerk, and I'm going to read."

On being thus rebuffed by Lunsford, the linguists presented to the House a resolution which asserted that the office of reading clerk was vacant and directed the House to proceed to elect an occupant for it.

When the resolution came up for House action, the linguists criticized Lunsford without mercy for his lapses in pronunciation and urged their colleagues to approve the resolution. With the endurance of a stoic, Lunsford sat in his seat in front of the speaker's dais throughout the proceedings and endured the vituperation in silence....One of the representatives most distressed by Lunsford's inadequacy was Union L. Spence, a perfectionist of Moore County, who was chairman of the Committee on Finance and one of the House's ablest members. He was the only member of the House who pronounced the word *finance* as 'fin-nance.' Representative Spence had made a somewhat bitter speech in favor of the resolution.

When I spoke, I told the House I opposed the resolution for two reasons. In the first place, I said the resolution alleges that the office of reading clerk is vacant. Pointing to Lunsford, I added, "That allegation is false. We have a reading clerk. He is sitting in his seat in front of the speaker's dais ready to perform his duty and read this resolution to the House as soon as the talking stops.

"My second reason for opposing the resolution arises out of my concern for my beloved friend, the gentleman from Moore. If the seats of all those in this chamber who pronounce "fin-ance" as if it were "fi-nance" should be declared to be vacant, all of the legislative burdens of the House would fall upon the gentleman from Moore. Although his shoulders are big and strong, I do not believe he ought to be compelled to carry such heavy burdens alone."

When the battle ended, the House overwhelmingly defeated the resolution and retained the reading clerk who allegedly could not read. Lunsford ameliorated the grief of the linguists somewhat in the future days by permitting his assistant, Phil Whitley, to read to the House the most complicated bills and resolutions.[31]

The controversy was precipitated, according to Lunsford, by his action in regard to a bill that was introduced by a lawmaker from a county where Lunsford had lived. The bill aimed to abolish the office of treasurer in the county and turn the county's financial business over to the legislator's father-in-law, a banker. Since the treasurer was a friend of Lunsford's, he sent a copy of the bill to him. When the legislator returned to the county on a weekend, the treasurer brandished the copy in his face. The legislator then rallied support for dismissal of Lunsford as a reading clerk. Some tried to get Lunsford to resign, but he refused. While Sam Ervin supported Lunsford, the speaker did not, and appointed several of Lunsford's supporters to attend a funeral on the afternoon the bill was to be debated and voted on. They stayed, however, to debate the bill. The arguments culminated with praise for Lunsford from Luther Hamilton, who later became a prominent North Carolina judge: "Lunsford, as I've said many times, is the best reading clerk that I've ever heard, and I've heard those in the U.S. House and Senate, but since I found out that he'll stick to his friends, I think more of him than I ever did."

The bill was defeated soundly, as was the bill that Lunsford alleged was the cause of the trouble, and Lunsford stayed on until the end of the session. At a final gathering, he was honored with the gift of a pen and pencil set from members of the House. He made a short speech about how it had looked for a time as if he wouldn't be around for the party, and then he quoted from one of his favorite poets, Joaquin Miller, lines he quoted often in extolling the human spirit:

Great is the man with sword undrawn,
And good is the man who refrains from wine;
But the man who fails and then fights on,
Lo, he is a twin born brother of mine.

As he said, "They gave me a great ovation. They just hollered. They had my picture in the paper—and said I had more influence than a governor." However, he did not seek the job again.[32]

In the late twenties a distinguished classical musician took notice of Lunsford's work. He was Lamar Stringfield, who had grown up at Mars Hill where Lunsford was born. A nationally recognized flutist, composer, and conductor, Stringfield's interest in folk music grew from his boyhood in Madison County, North Carolina. In 1928, he won a Pulitzer award for an orchestral suite, "From the Southern Mountains," and went on to write other works based on Appalachian folk music, including "The Legend of John Henry," "Moods of a Moonshiner," "From the Blue Ridge Mountains" and "The Mountain Song." He helped to found the North Carolina Symphony Orchestra and was its first conductor before moving on to conduct the Knoxville and Charlotte symphonies and the Radio City Music Hall orchestra.

Stringfield collaborated with Lunsford in a collection of ballads and other folk songs, published as *30 and 1 Folk Songs from the Southern Mountains*(Carl Fischer, Inc., 1929). Stringfield did the musical arrangements and notes from Lunsford's singing and playing of the songs. Lunsford's introduction and notes, as well as the selections, show his keen awareness of the value and the quantity of the traditional music available and the great problem in selecting 31 songs from the wealth of songs and their many variants that he knew.

Lunsford did not say much about his collaboration with Springfield, and so we can only speculate why he was drawn to it. Stringfield, when he was conductor of the North Carolina Symphony Orchestra, used Asheville as a summer rehearsal location. He was a colorful figure, and he was no doubt treated as an important cultural figure. Lunsford would have been flattered at Stringfield's interest in him and collaboration on the book of songs. Since Stringfield was from the mountains and was using folk material in his compositions, he and Bascom would have had a lot in common and each would have been valuable to the other. Lunsford, undoubtedly, saw an opportunity to do something important, and he knew that Stringfield's name would help in getting the book published and publicized and that the book would present him as a knowledgeable collector, rather than just a performer and festival promoter.

Another important scholarly contact for Lunsford was Dr. Dorothy Scarborough, professor of English at Columbia University, who came to the Blue Ridge Mountains in 1930 to collect folk songs and ballads. She was an essayist, novelist, short story writer and critic, but she, like Lunsford, had been bitten by the folklore bug and was ever on the trail of songs and ballads. She spent August of that year in Western North Carolina, with Asheville as her headquarters. "Before I unpacked my bags," she wrote, "I started in search of Bascom Lamar Lunsford, the folk-song enthusiast of Western North Carolina, the man who is doing more than any one else in the region to bring people to realize the interest and value of the native folk arts, singing, fiddle-playing, dancing, and so forth." She described him as, "a man in his forties, with boyish, open countenance, springy step, and in his eye that light of insanity which denotes the folklorist." She went on to describe him as "a sympathetic spirit, who would not jeer at me for spending my vacation in the arduous work of collecting old songs when I might have loafed." Lunsford offered his help, explaining that his law practice was slack in the summertime, "though with a twinkle in his eye he admitted that he was more active in the pursuit of folklore than of the law," Scarborough noted.

Lunsford was ready to take her to his best sources, though Scarborough protested that she did not wish to encroach on his sources or his songs, which she felt he should save for his own publication. After much wrangling, Lunsford agreed to accept a modest fee to cover expenses and some of his time, and they were off with a dictaphone and typewriter. Scarborough described his approach to a possible singer's house,announcing himself as "Bascom Lamar Lunsford from South Turkey Creek." Most people who did not already know him had heard of him, and they were welcomed.

The collection which Scarborough made in her journeys in the Blue Ridge was published as *A Song Catcher in the Southern Mountain* (Columbia University Press, 1935), in which she wrote several pages about her experiences with Lunsford in the areas around Asheville. They learned much from each other that August of 1930. It was Scarborough who later introduced Lunsford to Dr. George W. Hibbitt of the Columbia University Library. This contact in turn led to the 1935 recording of some 315 "memory collection" songs by Lunsford.

It is not clear just when Lunsford first met Dr. Frank C. Brown, the renowned North Carolina folklorist, for whom the monumental seven-volume *North*

Carolina Folklore was named, and to whom Lunsford contributed songs in 1922, or thereabouts. There is no record that Lunsford knew Brown at Trinity College while he was studying law there and Dr. Brown was teaching English. A fervent folklorist who founded the North Carolina Folklore Society (1913), of which Lunsford later became president, Brown had scoured the North Carolina hills for years in search of songs and other folk material. Lunsford mentions many contacts with Brown and the North Carolina Folklore Society, through which he also became acquainted with other folklorists, such as Dr. Arthur Palmer Hudson of the University of North Carolina. Lunsford was to be the co-recipient of the first Brown-Hudson Award, established by the Society in honor of these scholars.

Another important national folklore contact of Lunsford's was Sarah Gertrude Knott, founder and for many years director of the National Folk Festival. Knott, a Kentucky native, was no doubt influenced greatly by Lunsford. She attended the Mountain Dance and Folk Festival in 1934 and launched the National Folk Festival in St. Louis the following year. Although Knott was dependent on Lunsford (she said that she could not have done the National Folk Festival without his help),[33] she nevertheless brought him into contact with folk enthusiasts and scholars from all over the country (such as George and Rae Korson, B.A.Botkin, W.C. Handy, and George Pullen Jackson) and thus broadened his horizons.

By the early thirties, he was nationally known and was invited to speak, perform and present musicians and dancers to groups in many parts of the country. He was an apt student in all situations, learning from every experience, place and person. He was to a great extent a self-taught folklorist, but he had many great teachers from whom he learned many things that might not otherwise have occurred to him. But Bascom also knew a passel of things that his colleagues had not learned in universities so they taught one another.

NOTES

1. Harold H. Martin, "Minstrel Man of the Appalachians," *Saturday Evening Post*, Vol. 220, No 47, (May 22, 1948).

2. Author interview with Bascom Lamar Lunsford, West Asheville, N.C.., 7-27-71.

3. Anne Winsmore Beard, *The Personal Folk Song Collection of Bascom Lamar Lunsford*, unpublished master's thesis (Oxford, Ohio: Miami University), 1959, p. 11.

4. Newman Ivey White, gen. ed., *The Frank C. Brown Collection of North Carolina Folklore*, 7 vols. (Durham: Duke University Press), 1952-57.

5. Beard, *op. cit.*, pp. 23-24; Letter from Debora Kodish, 7-8-81.

6. John Angus McLeod, *Minstrel of the Appalachians*, unpublished biography of Lunsford in the Mars Hill College Library, 1973, p. 26.

7. Letter from Scott Wiseman, 12-3-73.

8. For more on Peer and Brockman see Bill C. Malone, *Country Music, U.S.A.* (Austin: University of Texas Press), 1968, Chapt. 2.

9. Beard, *op. cit.*, p. 22.

10. Martin, *op cit.*

11. For printed versions, see B.A. Botkin, *A Treasury of Southern Folklore* (New York: Crown Publishers), 1949, pp. 112-14, 250.

12. Letter from Fred Stanley, February 1974.

13. Interview with Lunsford, 7-27-71.

14. Wiseman letter.

15. From the singing of Tom O'Carroll, Dublin native, now a resident of Newburyport, Massachusetts.

16. Interviews with Tom O'Carroll and Grady McWhiney inRock Hill, South Carolina,November 19, 1983. Colm O Lochlainn includes a version called "That Real Old Mountain Dew" in his *Irish Street Ballads* (New York: Citadel Press, 1935), pp. 128-29, and notes that he first heard the song at "a meeting of newly released political prisoners in December, 1916." Other versions can be found in John A. and Alan Lomax's *American Ballads and Folk Songs* (New York: McMillan, 1934), pp. 180-82; *Sing Out*, Vol. 10, No. 4 (Dec. - Jan., 1960-61), p. 21; and in *The Clancy Brothers and Tommy Makem Song Book* (New York: Tiparm Music Publishers, 1964), p. 28. The Clancy Brothers and Tommy Makem also recorded the song on *Irish Folk Airs* (Tradition 2083) and *Irish Drinking Songs* (Tradition 2092).

17. Columbia University Recordings of Lunsford, 1935.

18. David Whisnant, 'Finding the Way Between the Old and the New: The Mountain Dance and Folk Festival and Bascom Lamar Lunsford's Work as a Citizen," *Appalachian Journal*, Vol. 7, No. 1-2 (Autumn-Winter 1979-80), pp. 136-137; *Asheville Citizen*, April 9 and May 27, 1928.

19. Whisnant, *op. cit.*, p. 137.

20. *Ibid.*, p. 127.

21. Thomas Wolfe, *Look Homeward, Angel* (New York: Charles Scribner's Sons), 1929, pp. 6-7.

22. Thomas Wolfe, *You Can't Go Home Again* (New York: Harper Brothers), 1940, pp. 109-10.

23. *Ibid.*, pp. 741-43.

24. *Ibid.*, pp. 112-13.

25. Martin, *op. cit.*

26. Whisnant, *op cit.*, p. 138.

27. *Asheville Citizen*, 6-6-28.

28. Whisnant, *op cit.*, p. 139.

29. McLeod, *op cit.*, p. 13; *New York Times.*, 10-30-48. p. 15.

30. McLeod, *op cit.*, p. 13; *New York Times*, 10-30-48, p. 23.

31. Sam J. Ervin, Jr. *Humor of a Country Lawyer* (Chapel Hill: University of North Carolina Press) 1983, pp. 132-35.

32. Interview with Lunsford, 7-21-71.

33. Interview with Sarah Gertrude Knott, Berea, Kentucky, 12-29-73.

CHAPTER 4

Fulfillment

The Mountain Dance and Folk Festival, and similar programs which Lunsford arranged, became his leading and consuming interest for the rest of his life. The festival was not just a program that he organized by writing a few letters and then managed as master of ceremonies. He worked at the festival the year round, always on the lookout for additional authentic talent. He scoured the mountains of Western North Carolina in a successsion of battered Nashes and Hudsons, driving absent-mindedly, perhaps with his mind on more important things, until stories of his driving mishaps became as well-known as his singing. One performer claimed Bascom mowed down all the mailboxes for a quarter of a mile on a country road.

Lunsford approached mountain musicians in a dignified way, assuming their own sense of dignity and their understanding of the value of their musical talents and repertories. He claimed, "The key to whatever success I've had has been in recognizing the value of the fine traditions of mountain people." One contact would usually lead to another. As Lunsford put it, "They'll say you ought to go see so and so. He knows so and so. Go see him. He's the funniest guy you ever saw." So he would clatter off to look up the suggested person to find out if he had something to offer the festival. If he was not yet ready for the festival, Lunsford might make suggestions for improvement, or he might help him get a better musical instrument. "I've lived this thing," he said of the festival, "I've met myself coming back."

"Knowing the proper approach has helped me a whole lot," he commented. "Knowing how the other man thinks about things and knowing what to depend on is important. In a festival you get as much good in as you can and keep as much bad out as you can. We keep it as genuine as we can. I find a fellow from the country that sings a song we want. We invite him to come and sing it. We may let him also sing something he wants to sing. We may or may not like it, but that's all right."

"In the very beginning," he wrote later, "ballad singers, fiddlers, mountain dancers, old and young, came from the Valley of the Cheoah, Laurel River, Bear Wallow, Watauga River, Soco Gap, Oconalufty River, Sandymush, Rabbitham and South Turkey Creek, or some 20 other mountain counties or communities where the old ballads have been sung at their best for years, where group dancing based on older figures movements, and childhood games and singing games, all spirited and moving, were never talked out by a sophisticated society as had been done elsewhere." He felt that the festival ought to be like a smorgasbord with something for everyone. He made sure that there was variety—fiddlers, pickers, harmonica players, singers, string bands, buck dancers, dancing groups and so on. But he had tested their quality before they came. He told of reading the Bible about separating the wheat from the chaff, "and that's what I've been trying to do with the festival. There ain't a performer here that won't entertain you."[1] Walter Parham described Lunsford as "one of the most intelligent talent hunters that's ever been in my time. He had a wonderful, wonderful memory. He could sing ballads I've never heard myself. He was a go-getter when it came to folk music, and when he got it he knew what to do with it."[2]

Other performers at past festivals admired Lunsford's skill in programming the different performers. He refused to print a program or to give a starting time for the program. "Along about sundown" was his time for starting, and that is as exact as he would get. He confessed that he liked slogans that stuck in people's minds, such as his for the starting time. But he had another reason for this impreciseness. Because he always liked to give young and inexperienced talent a chance, he would put them on first while the crowd was settling into the auditorium, rather than when the festival was fully under way. Also, he frequently put persons on early who were not quite what he wanted in his prime time, but whom he still wanted to perform. Because he had no exact starting time, performers could not later accuse him of having put them on before the festival actually began.

Mountain musicians attending the National Folk Festival with Lunsford (courtesy of Lunsford Collection, Mars Hill College)

"For forty-six years I've never had a written program," he said in 1972. "I knew the people, and knew what they played, knew how well they did it. The people are my program." He simply gave the nod to the right person at the appropriate moment. As Walter Parham said, "He knew when the program was dragging, and he had just the right person or group in mind to stir up the audience. He could keep about three groups ahead in his mind." Lunsford made it sound easy: "I'd go over and sit back stage and talk to my friends. I'd go out on stage just a little, to give it color."

No doubt he looked casual, but he always knew who was performing, how well the audience was responding, and he was thinking ahead for the most appropriate person to go on next. Jean Earnhardt described the scene in the Greensboro *Daily News*: "The performers gossip in the wings, swap tunes and wait for Lunsford to nod. The stage is not bare and cold. It is filled with chairs to seat performers, their families and friends....Lunsford shuffles his people on and off with unfailing intuition for what ought to come next....At the Asheville Auditorium there is a constant coming and going and spontaneous enthusiasm...no sharp division between listener and performer."[3]

The festival usually has been held the first Thursday, Friday and Saturday evenings in August since 1928. Since Asheville is a tourist town the festival soon became an important event to attract tourists from other states, as well as mountain people. Thus the festival became important to the Chamber of Commerce and its affiliated businesses. Since it runs from Thursday evening through Saturday evening, many people are in town for several days, staying in local hotels and motels and spending money in various establishments. Lunsford was not very much interested in the economic benefits of the festival, although he understood and appreciated the reasons the Chamber of Commerce was willing to back the venture. What he wanted was an audience to whom he could present the best of Appalachian culture. "My business was to draw attention to the fine cultural value of our traditional music and our dancing and the fine honor of our people. I was trying to perpetuate the real, true cultural worth of the mountain people. Our section, you know, has been slandered. People had the notion that it was somehow inferior. Now, they've turned around and found there might be something in it."

Having attracted the audience, Lunsford felt a real responsibility, not just to educate them, but to entertain them. "It is an entertainment....so far as I am concerned," he said, in response to those who criticized him for making music and dance a spectator event rather than a participatory event. Some folklorists and recreation people chided him for having competition rather than just having people sing and dance for enjoyment. There were those who felt that there should also be "audience participation," that folk music and dance should be a sharing experience and not a show. Lunsford rejected these arguments, so far as his festivals were concerned. He said, "When I am endeavoring to present the finest of our traditional American cultures to an audience with one of my own

Poster for Mountain Dance and Folk Festival
(courtesy of Lunsford Collection, Mars Hill College)

The traditional opening of the festival for many years:
Marcus Martin, Bill McElreath, and Aunt Samantha Bumgarner
(courtesy of Lunsford Collection, Mars Hill College)

Bascom leading the Festival square dancing
(courtesy of Lunsford Collection, Mars Hill College)

Cas Wallin and Rilla Ray (photo by Bob Lindsey, courtesy of Berea College Southern Appalachian Archives)

groups or even with a newly organized group, I can't see any place for a bunch of irresponsibles to come in to break into the continuity of the message I am trying to give." His response was over-drawn, but he had a point. The festival audiences were so large that they could not be meaningfully involved in either the singing or the dancing. "Now as to a dance, whether it be in a one-room cabin in the mountain coves or....in New York, the responsibility is on the promoter to please the patrons." He was especially critical of those who attempted to present authentic cultural programs in noisy auditoriums to large audiences attempting to participate, because he felt that the authentic qualities were lost as the uninitiated attempted to participate and the managers lost control of the program.

Opening night at the Festival
(courtesy of Lunsford Collection, Mars Hill College)

Bill McElreath and Rilla Ray demonstrate clog steps at the Festival
(courtesy of Berea College Southern Appalachian Archives)

This wish to entertain, no doubt, made Lunsford vulnerable to innovations away from traditional styles. While he steadfastly tried to hold the line on anything that he felt lacked authenticity, he had many pressures to include some modern "improvements," for example, clog steps in the regular figures of the square dance. The buck and clog-dance steps are without doubt traditional to the mountains. However, they were ordinarily individual expressions of exuberance, a lively response to the music. The usual step for mountain square dancing was the running step which had fascinated Cecil Sharp. A dancer might individually clog to the music, or break into a clog-step while running the sets, but in the old dances he did not continually clog. Probably because of the competitive element in the Mountain Dance and Folk Festival, some groups began using the clog-step, sometimes called the "hoedown," "flat-foot" or "double shuffle," as the standard step in the dance. There are many variations on this basic step, but one characteristic is that the dancer stomps with the heel or the flat of the foot rather than dancing on the toes. This step makes a great deal of noise when all of the dancers are in step. In order to get more sound , heel and toe taps were sometimes added. Colorful costumes also crept in. At the same time, a few electrically amplified instruments were introduced, partially, no doubt, so that the music could be heard over the clog noise.

However, after a time, both shoe taps and electric instruments were banned at the festival. The ban on amplified instruments was enforced; the one on toe and heel taps was not. In reference to electronic instruments, festival chairman Jerry Israel said, "We want musicians, not electricians." The banning of amplifiers was possibly an attempt to get back to more traditional forms, which was also part of the motivation for doing away with shoe taps. However, one judge commented that the banning of taps was mainly to cut down on noise so that dancers and spectators could hear the music.

The dance teams were always a popular and colorful part of the festival. Lunsford set the size of the dance teams at eight couples to give the best effect. Fewer couples, he thought, do not make a good symmetrical appearance, and more couples are too crowded on the platform.

Slick commercial costumes were not encouraged, especially big hats or western outfits. "We are mountain people," Lunsford said. "And we want to present ourselves and our heritage in a manner that is in keeping with the dignity of our forebears. Just wear the best you've got and be proud." However, coordinated dance costumes gradually became a part of most dance teams.

Groups were expected to bring their own string bands along, but there was usually a house band or plenty of other musicians to provide music if this was not possible. Eventually, local businessmen and corporations began to sponsor dance groups, but they were not allowed to use their company names. The groups had to be named after a community.

At the festival there was competition between the dance groups as well as between individuals and bands. Lunsford maintained that his purpose was never to standardize folk expression. "We try to get laymen, also mountaineers, also people of some prominence as judges, yet who have at some time in their lives attended the old mountain dances," he said. Lunsford depended on the competition to lure the dance groups and the musicians because he could not pay each one for performing. He paid a few of his tried and true performers a small amount, however, to insure a basic core of good traditional musicians. This caused hard feelings among those who were not paid.

The competition was felt keenly among those in the audience, who cheered favorite performers. The spirit of competition also led to occasional unpleasantness—arguments, or even fights, between members of the dance teams. According to Harold Martin in the *Saturday Evening Post,* Sam Queen, leader of the Soco Gap team, was attacked by a knife-wielding member of his own team because he had asked the man's sweetheart to be his dancing partner. Another young man who had been left off of the team set upon Queen, threatening to shoot him. "Sam knocked him backward off the platform, signaled the fiddlers....and sent the team whirling," Martin wrote.[4] Artus and Mabel Moser reported that Artus was threatened by a losing dance leader when they served as judges.

Lunsford himself was involved in a few unpleasant incidents: Martin wrote that some losers in the contests tried to take their disappointment out of his hide. "Bascom discouraged this by wearing a heavy ring on his hand, like a pair of knucks, when he sensed that trouble was afoot, and by keeping a wary eye on those who approached him in hot blood." Nor was it always festival participants who caused trouble. When the festival was young, a radio station in Asheville wanted to broadcast the program. Lunsford worked out an agreement by which he understood that the advertising during breaks would be done from the radio station. However, when the festival opened, a station announcer appeared on stage to read the advertisements. Lunsford refused to let the announcer read them. A struggle ensued in which the announcer broke Mr. Lunsford's glasses, and Lunsford laid the announcer out with a banjo. This ended the encroachment of the radio station on the festival.[5]

Some festival participants were rough, ready and sometimes rowdy mountain men. Lunsford had problems with those who "made too many trips out to the saddlebags," as the old saying goes. "You have to choose people you can depend on," he said. "You may have the finest musician in the world, but he may not be reliable. He may drink too much. You may have to choose somebody who's not as good a musician but who can be depended on." In spite of his care in choosing performers, however, a few were known for their fistfights in the joints along Asheville's Lexington Avenue. One of the festival's most talented and popular performers did time in the penitentiary for killing a man, according to some, after they had had a few drinks.

Lunsford also had problems in keeping the festival authentic. Although his sense of the appropriate was acute, his prejudices occasionally got in the way of

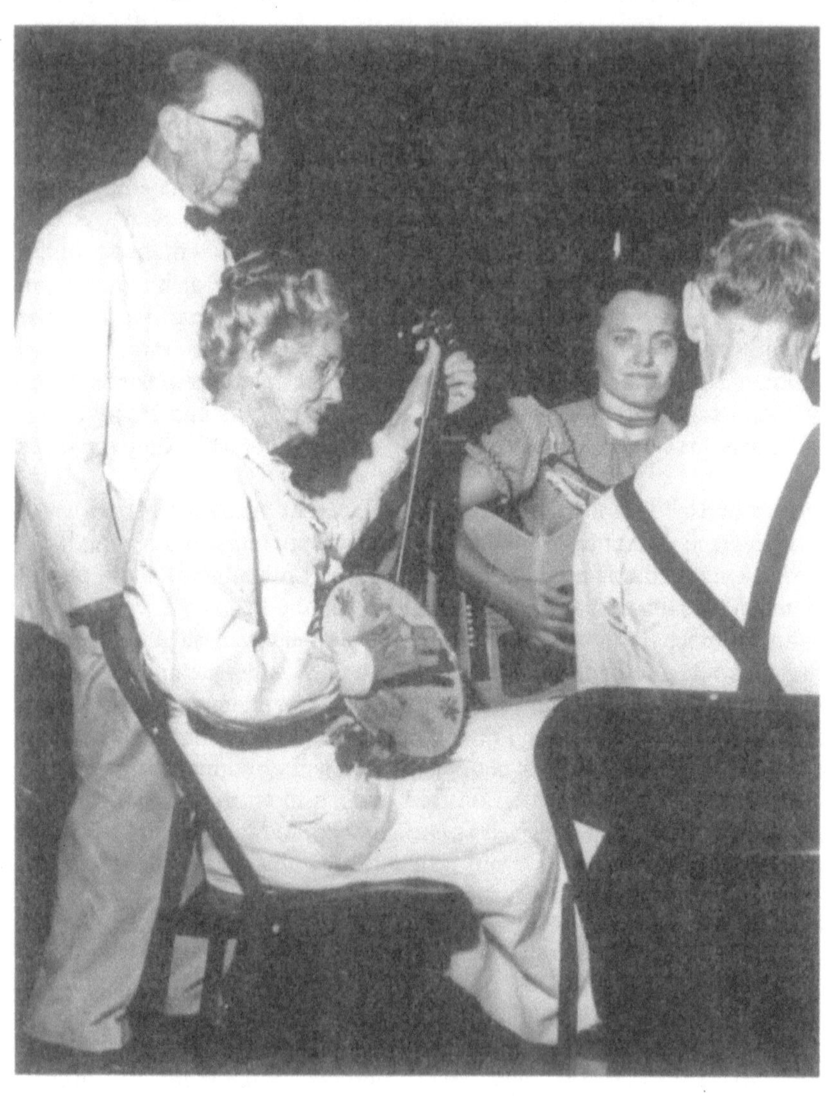

Bascom and Aunt Samantha Bumgarner
(courtesy of Lunsford Collection, Mars Hill College)

Bascom and the Burleson Sisters (courtesy of Lunsford Collection, Mars Hill College)

Sam Honeycutt, Bascom Lunsford, Bascom Hall, and G.P. Fisher (courtesy of Lunsford Collection, Mars Hill College)

Bascom receives the Burl Ives Award from Sarah Gertrude Knott (courtesy of Berea College Southern Appalachian Archive)

Dance team in the sixties (courtesy of Lunsford Collection, Mars Hill College)

Bascom dances with Lillie Lee Baker (courtesy of Lunsford Collection, Mars Hill College)

Bascom introduces Pleaz Mobley, Kentucky ballad singer (courtesy of Berea College Southern Appalachian Archive)

Byard Ray and Obray Ramsey, master musicians from Madison County, North Carolina (courtesy of Berea College Southern Appalachian Archive)

his judgment. He had trouble understanding all of the young people from far-off places who came to the festival with their beards, long hair, and blue jeans. His distrust for them was probably heightened during the McCarthy era in the 1950s when many people in the nation were concerned about communists and when folk music and politics sometimes shared the same bed.

Roger Sprung, a New York banjo player and folk singer, was bodily thrown off the show by Lunsford, early in the 1950s. Some say it was because of the kind of music Sprung was playing, although Sprung sings traditional music and is a fine frailing-type banjo picker as well as a bluegrass picker. Others say it was because Sprung performed at the festival for many years, uninvited, by joining other groups as a means of getting on stage. No doubt Lunsford did not like a New York banjo picker in a festival that was primarily an Appalachian or a North Carolina show. Sprung thinks the trouble came after Jack Elliott, another outside folk singer, questioned Lunsford about his relationship with Sprung and Pete Seeger, who at the time was in a hassle with the House Committee on Un-American Activities. But he adds that it might merely have been his blue jeans and checked shirt that set Lunsford off. Sprung agreed that while Lunsford might have thought jeans were all right on mountain farmers, he resented them on middle-class performers. At any rate, according to Sprung, Bascom heaved him off the stage by the checked collar and the seat of the jeans. Sprung, who does Lunsford the high compliment of imitating his singing style, reports that he later repaired Bascom's banjo and received a near apology, "Sometimes people do things a little hastily." Also, Lunsford later went out of his way to compliment Sprung on the way he and his wife sang the songs they had gotten from him. Sprung has been an occasional performer at the festival for the more than 20 years since that incident.[6]

Lunsford worked for Charles Seeger, a political leftist, in the Music Program of the Farm Settlement Administration during the thirties, and he later cordially received his activist son Pete Seeger (who took up the five-string banjo as a result of Bascom's influence), but in the 1950s he was curt with Pete's brother Mike who asked to use some of his songs. This rejection of Mike indicates that he had become more suspicious of outsiders by this time, especially those he assumed had radical social notions. He, no doubt, feared the influence that they might have on his festival, on mountain music, and indeed on mountain life. He had a degree of paranoia about certain outsiders and was at times inhospitable to them. That Pete and Mike Seeger and Roger Sprung speak in complimentary terms of Lunsford and his contributions is as much to their credit as it is to Lunsford himself.

There were many others Lunsford asked not to come to the festival again, or more politely, simply did not invite again. For a while he would not have George Pegram on the festival. Pegram became so popular that the crowd would often break into chants of "We want George," and Pegram, somewhat heady over this popularity, might just come forward without Lunsford's nod. This was the sort of thing that Lunsford, creator and boss of the festival, would not tolerate. However, Pegram held an affection and respect for Lunsford.

The pre-show, on which Lunsford presented the less admired groups and individuals, sometimes got completely away from the purposes of the festival. Once, Walter Parham reported, Bascom Hall, who helped with the festival, allowed a young lady banjo picker on stage wearing a hula skirt. Lunsford, back stage, heard a strange sound coming from his stage and came suspiciously forward. In a visible show of wrath and with quivering jaw, he shook his finger at Hall across the stage, took the offender by the arm, and escorted her off the stage. "If you are going to try and play on my show, you go home and put on some decent clothes like a lady is suppose to wear," he advised. "You are a disgrace to the five-string banjo."[7]

"One thing about him," Walter Parham said, "He was strict with his show. There was nothing unclean that got on his show. If anybody did something like that, the minute he caught it, he'd walk right up, take him by the arm and take him off stage. He'd tell him 'no dirty songs'."

Lunsford's reasons for discouraging certain musicians from performing were almost always sound. He had the interest of the festival and its audience at heart. The unpleasant scenes associated with his role as gatekeeper were rare. Usually he spoke softly and was the essence of the gentleman. He disliked exchanging unpleasant words with anyone, and it was only when the integrity of his festival was at stake that he resorted to unpleasantries.

There were frequently 300 or more performers at the festival, including dance teams and string bands. In addition to the prize money, trophies were also awarded.

The success of the Mountain Dance and Folk Festival led to national and international recognition and to new dimensions in Lunsford's activities. In 1934 he spent seven weeks in California as Asheville's roving ambassador of good will, publicizing the Land of the Sky and its climate. He made personal appearances in a number of schools, including the universities at Berkeley and Los Angeles. After every performance he was invited to return.

On his way back from California he attended the first National Folk Festival, held in St. Louis. Though the idea for a national folk festival was originated by Sarah Gertrude Knott, head of the Dramatic League of St. Louis, it was inspired by Lunsford's festival in Asheville. Miss Knott, a Kentuckian who was as energetic and indomitable a promoter as Bascom was, said that the first folk festival she ever attended was the 1933 Mountain Dance and Folk Festival. "No other person has had more influence on me," she wrote of Lunsford. Seventy-five mountain singers, dancers and musicians met Lunsford in St. Louis for the first festival. The next year he took 100 to Chattanooga for the second National Folk Festival. Aunt Samantha Bumgarner, Fiddling Bill Hensley and Sam Queen with his Soco Gap dancers were for many years fixtures at the national festival.[8]

"We couldn't have gotten a National Folk Festival started without Bascom," Sarah Gertrude Knott said. "For the first six or eight years he came to the festival city a week or more in advance to teach the folk dances in groups and to give programs of folk songs. He was the greatest possible influence in helping us to show what the folk festival was to be like. His informality and natural real mountain dignity and wit did much to help us to establish the right mood for the festival. He was on hand before it became a fad. It was real with him." Bascom himself wrote, "It has been my pleasure and my duty to go each year about a month before the festival to engage in promotional work leading up to the festival where I would visit schools and colleges and various dance groups to 'spread the gospel' of the value of 'our Traditional American Cultures.' I have tried to do my part of it as seemed best at the time."

Lunsford served on the National Folk Festival Board down through the years, along with such notables in folklore and related arts as B.A. Botkin, Frank C. Brown, Josiah Combs, Arthur Kyle Davis, J. Frank Dobie, May Gadd, Patrick Gainer, Paul Green, W.C. Handy, George W. Hibbitt, George Pullen

Jackson, Gladys Jameson, George L. Kittridge, Frederick H. Koch, George Korson, John Lair, Vance Randolph, Stith Thompson, Gordon Wilson and Grant Wood. The festivals took him and his performers to such places as Dallas, where more than 9,000 performers gathered; Chicago, where 27 states were represented; and New York, where the audience numbered 16,000. From its beginning, the National Folk Festival was a success.

At the suggestion of Dorothy Scarborough, three members of the English Department at Columbia University—George Hibbitts, Henry K. Dick and Walter C. Garrick—invited Lunsford to New York to record his memory collection. This set of recordings was made possible by the Manners Fund and was intended primarily for the use of the English Department. Lunsford arrived at Columbia in late February of 1935 and set to work recording all of the ballads, songs, hymns, singing games, square dance calls and stories that he could remember and that he thought were worthy—about 315 items—on 80 twelve-inch aluminum discs (See Appendix II for listing). It took him two weeks. Lunsford dedicated his memory collection recordings to his wife:

> I dedicate this personal memory collection of ballads and folk songs to Nellie Triplett Lunsford, who was my playmate in childhood, my classmate in grammar school and high school, and has been since a loyal, devoted and affectionate wife since our marriage Saturday, June 2, 1906, and who is the mother of my seven children, Kern, Lamar, Ellen, Lynn, Nelle, Merton and Josefa.

Along with the songs and other material, Lunsford gave oral notes, including, if possible, from whom he had learned each item and the date and special circumstance. He was 52 years old at the time, and his voice was probably at its best. The recordings are a priceless legacy that reflected the scope of Appalachian folklore but also the personal interests and aesthetic of one remarkable man. It was the largest repertory ever recorded by one person, although several artists have claimed to perform more material than he recorded.

Also in 1935, Lunsford was appointed to a position with the New Deal Works Progress Administration. He was asked by Erle Stapleton of Greensboro, state director of the music unit of the Special Skills Division of WPA, to organize a folk music unit in North Carolina. In 1936, he transferred to another New Deal program, the Resettlement Administration, where he worked in the Music Program, directed by Charles Seeger.[9] "I asked them what they wanted me to do. They said do just the same thing you've been doing in the music unit of WPA." This move widened the territory that he could serve. After a month's orientation session in Washington, Lunsford went to Scottsboro, Alabama, in the Appalachian foothills, to work with the Skyline Farms Foundation, a project of the Resettlement Administration. There he scouted for traditional music and musicians, coached teams of dancers and musicians who put on programs as part of the project and who participated in programs elsewhere. He also helped with other gatherings and encouraged festivals elsewhere as a part of this work.

Dancing in Lunsford's home on South Turkey Creek
(courtesy of Lunsford Collection, Mars Hill College)

Lunsford had long dreamed of a house big enough to accommodate guests for musical entertainment and square dancing, but it was not until 1935 that he felt financially able to start a new home. As he had gotten more involved in festivals and related work, he neglected his law practice except for friends and old clients, and with the Depression, money was in short supply at the Lunsfords'. However, there was ample timber on Nellie's place to provide lumber for the building, and he arranged to have it cut and sawn. The site he selected was alongside the road on South Turkey Creek, just north of 3,197-foot Hanlon Mountain, a local landmark, on the side of which he and Nellie had lived when they were first married. On up the South Turkey Creek valley to the southwest was Newfound Mountain, rising to 4,000 feet. It was a lovely spot, located not far from Asheville and just south of Madison County where lived so many of the musicians whom Bascom admired.

The house he built was modest in size and design, except for the oversized living room which took up all of the front part of the structure. The room had hardwood floors and a commanding fireplace, perhaps four feet by four with sturdy andirons to accommodate huge logs. The house itself was two stories, with both front and side porches which sported the only decoration: fancy-turned posts and bannisters on the porch roofs above to form balconies.

The Lunsford house on South Turkey Creek
(courtesy of Lunsford Collection, Mars Hill College)

The practice platform at South Turkey Creek
(courtesy of Lunsford Collection, Mars Hill College)

Lunsford planted shrubs, rosebushes and trees around the house and later built an outdoor dance pavilion nearby. The place was a working farm, but most of Bascom's creative energy went into making it a gathering place for music and dancing. Later, George W. McCoy, editor of *The Asheville Citizen*, described the Lunsford home in an article as "The House the Five-string Banjo Built."

Lunsford first met John Lair, a Kentucky student of the origins of American folk music, at one of the Asheville folk festivals. Lair doesn't remember the year. When Lunsford attended the National Folk Festival in Chicago in 1937, he visited with Lair, who had formerly been musical director for WLS in Chicago and who had introduced to radio audiences such Kentucky talent as the Ledford Sisters, Karl Davis and Hartford Taylor (Karl and Harty), Slim Miller, Red Foley and Doc Hopkins. At the time of their Chicago meeting, Lair was working for WLW in Cincinnati, from which he originated the Renfro Valley Barn Dance. He later moved this show to Renfro Valley, Kentucky, where it was broadcast over WHAS in Louisville and became popular on the CBS network for many years.

Lair knew that many other mountain people like himself had moved north of the Ohio River seeking employment. He asked Lunsford to work with WLW to discover and engage talent for the folk programs broadcast over the station. He also wanted him to teach square dancing, as a free service of WLW, to various clubs in the Ohio Valley. The aim was to create a bigger audience for the Barn Dance show. Thus, the Ohio Valley Folk Festival was born. Lunsford found talent for the festival in southern Ohio and in Kentucky, and the best of the talent was used on the radio programs. Lair loaned him the popular Coon Creek Girls and Red Foley from his show.[10]

The Cincinnati Times-Star (March 13, 1938) announced that Lunsford would direct the Ohio Valley Folk Festival sponsored by WLW, to be held in the Cincinnati Music Hall on March 27. The article also stated that Harold Spivacke, chief of the music division of the Library of Congress, had authorized that the mountain music played and sung at the festival be recorded for the permanent records of the library. Alan Lomax of the library music staff was dispatched to Cincinnati to make recordings.

While working for WLW, Lunsford performed regularly on the station's Saturday night broadcasts. Lair remembers that he was also a big hit with clubs and similar groups in the area. "Everybody liked him. He was an affable sort of fellow—never quarrelsome about anything. If he didn't like anything, he kept it to himself. As a musician, he was just fair. His value was all in his recollection—in his knowledge of the songs—and not in the way he presented them. He had an authenticity about him. People didn't doubt him. People like anything that is genuine."

Lair was impressed with Lunsford's instinct for performers.

> Let me tell you what he did to me in Cincinnati. He had a fiddler that he wanted to bring up there. He kept telling me how good he was, and I finally let him bring him up.

> He was a tall red-headed boy. We got back of the stage and rehearsed a few numbers with him, and I thought he wasn't worth a dime. I wasn't going to go out there on the stage and put him on. I told Whitey Ford, who was helping me emcee the show, "I don't want you to put him on. Let Lunsford put him on. He brought him up here." So, I said, "Bascom, you're going to have the honor of introducing your own guest tonight," That pleased him. He got out there and told about this boy and sent him out there. He started to fiddle. He hit about four licks and laid his head back and started bellowing out a song, and he just absolutely, completely swept the house. We couldn't get him off the stage to let the other acts on for ten minutes. We missed the boat. He was the biggest hit of the night, and we didn't want to be associated with him.[11]

Lair gives an interesting side of the story about the Music Hall show, which was presented in one of the three auditoriums in the Hall. Occasionally the Cincinnati Symphony would play in another auditorium. "The wives of the symphony men, and some of the society people too, would come and sit in their boxes while the lights were on, but as soon as the lights went down, they would come over to the Barn Dance, watch their watches, and get back by the time the lights came up again."

Undoubtedly the highlight of Lunsford's career was the 1939 invitation from President and Mrs. Roosevelt to perform at the White House for King George VI and Queen Elizabeth. Mrs. Roosevelt wanted to give the royal couple a cross section of the music of America. Along with Lunsford they invited Marian Anderson, the renowned concert contralto; opera baritone Lawrence Tibbett; popular singer Kate Smith; folklorist Alan Lomax; John Lair and the Coon Creek Girls. Lunsford took along Sam Queen and his Soco Gap Dancers and the Skyline Farms dancers from Scottsboro, Alabama. The following recollections of events are from Lunsford, John Lair and Lily May Ledford Pennington, one of the Coon Creek Girls.[12]

"Mrs. Roosevelt knew Lunsford," Lair reported. "When we were in the reception line to meet the King and Queen and President and Mrs. Roosevelt, Lunsford told us how well he knew Mrs. Roosevelt. She'd met him down at the White Top Festival in Virginia. But as we began to get close, he got cold feet, and he said, 'Now, John, she may not remember me. It's been some time and she may not remember me at all.' When we got up close to her, she looked up and saw him, and she said, 'Why Bascom.' She threw both arms around his neck and pulled him over. I thought he was going to faint, he was shaking so."

Lily May Pennington remembered that Lair had had a hard time getting in, because the security was so strict. "He was carrying the bass fiddle, so they finally let him in because of that."

"They didn't give us programs," Mrs. Pennington said. "But Mr. Lair stole two out of the pockets of servants. We still have one—very pretty, all tied, with a ribbon."

Mrs. Pennington also reported another interesting episode. "We went over early for a rehearsal. The people in charge wanted us to run through what we were going to do that night. We went through all of it. A distinguished looking

The photograph presented by the Roosevelts to Lunsford and the Soco Dance Team as a memento of the 1939 concert at the White House (courtesy of Lunsford Collection, Mars Hill College)

gentleman came to the door and listened for awhile. He asked me, 'How long have you been playing?' I said that I had been playing for a long time. He said, 'I play a little myself. Could we play some together? Let me go get my fiddle. I'll be right back.

"He introduced himself. He said, 'I'm Cactus Jack.' That's all he said, so that's what I called him—Cactus Jack. We went over to another room. He'd play a tune, and I'd play one, and then we'd play one together, for quite a long time. It was later I found out—I guess Mr. Lair told me—that that was the Vice President, John Nance Garner. That was Cactus Jack."

"I knew who he was. I don't know whether any of the others did or not," Lair remembered. "We like to have never got him out of there in time for the show. He wanted to sit there and fiddle for Lily May. He was a pretty good old country fiddler."

Lair was quite taken by the Queen. "The person who put the most into her expression was the Queen, incidentally one of the few actually beautiful women I've ever seen. She had a complexion out of this world. She had real charm and beauty. She was all smiles and gracious. The King never changed expression. He had lost the key. He didn't know how to change it."

Lily May described the performance of the Coon Creek Girls. "When we went on I decided that this was not the same thing as playing school houses. The platform was all ringed with ferns and the lights were in our eyes. I looked for the King and Queen, and there they were right under me. I felt pretty good until I looked at the King. He looked pretty sour. President Roosevelt wanted us to do "Cindy," and we did. I looked at the King and he was patting his foot and I knew I had him."

Lunsford stood in the crook of the gold piano and picked the banjo with the string band while Sam Queen led his dancers through such figures as Dive and Shoot the Owl, London Bridge and King's Highway. Lair was especially impressed by the Soco Gap Dancers. "They were the most graceful dancers I've ever seen in my life. They had a graceful, easy swing, and it was a sight to behold."

Lunsford remembered that Cordell Hull, Secretary of State and former congressman from East Tennessee, came up after the program and bragged that he could dance any figure that Lunsford or Queen could call. Lair remembered that one of the musicians or dancers Lunsford had brought knew Hull and addressed him by his first name. "Hull was familiar with him, so he got such a big kick out of this that he got some staid and dignified man and brought him over and introduced him to the boy. Everybody they would bring in, he'd talk to them and call them by their first names just like he was down home."

Nothing could have pleased Lunsford more than presenting music and dances from the Appalachians to the King and Queen of the empire to which most Appalachians trace their origins. It was one of his most cherished memories.

Later, in 1946, after John Lair moved his Renfro Valley Barn Dance to his place of birth in the Renfro Valley of Rockcastle County, Kentucky, he invited Lunsford to start a festival there. The resulting Red Bud Festival began in 1946. On the programs Lunsford had such personalities as Pleaz Mobley, the Manchester, Kentucky, attorney, politician and ballad singer, and Jean Ritchie. "I claim credit for discovering her. There was a boy down there in the agricultural field. He told me about having a friend in Lexington named Jean Ritchie who could sing a lot of songs. I went up there and saw Jean Ritchie. I invited her to be on the program, and she came down later and sang on the festival. Well, she's made quite a reputation. Fine family, the Ritchies." Pleaz Mobley and Jean Ritchie were recorded at the Red Bud Festival by Artus Moser for the Library of Congress. Moser also recorded Lunsford at Renfro Valley as well as at his home on South Turkey Creek for the Archive of Folk Song.

Lair commented recently on the Red Bud Festival. "Lunsford didn't do all of the work, but he was head of it. We gave him credit for being head because festivals were his business. We made arrangements through a publicity girl in New York, who was working for our sponsor, General Foods." Lunsford was at Renfro Valley for six months or more initially and directed the festival for three years. Perhaps it failed partially because Lunsford, by that time, had too many irons in the fire. But Lair has another opinion. "I'll tell you what broke up the

Mural by Bert Mullins, commemorating Lunsford's work with the Red Bud Festival at Renfro Valley, Kentucky

Red Bud Festival. The red bud trees were so inconsiderate that they never gave you an exact time for blooming. They'll vary two or three weeks every year. We were going to have all the candidates for queen to be redheaded. We got a lot of publicity, but we just couldn't keep it up."

The Renfro Valley Barn Dance, however, goes on. Lair sold it several years ago to Nashville interests, but when he saw its old-time flavor diminishing, he and two partners bought it back in 1976 and restored its country folk flavor. Through the years it had featured traditional singers and musicians such as Pleaz Mobley, Roy Starkey, and the Ledford Sisters (the Coon Creek Girls), as a continuing influence of the Lunsford-Lair team. Hanging in the Renfro Valley studio are portraits of Lunsford, John Lair, Bradley Kincaid and John Jacob Niles, and a mural depicting the history of man and music, done by the late local artist Bert Mullins.

Lunsford and Lair, both super promoters, had great respect for one another but did not always see eye to eye on how to do things. Lunsford was the director, but Lair had his own ideas about the Red Bud Festival. Lair tells of walking one evening by the room where Lunsford was staying and hearing the Carolinian's voice coming through the open window. Stopping to listen, Lair found that he was talking to himself, "Well, that's not the way I want to do it, but it's his place and I'll just have to do it his way. Well, he may be right, but I don't think he is."

"He was quite a character, and you miss him," Lair says. "I could never get him to wear a checked shirt or anything like that. He dressed like a lawyer. He wasn't going to be country. He wanted to be the man who told you about it, but he didn't want to be it. I appreciated Lunsford a lot. He was a fine fellow, and he was so sincere in his work. You had to say that about him."

In 1948, Lunsford was invited by Dr.Ralph Steele Boggs of the English Department to start a folk festival at the University of North Carolina at Chapel Hill which was held in June. In the same year Lunsford also established a festival for the North Carolina State Fair in Raleigh, in the month of August. Both of these festivals became popular events and made it necessary for Lunsford to locate new performers from places in North Carolina other than his native mountains. He traveled the hot and dusty roads of the Piedmont and Coastal Plain of the Old North State, seeking talent for his new festivals. He still relied on his tried and true mountaineers, however, for his basic program. Also, he persuaded several black groups to perform at these festivals.

The Carolina Folk Festival at Chapel Hill lasted until 1956. Dr. Arthur Palmar Hudson, folklorist at the University, explained some of its problems in 1955. A major problem, Hudson thought, was its stadium home where it was frequently rained out. "Disgusting rowdyism in the audience, quelled at last by the firmness and the evident fighting spirit of Director Bascom Lamar Lunsford, gave a sour note to the finale and made the performers nervous and the well-behaved portion of the audience somewhat dubious about the future of the folk festival."

Hudson went on to say that the festival was "uneven, ragged, imperfectly disciplined and over-exuberant....much was lacking in the authentic folk note....the talent was there but it did not choose the right pieces." Of Lunsford, he said, "This year he got together too much. It was not properly screened and processed and monitored. It is doubtful that one man can do all that. He needs help."[13] Perhaps, with three major festivals in one year and numerous other commitments, Lunsford had taken on too much. Hudson mentioned also that the festival's audiences had dwindled and that university students and Chapel Hill residents were not supporting the festival. Perhaps this indicates that Chapel Hill was too sophisticated, too modern, to be an ideal home for a traditional festival.

The State Fair Festival has continued, bolstered by a guaranteed audience. After Bascom, it was directed for fourteen years by Ruth Jewell, supervisor of Music for the North Carolina Department of Public Instruction, and is presently directed by Jim Hall, former director of the Cultural Arts Division of the Department of Public Instruction. The festival operates as an important part of the fair, with three shows daily for nine days, drawing 500 persons per show. It will be moved next year into a tent to accommodate more people. It has competitive

Ruby Lovingood Lunsford, Marcus Martin, Lamar Lunsford, George Pegram, and Clegg Gaines perform at the Carolina Folk Festival at Chapel Hill (courtesy of Lunsford Collection, Mars Hill College)

events for string bands, individual musicians and square dance teams. Like the Asheville festival it has wandered away from Bascom's standards for folk music, but its current director is attempting to bring it back to more traditional styles. He will have his work cut out for him, since bluegrass and country music-oriented styles are stronger than traditional strains in current times.[14]

Lunsford started other festivals—at Charlottesville and Virginia Beach in Virginia, Cherokee (in connection with the Cherokee Indian Fair), Winston Salem and Burlington in North Carolina, and in Clinton,South Carolina—that did not do so well as the Mountain Dance and Folk Festival and the State Fair Festival. During his busy life he probably helped with many other such programs, now forgotten.

In 1949, Duncan Emrich, head of the Archive of Folk Song at the Library of Congress, invited Lunsford to re-record his memory collection, for the purpose of getting better technical recordings than was possible at Columbia University with the equipment available in 1935. Bascom went to Washington on March 7, and even though he indicated on several occasions that he recorded his memory collection in a week, he states on the recording dedication that he finished on March 25. He was 67 years old. The new recordings, on 16-inch discs, were not that much better in quality than the Columbia recordings and some discs were of poorer quality. Since Lunsford was only 53 in 1935, his voice and musicianship are better on the earlier recordings. His daughter Kern felt that "his banjo playing on the Columbia recordings has more variation, his voice sounds better, and he does not stumble over a word as often as he did in 1949."[15]

The Archive of Folk Song lists 317 songs, variants, fiddle tunes, dance calls, tales, and comments recorded in this session, although Lunsford spoke of 350 items. Emrich called it the largest repertory ever recorded by one person; in fact, he said no one else had recorded a seventh of what Lunsford had.[16] While the session was planned to re-record the material from the Columbia recordings, there are some variations in the two sets of recordings (see Appendices II and III). Each contains material not included in the other. A comparison, plus other songs Lunsford was known to sing, shows that Lunsford's memory collection contained a total of some 350 items. One other difference in the two recordings is that in the latter one he used a banjo-mandolin—an instrument with a wooden body like a mandolin and a banjo neck with five strings—rather than his usual banjo, for some of his numbers. While he played the instrument in his usual two-finger picking style, it produced a mellower tone, somewhat like a guitar. The banjo-mandolin, along with his Gibson banjo and home-made fiddle, are on display in the Lunsford Collection in the Mars Hill College Library. Apparently, Lunsford had become fascinated with the different sound made by the mandolin-banjo and decided to use it for some of the recordings. He soon abandoned this bastardized instrument and returned to his beloved banjo. Another note, his Columbia recordings were made with an old-fashioned open-back banjo, but in the 1949 recordings he used his Gibson banjo with resonator. The homemade fiddle he used was oddly shaped, in that it lacked the U-shaped scroll effect on each side and instead was shaped more like a guitar. He called it his "de-horned fiddle."

Other collectors who recorded Lunsford for the Library of Congress, in addition to Robert W. Gordon in 1925, are: Sidney Robertson (Cowell) at Leicester, N.C. in November of 1936, Washington, D.C. in March of 1937; Alan Lomax, Jerome Wiesner and Joseph Liss at the Mountain Dance and Folk Festival in Asheville in 1941; Artus Moser at Leicester, N.C., Asheville, and Renfro Valley, Ky., in 1946; Ralph Auf der Heide in Los Angeles about 1947; Benjamin A. Botkin in Asheville around 1949 (probably including some of Artus Moser's recordings, according to the Archive of Folk Song), and James Scancerelli at South Turkey Creek in 1966 (See Appendix IV for preliminary list Library of Congress recordings of Lunsford). Duncan Emrich also interviewed Lunsford while he was in Washington for the 1949 recordings. As mentioned before, the Columbia University recordings were made available to the Archive of Folk Song, apparently copied in 1937 by the Music Program of the Resettlement Administration, as well as the 32 items recorded by Frank C. Brown in Buncombe County, N.C., around 1922, which were transferred from cylinders to discs in the 1940's.[17]

Lunsford in Washington to record for the Library of Congress in 1949. Sen. Frank P. Graham from N.C.; his aide, Richard Queen; Lunsford; and Dr. Duncan Emrich, Head of the Archive of American Folksong at the Library of Congress (courtesy of Lunsford Collection, Mars Hill College)

A letter in the Lunsford family collection from fellow Tar Heel L. Quincy Mumford, Librarian of Congress from 1954 to 1974, attributes "nearly 750 items of music and commentary during the years 1925-1949" to Lunsford. Mumford, no doubt, has totaled material from the various recordings and has not allowed for duplication.

In addition to the Columbia and Library of Congress recordings, Lunsford recorded extensively for Professor John Ball of Miami University and one of his graduate students, Anne Beard, whose master's thesis on Lunsford is quoted elsewhere in this work. The recordings took place at Miami University, Oxford, Ohio, in 1958. They were deposited with the Music Library at Miami University after Professor Ball's death but were apparently discarded later. No trace of them can be found.[18] The author was unable to locate Anne Beard to determine if she has copies.

The legacy Lunsford left on cylinders, tapes and discs is not likely ever to be equalled or exceeded by any other individual. These recordings contain not only the words and tunes in Lunsford's inimitable style with voice and instrument, but also occasional variants and verbal notes about most of the songs—where they come from, who contributed them, and often special comments about the contributors. The recordings preserve the repertory and aesthetic of Bascom Lamar Lunsford.

Lunsford's three commercial LP recordings need to be mentioned. He was one of the very few persons who recorded on wax cylinders, then on commercial acoustical 78 rpms and who lived on to record long-playing 33 1/3 albums.

His first LP was a 10-inch album, *Smoky Mt. Ballads Sung by Bascom Lamar Lunsford with Banjo,* released by Folkways as FA 2040 in 1953. The origin of the recording is obscure. Moses Asch, president of Folkways, does not remember how he acquired the recordings. Neither Pete Seeger nor Bertrand Bronson, who contributed to the notes, could remember who had recorded Lunsford. Archie Green, fascinated by the problem, has discovered that the recordings were made in Los Angeles on April 14, 1947, by Ralph Auf der Heide and probably Frances Lynne (a Los Angeles publicist who wrote an introduction to the folkways album) for Eagle records which went broke shortly after printing record labels but before the records were released. Green concludes that Lynne or Auf der Heide, or perhaps Lunsford himself, sent the tapes to Folkways. Even though Lunsford is credited with writing the notes to the songs, he obviously did not provide the words, since they show many errors, indicating that someone unfamiliar with Lunsford's Appalachian speech transcribed them from the recordings.[19]

Material for a 12-inch LP on Riverside (*Bascom Lamar Lunsford: Minstrel of the Appalachians*, RLP 12-645) was recorded by Paul Clayton, apparently in Asheville, or South Turkey Creek, in 1956. Kenneth Goldstein, who was free-lancing with several record companies at the time, produced the album and prepared the notes. It includes Freda English who sang on two numbers and also provided guitar backup. (Mrs. English later became Lunsford's second wife.)

This album, which was in Riverside's folklore series, carries no copyright date but was probably released in 1957.

The third LP was released by Rounder Records in 1976 from tapes made by Kenneth Goldstein in 1956. Goldstein, incidentally, worked in North Carolina during the summers of 1952-58, with Bascom's help in interviewing and taping local musicians, including George Pegram, Walter Parham and Obray Ramsey, with whom he produced several albums. This album featured Lunsford on Side 1 and Pegram and Parham on Side 2. It is entitled *Music from South Turkey Creek*. This writer wrote the liner notes as well as notes for each of the songs. However, only the descriptive notes about South Turkey Creek and the three musicians were used.[20]

For Lunsford the most exciting festival, other than the Asheville festival, was the International Folk Festival in Venice, Italy, in 1949. He attended as a U.S. representative, appointed by Duncan Emrich. A particular pleasure for Lunsford was riding in the stratocruiser at 35,000 feet and picking "Sourwood Mountain" on the banjo. "I reckon that's about the highest that tune has ever been played," he said. He took Henry Hudson, a fiddler, and Mrs. Lillie Lee Baker, a Texas dance leader, with him to Venice.

He told an interesting story about Venice:

> We had a hard way to get there because the fellow who was with me (presumably Hudson) had broken four ribs the night before and was in pain. I had to see about our luggage every time we changed planes. Finally we got there to the depot at Venice, and the burden just rolled off me, and I had a spiritual reaction that I couldn't account for. But a lady there accounted for it for me. She showed us about the city, showed us St. Mark's cathedral, St. Mark's Square where the festival was to be held, and I told her how I felt when I came there. She said St. Mark requested to be buried there in Venice because when he came there his burdens were all lifted away. Now, how about that? That's a true story.[21]

Mrs. Beatrice McLain, former director of the Southern Folklife Center at the University of Alabama, remembers Lunsford's leading an Appalachian square dance in St. Mark's Square while somewhat bewildered Venetians stood around trying to find out what was happening. He was determined to leave a bit of Appalachia there.

One of the greatest thrills on the trip was Lunsford's chance to visit England. As Jonathan Gordon commented, "Although he can talk for hours about England, he remembers almost nothing of Italy; it's as if a non-English speaking country, where everything was so different from what he knew....just dropped out of his mind. He remembers the monument to Shakespeare in Stratford: 'There was Prince Hal with the crown just above his head; and Lady MacBeth, rubbin' her hands and sayin' all the water in China couldn't make these little hands clean.' "[22] He could indeed quote Shakespeare: "I care not for the bulk or the bigness of a man; give me his spirit." He remembered the inscription on Shakespeare's tomb:

> Blessed be the man that spares these stones
> But cursed be he who moves my bones.

While in London, he gave a program at the Cecil Sharp House, an event in which he took much pride. The festival trip was a great bonus for him, as Gordon pointed out, because it gave him a chance to visit the fount of his people and their songs.

Although Lunsford spoke with great authority on the subjects dear to his heart, he wrote relatively little. When asked, he would contribute articles explaining his work, especially the Mountain Dance and Folk Festival, as he did for the *Disc Collector* around 1961, and for a time he wrote a regular column in *The Asheville Citizen*. He was proud of *30 and 1 Folk Songs from the Southern Mountains* prepared with Lamar Stringfield. Lunsford's second book was a small paperback called *It's Fun to Square Dance*. His co-author was George Myers Stephens, a long-time admirer. The book, published by the Stephens Press of Asheville in 1942, went into many printings. It was a well-illustrated book on how to square dance.

In 1966, Pete Gilpin and George Stephens wrote *Bascom Lamar Lunsford: 'Minstrel of the Appalachians,'* published by the Stephens Press of Asheville. Illustrated with many pictures, this slender book describes Lunsford's accomplishments and includes some of his favorite songs. As its middle section it reprints the square dance instructions from *It's Fun to Square Dance*.

Lunsford's personality, his special knowledge fired with his own unique zeal, shone through everything he did, and through his remarkable personality shone also the special quality of the Appalachian people and their culture. He maintained control of his festival programs and his recording sessions so that he could present what he wanted his audiences to see and hear about what he called "the great Appalachian people."

His relationship with newspaper and magazine writers was good. He was colorful, and he was constantly creating news and adding to the legend of the Squire of South Turkey Creek. Few writers could resist his charm and enthusiasm. Therefore, they were willing participants in his work. Articles about him and his activities appeared almost yearly in the major North Carolina newspapers. National papers, such as *The New York Times, The Washington Post,* and *The Chicago Daily News* carried stories about him, as did *The Saturday Evening Post, Life* and *Newsweek*.

Festivals, recordings and the printed page, then, were his media. He did not however, manage so well with radio, television, and film. The difficulty here was the intrusion of the popular stereotype of "hillbilly" music and the problems of Appalachia. From the time of the altercation at the festival in Asheville when the announcer tried to take over the festival, Lunsford had trouble with broadcast shows. Perhaps most of the problem was that he was expected to fit into someone else's show.

His eldest daughter Kern reflected on this problem. "Over the years, if he had occasion to be on radio, they would have a script written for him—filled with countrified talk and grammatical errors. He wouldn't have that, and it proved to

Bascom visits the Cecil Sharp House in London (courtesy of Lunsford Collection, Mars Hill College)

be an impassable barrier for him in that type of entertainment. We have to admire him for not giving in to any degree. He wore a business suit, a white shirt, and spoke like an educated man—and that was that!" Kern remembered also when her father was on the national television show "Wide Wide World." The setting was supposedly a family Sunday dinner. The script called for a person whom Lunsford didn't know to offer a prayer. Growing suspicious, he asked to see the script, which read something to the effect, "O, Lord bless this food for it's cold as hell." Lunsford said firmly, "No, that won't do," and he designated a member of his group to give a suitable prayer. Kern remembers, though, that they had him take off his coat, unbutton his vest, and push up his sleeves. "They just *couldn't* let him be himself! This was a national program, and a very important one, so he had to give a little, but I know it was hard to do."[23]

His most trying time came in 1964 when he agreed to assist a couple of film makers, David Hoffman and Jonathan Gordon, in a movie for National Educational Television on the music and musicians of the Blue Ridge Country. As Gordon's *Diplomat* article stated, "At eighty-three, when most men are either dead or useless, he actively collaborated with two men almost a quarter of his age on one of the newest art forms of our time." But the film makers had their own ideas about what they wanted to film. Lunsford complained, "I showed them the best we had, and they chose the worst." They worked some 15 hours of film into a one-hour movie,*Music Makers of the Blue Ridge, Featuring Bascom Lamar Lunsford*. When the film was released, he was disappointed with the results, considering it misrepresentative to the point of slander. He thought it portrayed, in the worst tradition, the people of the last century against a sordid background, omitting the more beautiful and picturesque settings.[24]

The film makers had their side of the story also. Actually, they seemed extremely fond of Lunsford and were certainly in awe of his knowledge and stamina. They were, nevertheless, condescending toward him and other mountain people and seemed to have a great deal of fun at his expense. For example, Gordon's *Diplomat* article threw doubt on Lunsford's authorship of "Mountain Dew."

Gordon also felt that Lunsford had a feudal paternalism toward those he called "my people." Perhaps this view was shared by a few mountaineers also. Gordon quotes one musician who reacted to their questions about Lunsford's accomplishments by saying, "Hell, I love Bascom, he knows that, but goddammit he didn't perserve the music for us, we preserved it for him." Of course the business of preserving cuts both ways. But, more to the point, Bascom had mentioned a fiddler along with other musicians as likely subjects for the movie, but he later refused to take Gordon and Hoffman to see him. He explained, according to Gordon, that the man ran with a rough crowd, that his family was "funny-looking" and that he might cast discredit on mountain people if he were filmed. Nothing could stop them then, of course, so they got another man to take them to the fiddler's house. "The whole thing was like something out of Li'l Abner....," Gordon explained, giving evidence that Bascom was more concerned about how the film makers would see the man than about the man per se, "and we filmed one of the best sequences in the movie."

The penchant that many outsiders have for seeking out and portraying the poverty of the people is evident in most of the Appalachian films made in the past two decades. Certainly, Gordon and Huffman wanted to get some of the "poverty stuff" in, and they appeared to want a few mountaineers who fitted the mountain stereotypes to a greater extent than did Bascom and his favorite musicians. Gordon's own statement is especially revealing: "Let me point out here that Bascom was not really a mountaineer; he wore a suit and he had lived in the city and was at home with its ways. His education, relatively speaking, was considerable." This curious notion about what a mountaineer is, a general one outside the region, has caused much outrage, not only in Lunsford, but also in other mountaineers who do not fit the stereotype.

When compared with other movies made in recent years aimed at highlighting the problems of the region, *Music Makers of the Blue Ridge* is much better than Lunsford thought it was. It has some good scenes with Bascom and Freda, his second wife, of Obray Ramsey, Red Parham and others making music, of the legendary Bill McElreath buck dancing, and it shows some nice slices of life in Madison and Buncombe Counties. It is evident that Gordon and Hoffman loved the music, even if they did view Lunsford and his friends with some condescending amusement.

Members of the Lunsford family are still somewhat bitter toward Hoffman and Gordon; they feel that the long hours and some unpleasantness during the making of the film may have contributed to Lunsford's stroke a few weeks later when he was in Madison County on business. There was, however, no lack of concern on the part of Gordon and Hoffman. Both went to see him after his stroke, and Gordon visited him again in 1966.[25]

It was not always easy sledding for the Mountain Dance and Folk Festival. By the 1960s attendance was dwindling. The local press had lost interest in the event, and Lunsford was beginning his eighth decade. The Chamber of Commerce threw its support behind the competitive Festival of American Folklore in 1963, no doubt with visions of Asheville as the folk music capital of the world. This new festival went on in June of that year with such performers as Pete Seeger, Jean Ritchie, Doc Watson, the Weavers, Frank Proffitt and Judy Collins. The Festival of American Folklore was well-organized and promoted, but it was a financial disaster and was never held again. Lunsford, typically, had kept his own counsel about this development and did not comment on it in public.

Officials of the Chamber of Commerce were getting restless about the leadership of the Mountain Dance and Folk Festvial (one reason they supported the new festival). Feeling that Lunsford was getting too old to manage it effectively, they were looking around for someone to rejuvenate his festival.

However, in 1963, Bob Lindsey came to the Chamber of Commerce as its travel promotion manager, and the festival was dumped in his lap for study and reorganization. The word he got was that the festival needed new blood and a new approach to publicity. Lunsford, he was told, had always been hard to work with, and his age had not improved him. Lindsey did not know Lunsford but had observed him at the Singing on the Mountain at Grandfather Mountain and had photographed him there. "He did not press forward, did not mix or mingle," Lindsey remembered. "It was as though he sat and whittled, listened, observed and quietly talked with those who passed his door."

George M. Stephens, always concerned for Lunsford and the festival and aware of the disenchantment with Lunsford's leadership, brought him and Lindsey together for lunch. "It was a quiet revelation for me based on what had been painted for me earlier." Lindsey wrote, "He was vigorous, humorous, much interested in gauging me, and we had a rather swift blending. He was a promoter. He instinctively recognized news and publicity values. Publicity was my job. I wanted to get to know his people, his performers. He wanted me to know them as swiftly as possible."

Lindsey recommended to the Chamber that they obtain more advance publicity for the festival and that they retain Lunsford and build publicity around him. He argued that Lunsford was irreplaceable. The Chamber agreed to wait and see.

"Lunsford always valued his Chamber relationship," Lindsey noted. "He came rather quickly to prize me, initially because stories followed conversations. He never pushed for stories but merely guided me toward material or "recalled" important things. In the execution of my job he was invaluable to me. Always a resource. Always colorful, interesting, authentic of the mountains. Routing a writer through South Turkey Creek was to guarantee good copy for Asheville and Western North Carolina."

Attendance at the festival jumped that year and continued to grow in subsequent years. There was no further talk of replacing Lunsford.

Lindsey's considerable contribution to the festival was in getting the local press again to value Lunsford and the festival. Lindsey began to call him "Mr. Bascom," another title that stuck. He also began to refer to him as a folklorist, an elder statesman of folklore. "Increased use of the title 'folklorist' helped," according to Lindsey. "He (Lunsford) was pleased to have it used locally, and would almost chuckle gleefully over it and roll it over his tongue, as though it was a private joke between us."[26]

Bob Lindsey was an important figure in the festival during the 1960s as attested to by several persons. He held things together and was largely responsible for the 1965 festival when Lunsford suffered a stroke.

Lunsford stayed busy until his stroke and loved every minute of it. His main interest in later years was the Asheville festival. He traveled from coast to coast from universities in California to the Waldorf. Harold Martin wrote in *The Saturday Evening Post* of how Lunsford, Sam Queen and the Soco Gap Dancers, "so stirred the emotions of a glittering assembly at the Waldorf Astoria that assorted elegants left their tables to tread a romping measure to the fiddle tune called "Billy in the Low Ground.' " Lunsford remembers being invited by Senator Robert Taft to a Washington hotel to lead square dancing and perform for a group called the Ohio Society, only to have the senator forget his name when he started to introduce him.

In fulfilling what he considered his calling, he received his share of recognition, much applause, and only a smattering of criticism. Personal letters came to him from individuals and groups before whom he appeared. *Who's Who in Music* (Fifth Edition, 1951) included a biographical sketch of him, and folklore publications mentioned his work. For 12 years he was on the Board of Directors of the National Folk Festival Association, and in 1951 he was elected president of the North Carolina Folklore Society.

A prized possession of Lunsford's was a 10 x 12 photograph of President and Mrs. Franklin D. Roosevelt, autographed with a note by the president. This framed photograph is on display at the Mars Hill College Memorial Library, along with other citations and awards. Among these are the Burl Ives Award, presented at the National Folk Festival in 1964; an engraved plaque from Mars Hill College, given in 1967 on the 40th anniversary of the Mountain Dance and Folk Festival; The Distinguished Citizen Award, awarded by N.C. Governor Robert W. Scott "in appreciation of the music you have given us," and the Brown-Hudson Award, presented to him in 1970 by the North Carolina Folklore Society.

On November 22, 1966, while he was still living on South Turkey Creek, Mr. Lunsford was honored at his home by his neighbors with a kind of "This Is Your Life" program. John Parris of Sylva, North Carolina, noted author and columnist for *The Asheville Citizen* who has written extensively on the history and traditions of his native mountains, was one of the speakers. He said of the honoree, "For most of sixty-four years he has been a fiddle-playing, a banjo-picking man, a ballad-singing man and a dancing man....He is more than a mountain troubadour. He is a folklore scholar who has appeared before learned groups to talk of mountain music."

September 6, 1969, was declared Bascom Lamar Lunsford Day at Mars Hill, his birthplace, "....as an expression of gratitude for his valuable contribution to the music of the region." Mayor William Powell named him honorary mayor for the day. In the evening a folk festival, patterned after the one he had directed in Asheville for 41 years, was held in the college gymnasium. The arrangements were made by Ed Howard, a local pharmacist, who invited old timers, youthful musicians, and dance teams to participate. The performers responded in large numbers, and crowds poured in. The festival was such a roaring success that it was decided, with Lunsford's consent, to make it an annual event. The next year it was moved from the gymnasium to the 1,800-seat Moore Auditorium, where it has remained a popular affair the first week in October of each year. In 1970, on Bascom Lamar Lunsford Day at Mars Hill, Lunsford was installed, along with Fiddling Bill Hensley, in the Mountain Music Hall of Fame, an honor created by Mars Hill College.

Probably because of his affection for Mars Hill College and because it was virtually the only regional college to show much interest in his work, Lunsford gave his collection of materials to Mars Hill in his will, dated January 11, 1968. It included his personal papers, his folksong collection on paper and tape, the Columbia University and commercial recordings, his notes and the enormous scrapbook that Lunsford and his children had put together from news clippings, magazine articles and other memorabilia, his books and photographs. It is housed in a special room in the college library.

On October 10, 1971, Lunsford was present at a meeting of the Appalachian Consortium (of colleges, universities and other agencies in North Carolina,

Virginia and Tennessee) at Mars Hill and was elated by the prospect that the colleges and universities of the area were manifesting a joint interest in perpetuating and expanding the cause in which he had expended most of his life and talents. Dr. Cratis Williams of Appalachian State University, a leading advocate of the preservation of basic mountain culture, said on the occasion that modern America was in danger of losing its roots, but that preserving the mountain heritage could help all Americans to re-establish their identity.

Lunsford was pleased to see the new academic interest in the region. "I'm glad to see the colleges taking an interest in traditional culture. They ought to teach it right along with art culture. Traditional culture is more lasting and more powerful than art culture and a person ought to know something about traditional culture—ought to know traditions and history. We people of the mountains have in a way been slandered, and most systematically. Here in the Appalachian region the people are sturdy and they are fine, and they have held to their traditions very well, and they are worthwhile." He added another thought, quoting a line of poetry, " 'We are heir to all the ages from the files of time.' We heir it all. We heir the mistakes and all. We heir the victories, and we get inspiration from them. We heir the mistakes and hope for judgment to correct ourselves accordingly. And so there it is. It is ours through tradition, and we can get it through tradition better than anywhere else."[27]

When he turned 90, the Chamber of Commerce's Folk Heritage Committee gave him a birthday party at the University of North Carolina at Asheville. That year Mars Hill College also gave him a party to coincide with the completion of the cataloguing of his collection there. On both occasions he made speeches about the value of mountain traditions.

His last award, on May 5, 1973, was from the Western North Carolina Historical Association. In part the citation read:

> At a time of rapid urbanization of the area, when its rich heritage was in danger of being lost, when the lore and customs of our ancestors were threatened by commercialism and contemporary modes of life and their music was being parodied and drowned out by current sounds, he proved to be the right man, in the right place, at the right time.

NOTES

1. Author's interview with Bascom Lamar Lunsford, West Asheville, N.C., 7-27-71.
2. Author's interview with Walter Parham and George Pegram, Berea, Ky., 7-2-74.
3. *Greensboro Daily News*, 5-7-64.
4. Harold Martin, "Minstrel Man of the Appalachians," *Saturday Evening Post*, Vol. 220, No. 47 (May 22, 1948).

5. Reported by two persons. No other record of event.

6. Telephone interview with Roger Sprung, July 1975.

7. Interview with Parham and Pegram.

8. Letters from Sarah Gertrude Knott, 1-12-74, 1-23-75.

9. John Angus McLeod, *Minstrel of the Appalachians*, unpublished biography of Lunsford in the Mars Hill College Library, 1973, pp. 29-30.

10. Author's interview with John Lair, Renfro Valley, Ky., 4-30-74.

11. *Ibid.*

12. *Ibid.*; Interview with Lily May Ledford, Berea, Ky., 6-25-75.

13. "Hudson Tells What Ails the Folk Festival," *The Chapel Hill Weekly*, 6-17-55.

14. Telephone interview with Jim Hall, 12-22-81.

15. Letter from Kern Lunsford, 9-10-72.

16. "Tar Heel of the Week, Bascom L. Lunsford," *Raleigh News & Observer*, 6-5-55, Sec. IV, p. 3.

17. From materials supplied by the Archive of Folk Song, Library of Congress.

18. Letter from Joseph C. Hickerson, 11-22-83; telephone conversations with Edith Miller, Music Librarian, Miami University, 11-23 and 29-83, and Helen Ball, Director of Archives, Miami University, 12-7-83.

19. Telephone interview with Moses Asch in 1981 and with Bertrand Bronson, November 16, 1983. Note from Pete Seeger, December, 1978.

20. Information on both the Riverside and Rounder discs was obtained primarily from interviews with Kenneth Goldstein, November 16, 1978 in Washington, D.C. and November 16, 1983 by telephone.

21. Interview with Lunsford, 7-27-71.

22. Letter from Kern Lunsford, 6-14-72.

23. Interview with Lunsford 7-27-71.

24. Jonathan Gordon, *Diplomat, August, 1966.*

25. Interviews and correspondence with Lunsford's daughters, Kern Lunsford, Nelle Lunsford Greenawald, Jo Lunsford Herron, Lynn Lunsford Hadley and Merton Lunsford Brown.

26. Letter from Bob Lindsey, 3-12-75; author interview with George M. Stephens, Asheville, N.C. 8-6-74.

27. Interview with Lunsford, 7-27-71.

CHAPTER 5

Mostly Personal

When Harold H. Martin wrote in *The Saturday Evening Post* that Bascom "walks all reared back....stands all reared back, like a man of substance..with dignity," he captured Lunsford's personal appearance as well as it can be put on paper. Of course, one has to realize that the "substance" giving Bascom his feeling and appearance of aplomb was not of land and cattle and money in the bank. It was something more ethereal, harder to grasp, and harder still to hang on to in changing times and values, but it was worth more to Bascom than property and cash.

He was a small man, five feet six inches in height. In his prime he weighed 160 pounds. He had black hair and brown eyes that flashed and sparkled behind rimless glasses. He smiled constantly out of a ruddy complexion that looked as if it should belong to a red-haired man. He had full lips and a thin, well-shaped nose. His face was constantly expressive, reflecting the rapid movement of his imagination. His countenance was lightened by his zeal.

He was always dapper. Usually short of money, his family of teachers had always been concerned about their appearance. A saying of the family reflected their character in hard times: "mend it, starch it, iron it and then go on." Bascom's brother Blackwell, a school principal, was seldom seen at the dinner table without a coat. Once a member of the family visited Blackwell and found him digging a ditch barefoot to save his shoes from the mud. When dinner time came, he washed up, put on his coat and came to the table barefoot.

In the beginning, Bascom had dressed in a swallow-tail coat— for a performance or two and to have his picture made—but he shortly decided that this was going too far. He remembered a time, though, when the long-tailed coat had come in handy. While returning from a performance, he had a flat tire, and on looking in his trunk, he found he had no jack. A man came along and insisted on changing the tire for him, assuming by his dress that he was a preacher.

At his festivals, he usually wore a white suit or dark coat and light trousers with a dark tie, although a dancer at the State Fair Festival in Raleigh remembers him dressing in a blue pinstriped suit, green hat, and green suede shoes! He insisted that the groups he directed dress properly. He was sometimes urged to dress people in phony hillbilly or western garb to promote his festivals, but he discouraged such attire, saying everything should be genuine and natural. He quoted John Lair of the Renfro Valley Barn Dance as saying that he was the only man Lair could never get to put on a checked shirt and an odd hat. "I said no,

I'm just doing my work as a citizen, and just because I'm going to sing a song or call a dance I learned from my great-granddaddy, why should I have to change my costume?"

He was often called a ladies' man, but without the improper connotations. He liked to talk to women and loved to dance with them, and was always courtly, witty and attentive around them. He cut a dashing figure, for while he was a man of the mountains, he was also a man of the world. This does not, however, mean he was not a man's man. Artus Moser remembers "he was just a typical mountain man. He admired other mountain people. He liked to get into nature. He loved to camp and go bear hunting. He would go hunting regularly—get with mountaineers and go through the terrific strain of staying out a week and running after bears with bear dogs. I don't think he was such a great deer hunter, but he did love to chase the bears."[1]

Byard Ray, master fiddler from Madison County, relates a hunting story about Bascom. "It was his first trip on a deer hunt. We were going down this creek to get to a deer stand. Somebody had a cow across the creek, and when she turned toward the light, her eyes shined. Bascom was trying to get his rifle around to shoot the cow. I said, 'Don't shoot that man's cow. That'd be a penitentiary crime.' I guess he got excited." While friends such as Ray held great affection and respect for Lunsford, they were not above making him the butt of practical jokes or anecdotes. His old friend Obray Ramsey once offered to carry him across the Laurel River when they were bear hunting on an icy day, only to drop him in the river halfway across. Lunsford reportedly accepted these pranks as part of his involvement in masculine enterprises.[2]

"He liked the good old-fashioned whiskey that they made back in the mountains—the genuine article," Artus Moser continued. "When Dr. Emrich, the director of the folklore section of the Library of Congress came down to visit his festival, Bascom presented him with a pint of 'that good old mountain dew.' He (Lunsford) would take a nip, but he was not a drinker. He would not get drunk, but he would take a nip all right." Lunsford sometimes mentioned drinking to be sociable, but he had little use for people who could not control their drinking, especially musicians who couldn't be depended on. "Alcoholic beverages were on his list of taboos...other than a little eggnog at Christmas," his daughter wrote. "He used to say that a fellow did not have much on the ball if he had to depend on whiskey to have a good time or express himself. He loved people, all people. He got his 'highs' from being with them and sharing music and dancing and yarns."

Another story relating to whiskey was told by Davis G. Lunsford, Bascom's nephew (Gudger's son), of Baton Rouge, Louisiana:

> A vivid recollection of Uncle Bascom is an incident on one of his visits here. My father-in-law and I took him to New Orleans to the bus station on his return to Asheville. He noticed a flamboyant display at a cut-rate liquor store across Canal Street and said, "I'd like to go over there and look around, as we still have some time

to kill before the bus leaves." We walked over and he shopped around for a few minutes, then bought a few half-pint bottles of bourbon. As he tucked them into his bag back at the bus station, I could restrain my curiosity no longer and asked, "Uncle Bascom, you could have gotten almost twice as much liquor for the same money if you had bought bigger bottles—why all the half-pints?"

He responded, "Well, D.G., along about Christmas we'll be having folks come in right often for some music and dancing, and while we're taking a little rest someone is sure to say, 'Sure would be fittin' if we had a little Christmas spirit to pass around about now.' So, if it's about the right time of the evening, I'll say, 'Well, let me look in the closet. I might just have a drap of spirit left!' "

He continued, "Now if I brought a quart bottle, by the end of the evening, all of it would be gone, and nothing left for the next time. And occasionally one of the boys gets too much and kinda spoils all the fun. Now if I bring out a half-pint everybody is glad and satisfied they had a drap of spirit to properly celebrate the season. It livens up the party by way of conversation more than the booze, and nobody gets too much."[3]

This story illustrates Lunsford's understanding of human nature as well as his belief in keeping alcoholic spirits in their place.

One thing to remember about Lunsford was that he could relate to almost any person. Bob Terrell in an *Asheville Citizen* (March 19, 1973) article wrote, "He has met with the mighty and the most humble and has treated them with the same respect." Byard Ray was impressed by the same quality.

He was well-liked. He had a lot of personality about him. He was the best in the world for mixing and mingling. He could fit 'most any crowd. He'd take a social drink with them, or attend religious services with them, or he'd pick and play with them. He'd help them string beans, hoe tobacco, 'most anything—help them kill a hog. He was that kind of fellow. When he came into a community everyone was glad to see him come. He was an old-timer. He'd come up the old way and was born right in the midst of things. No trouble mixing and mingling. He knew just how to do. He could get along with the elites too. He could talk to the Chamber of Commerce because he was an attorney. Bascom was a wide-ranger in his field.

"He could meet anyone," Artus Moser felt. "He could find his social position among any group of people—high or low."

George M. Stephens, a long-time personal friend, commented, "The special meaning of his life was that he had the wonderful talent for reaching both the scholars and the humble people back in the mountains, and they all understood him." Stephens quoted another friend, Richard B. Wynne, publisher of *The Asheville Citizen-Times*: "The humblest man knows that Mr. Lunsford's work is a part of his life and his heritage. So every man identifies himself with Mr. Lunsford, even though he was an outstanding scholar as well. The people could always understand what he meant and said so readily. So it was just like Abraham Lincoln's quality, wasn't it?"[4]

Kern, Lunsford's oldest daughter, adds, "One thing we learned from Dad was always to meet people on their own level, though he didn't teach us that in so many words. I met a man at Mt. Mitchell who had known Dad and had gone with him to collect some songs. He was very impressed with the way Dad had drawn the people out and got them to sing their songs."

Lunsford was amused and somewhat puzzled at his educated friends who marveled at his ability to relate to and communicate with the people of the mountains. He just couldn't understand people, especially those from the mountains, who had moved so far from their roots that they couldn't talk with country people. Perhaps his key was the respect he felt for everyone and the appreciation of the cultural heritage of the mountains that he shared with them. Only part of the success was due to his warm and friendly way. He commented that he learned the different greetings in various parts of the mountains, and he took the trouble to know about crops, weather and other such lore so that he was a knowledgeable conversationalist. However, his ability to talk with all people was not an acquired characteristic. It was the basic foundation of his character and philosophy. It related directly to his work as a collector and promoter of traditional practices, for he instinctively knew that the traditions he loved belonged primarily to the common people and that it was they who had kept them alive through the centuries. Although he admired the folklore scholars, he saw them as servants of the people. Furthermore, he knew that without the common people the "collections" of the folklorists became merely relics of the past. He never forgot those who were vital to living folk tradition.

"If I were to describe him in one word," said Earl Ward, who currently assists his wife Jackie in running the Mountain Dance and Folk Festival, as well as the Shindig on the Green, a folk music get-together held each summer Saturday evening in Asheville, "it would be that he was *real*." John Lair, Artus Moser and Jerry Israel also commented on his genuineness. People at all levels could readily see that there was no sham about him, that his word was good, and that he was sincere about whatever he was talking about. Perhaps these are qualities possessed by all who rise above the ordinary.

In some ways a modest man, Bascom nevertheless possessed his share of vanity. He collected information on and suggested that he was a descendant of Sir Thomas Lunsford, a colorful and impetuous nobleman, both honored and imprisoned during the English Civil War in the last days of Charles I. He was outlawed by the Star Chamber for poaching a deer and then trying to kill the deer's owner but escaped to France and a six-year tour in the French army. Returning, he was appointed by Charles I as Lieutenant of the Tower but was later imprisoned there for treason and when called before the House of Commons to answer charges, he engaged in a fistfight with members. Charles knighted him and he fought many of his battles as colonel of a regiment. He escaped to Virginia with his wife and children in 1649, after Charles was beheaded. However, his only recorded children were three daughters. There appears no proof of a direct connection between Sir Thomas and Bascom, but it suited Bascom's fancy to claim such kinship and to dwell on Sir Thomas' exploits.[5]

Bascom was bothered somewhat by his vanity. "It's hard to talk about things without appearing to be too chesty, of blowing my own horn," he commented and then went on to tell the following story that shows how acutely aware he was of his own personality and his relationship with others.

> Dr. Frank C. Brown wanted me to go down to Raleigh and appear at the North Carolina Folklore Society meeting, and I did. The next morning I wanted to get a paper and see how well I did. I was going back to South Turkey Creek, you know, and I knew if I didn't get one there I wouldn't get it at all. I got the paper, and it had a story—pretty good for Bascom.
>
> There was a fellow, Walter Garwick, who managed the recordings I did at Columbia University. Next year he came to North Carolina and talked with Dr. Brown. He asked Brown if he knew me. "Yes, he's the kind of man who likes to see his name in print," he said. I went down in December (1967) to take the Brown-Hudson Award. I was called on to talk some, but I didn't tell that on Dr. Brown because Dr. Brown had gone on. The joke was really on Bascom.

He then explained his particular problem: "I had to be my own press agent so much of the time—a disinterested third person standing by to see what I did and what place I ought to fill. I measured my efforts by mistakes of the past."[6]

He was successful as his own press agent, a fact that did not escape careful observers. In an article in *The Greensboro Daily News* (March 19, 1972), Jerry Bledsoe wrote, "He could always stir an audience. He knew what they wanted. And he had a flair for promotion. He would latch onto little things like being called the Minstrel of the Appalachians or the Squire of South Turkey Creek....and really promote them. He was never bashful about promoting himself—he figured he had to if he were to accomplish his goals—and he was quite successful at it. He and his festival got attention around the world, and he never spent a cent on advertising."

Lunsford said, "I am known as the Minstrel of the Appalachians and there's a good ring to the words. I used them for all they were worth. The proper use of words and expressions can take you a long way. I always started the festival 'along about sundown' because expressions like that will stick in a person's memory." The "Squire" title apparently grew out of a little tongue-in-cheek humor. He was often on programs with important-sounding persons, introduced as Doctor, or Professor, or Reverend so-and-so, from this or that university or city. When asked once how he wanted to be introduced, he replied, "As Bascom Lamar Lunsford from South Turkey Creek, North Carolina." Later he sometimes said he was the "Squire of South Turkey Creek" or the "Minstrel of the Appalachians from South Turkey Creek." No doubt this began in fun, but he soon saw the advantage of using titles or slogans that stuck in the mind. "I did it from the standpoint of the folk tradition. It pays off," he said. The best proof of his theory was his receipt of a letter addressed to him at South Turkey Creek, even though there is no such post office.

Another statement he liked to make was, "I've spent the night in more homes from Harper's Ferry to Iron Mountain, Alabama, than anybody." Since no one ever challenged him, this in time became part of the legend about him.

Jerry Israel, chairman of the Folk Heritage Committee, commented, "There were all of these pet phrases that he used, and they might not all have been accurate, but it eventually got to the place that we all believed them. You can't hear something for nearly 50 years without beginning to believe the myths, like 'Minstrel of the Appalachians.' Some newspaper lady used that little phrase and Bascom latched on to that like a leech. It was good and it served the purpose.

"He was a very strong, very dominant personality without question," Israel continued on another tack. "If there's anything significant about Bascom it was that he did something that was not at all popular at the time, and he was successful at it. He maintained that if anybody ever had a calling, he had a calling."[7]

Lynn, his daughter added,

> Of the myriad facets of Daddy's life and character none was more striking than his singleness of purpose. The mountains of glowing tributes in newspapers, magazines and other media through the years never touched on the quality I knew him best for, the part that really made him tick. Daddy was not always famous and so highly honored and it was not for this purpose that he so doggedly pursued his dream. I quite vividly remember when some considered him lazy and shiftless because he picked the banjo and sang, neglecting his law practice to "run all over the country collecting songs and square dancing." However, this never seemed to bother him. He continued, undaunted in his quest for what he believed in, despite the criticism. Being a teenager during some of this I was extremely sensitive about it. Looking back in later years I began to realize this was one of the qualities which made him great. To do anything for financial gains only was considered by him a complete waste of time.

Mrs. C.P. Wells from South Turkey Creek said, "You couldn't get ahead of Bascom," which she meant as a compliment. Mr. Wells remembered meeting a fellow in Asheville who, on learning that he lived near Bascom, asked if he knew Lunsford. He then told about a train trip he took with him once into Tennessee, probably in connection with a music or dance program. Bascom inquired of the conductor just when the train would arrive at their destination. The conductor informed him that the train didn't stop there. "Well, that's where we're getting off," Bascom said, and when they reached the place, Bascom pulled the emergency bar. The train stopped, and they both got off.[8]

"He always said, 'Make very few promises and keep the ones that you make',"Jerry Israel remembered. "This was a constant admonition."

> He felt a great deal of responsibility, not only toward the people he was working with, the heritage and dignity of his people, but also toward himself. He used to tell us, "Decide what you want to do and then do it the best you can. You might have to make some arrangements along the way," or as we always put it, grease the wheels of progress, "but you've got a goal in mind. You're trying to do something, and you make your adjustments. You might have to step on some toes and you might get someone mad at you for the rest of your life, but if what you are doing is important enough, it is justified."
>
> He made, especially in his later years, about as many enemies as he did friends over the Mountain Dance and Folk Festival, trying to keep it traditional or trying to keep one person, and that means he automatically had to exclude another one. The

thing to keep in mind when you realize that he made as many enemies as friends is that the people who play traditional music, who are involved in it as a major part of their lives, they are jealous as hell. Their way is traditional and everyone else is just out of it.

As this statement indicates, Bascom did ruffle some feelings as he followed his calling. He annoyed other folk enthusiasts, such as those in the private settlement schools, who tended to be purists and who generally disapproved of his festival, and he alienated the performers who wanted to be in the festival but who were not always invited. Bascom also had to deal with the petty jealousies between his performers. For example, one performer, George Pegram, was extremely competitive and had won in his class for several years. Then his position was challenged by Freda English who later became Bascom's second wife, and her instrument suddenly started getting out of tune, wandering, and then disappearing altogether. Consequently, Lunsford banished Pegram for a time.[9] Usually, though, his manner of dealing with such problems was smooth. He never talked behind other people's backs but chose to keep the matter between him and the other person. He was firm and effective, however, in getting what he wanted, and his word could be depended on. For this reason, those with whom he came in conflict appeared to bear no animosity; rather they, including George Pegram, appeared to respect Lunsford for his principles.

George Stephens remembers that Lunsford was always dependable in money matters, that his debts were usually paid on time. "It is unusual in a person who is driven first and foremost by the artistic impulse—very often the regularity and dependability get lost somewhere—but it was not so in his case. This is not the main thing, but it is nice that it was a part of his character always."

The financial arrangement with the Chamber of Commerce was that he would receive half of the profits as payment for promoting and directing the festival. The Chamber used the remaining half to furnish prizes and to pay Chamber expenses for promoting and administering the festival. The stipend from the Chamber of Commerce ranged from $600.00 in 1944 to $2,054 in 1954, dropped to $713 in 1961 (reflecting the diminshed interest in the festival) and then climbed to $1,603 in 1969. This was meager pay for the energy and imagination that he put into the festivals.

"The Chamber performed a very useful function," George Stephens commented. "It was too big a job for Bascom to do as a management job. But the Chamber was proverbially short on funds, and they took all they could for operations."[10]

One daughter remembers that the Department of Internal Revenue became suspicious of their income tax return since Lunsford was a lawyer, and the Department had noticed that lawyers usually have high incomes. They sent auditors to South Turkey Creek to look into the matter. They went away shaking their heads that the family lived so well on such a limited income.

Although some of his critics accused him of profiting excessively from his festival work, their criticism appears to be unfounded. He received some pay for his work with other festivals, programs at the Cherokee Indian Fair at Cherokee, and for lectures and concerts, and he received a small royalty from "Mountain Dew" and the Folkways and Riverside commercial records. He no doubt also had income from the farm, perhaps from property he owned in Madison County, and from occasional legal work. By most accounts, however, Lunsford's income was always modest, proving that he was motivated by the "call" of his work rather than by the financial returns.

He held his share of personal prejudices and biases. He had no time for anything or anybody who appeared to be phony, for he hated sham. He was also suspicious of outsiders, especially those from the city, particularly New York. Several people mentioned that he was concerned about communists. Artus Moser doubts that the McCarthy era had much effect on him, however, explaining:

> People here in the mountains are very patriotic. We love this region, and we don't want anyone coming in and tearing down our government. And Lunsford inherited a double dose of that feeling. He was very patriotic. He ran for the legislature, you know. I think he had the characteristics of a typical mountaineer, which we can't help from assessing. If a stranger comes in, we want to know who he is. We'll say, "What might be your name? Where do you live? What do you do for a living?" We want to know about him, and I don't see anything wrong with that. But people outside were sensitive about that.

Dr. Jim Wayne Miller, a university professor and poet who grew up on North Turkey Creek, tells of a time he went home to visit in the late 1950s:

> I saw two scruffy-looking characters in front of the Leicester post office with their thumbs out. They were dressed in blue-jeans and denim jackets and had bed rolls and back packs. They had long hair and beards. The word "hippy" wasn't current. Then they were beatniks.
>
> I stopped and offered them a ride. It turned out they were looking for Mr. Lunsford. They said they were representing a magazine and were getting information on mountain music and musicians. I said I knew where Mr. Lunsford lived and would drop them off there. So we drove on out of Leicester, past the school, past Camp Forest, and turned left at Hal Wells' store, up South Turkey Creek. When we pulled off at the house, Lunsford was just coming out of the door. It was clear from his manner that he was in a hurry and that he wasn't favorably disposed toward the two hairy guys I had with me. Briefly they told him what they were after, which was a leisurely tape-recording session in which they could put a lot of questions to him and (maybe) even get him to pick and sing a few things. Lunsford was not rude to them; in fact, a gentleness came into his voice as he explained that he was in pretty much of a hurry, had to get to Asheville (I don't remember his exact words, of course), but I believe he tried to soften the turn-down by saying something humorous like "I've got to see a man about a dog," which around Leicester would mean a fairly urgent appointment of a) either no particular consequence or b) the substance of which I don't care to reveal to you.
>
> I don't know whether or not the two hitchhikers ever got an interview. I remember thinking at the time that they seemed to have a simplistic notion that mountain musi-

cians could be encountered sitting on a stump somewhere making music, with nothing else in the world to do but to give an interview.[11]

In their book, Pete Gilpin and George Stephens discuss Lunsford's feelings about using folk music for political purposes. Lunsford thought is was all right for folk singers to make money from hootenannies and other commercial ventures: " 'If that's what they want to do, fine, but it's not for me.' But one request to add his name to a group of folksingers opposing U.S. policies in Vietnam riled him good. He couldn't disguise it. Lunsford says folk music often has patriotic themes and he went on to criticize those who would use it for political motives, particularly in opposition to their country." Lunsford was not the only folksinger to have problems with the role of folk music in the protest movement. Buell Kazee, Kentucky Baptist preacher, banjo picker and balladeer, expressed discomfort at being on the Newport Folk Festival program with such activists as Joan Baez and Pete Seeger in the 1960s.[12]

At any rate, Lunsford had trouble with the beatnik, hippy and others of the counterculture. He didn't understand them, and was thus suspicious of them and their motives. Some outsiders, such as Pete Seeger, were willing to relate to him on a purely musical basis. Others were not able to relate to him at all, or perhaps he simply refused to have anything to do with them. He particularly disapproved strongly of clothing that made one appear to be what he was not; he thought this was a put-on, a striving for an image that was not real.

On the other hand, some outsiders were turned off by Lunsford. They believed that anyone who sang the songs and played the instruments that had become part of a protest movement must surely share some of their social and political ideas. Usually Lunsford did not.

Lunsford was a gentleman in the Stoic tradition. That is, he was a man of some authority and influence who felt it was his duty to set a good example and to treat others in a gentlemanly fashion. Of course, he would never have indicated that he felt he was better than others, for this would have been completely out of character. Rather, he treated everyone as a peer. "When you go into a mountain home, you treat them like ladies and gentlemen," he had said. He was of the mountain culture—unlike the larger South—a society of levelers, of people who believed one man is as good as another, but no better. Yet he was of the South as well. A Democrat of the southern variety, he had taken after his father, the old Confederate and Democrat, rather than after his mother's folks, the Deavers, Unionists and Radical Republicans. Thus he was saddled with many of the provincial fears and prejudices of southern people of his time—suspicion of outsiders and their ideas, and guilt and uneasiness about black-white relations. He was, however, a genuine and very humane person, and he appreciated genuine qualities in all people, outsiders or insiders, black or white.

He collected songs in the Negro schools and churches of the mountains. His papers contain sheafs of songs black children had written for him. Lunsford did not have black performers on his Mountain Dance and Folk Festival, but he welcomed such groups to the Chapel Hill and State Fair Festival. When Lunsford commercially recorded *Speaking the Truth* in 1930, he used the word "nigger" as had, no doubt, those from whom he had learned it, but in 1935, when he recorded for Columbia University Library, the word does not appear. This change shows sensitivity on Lunsford's part because on the market at the time were numerous records containing racial slurs. Lunsford frequently spoke highly of black singers and speakers he had met on his collecting trips to black churches and schools.

A product of old-time education, Lunsford had studied Latin and had read the classics. He was much interested in poetry and frequently quoted Shakespeare and Burns. He loved a good turn of phrase and admired ballads and folk songs containing good poetry. He felt that the really good ballads and songs were equal to the lines of a Shakespeare or a Burns. He would quote from *Hamlet*, "Some say that ever 'gainst that season comes, wherein my Savior's birth is celebrated, the bird of dawning singeth all night long." Then he'd say, "Not one man in a million would have expressed it that way, one in a million." He would talk about modern songs and complain that they did not have good poetry.

> Why there's nothing poetic in:
> Put your sweet lips a little closer to the phone
> Let's pretend that we're together all alone.
> I'll tell the man to turn the jukebox way down low
> And you can tell your friend there with you
> He'll have to go.[13]
>
> But you take these lines from Jesse James:
> Robert Ford caught his eye,
> And he shot him on the sly.
> The people said he was brave,
> But he ate of Jesse's bread,
> And he slept in Jesse's bed,
> Yet he laid poor Jesse in his grave.
>
> That's pretty strong language. Folk poetry can be as strong as Shakespeare's. We're at a disadvantage today. We had more poetic things to think about back in those days than we have now. Now when Burns wrote:
>
> The banks and braes around the
> castle of Montgomery
> Green be your wood, fair your
> flowers
> Your waters never drumlie.
> There summer first unfolds her
> robes
> And there the longest tarry.
> There I took the last farewell
> From my sweet Highland Mary.

> Those are poetic terms about poetic subjects. We're at a disadvantage about making good poetry today. A lot of the songs today are pretty good—pretty good singers too—but the poetry is nothing like the old songs, from the literary standpoint.

Lunsford was not always well received in his own community. Some of his neighbors on South Turkey Creek did not take too kindly to his music and dancing. Some accused him of neglecting his law practice, his farm, and even his family while fiddling around and gallivanting about the country. His thrifty father-in-law confided that he did not think Nellie's husband would ever get ahead in the world. It is hard to tell whether neighbors were more affronted by the worldliness of Lunsford's pursuits or by his disinclination to "get ahead" financially. Some commented about being unable to understand how a man of his education and standing as a lawyer could fritter away his time on music and dance. The attitudes toward Lunsford are similar to attitudes toward musicians elsewhere. Folk musicians are generally liked and enjoyed but are not highly regarded in the social structure of the community because they are assumed to be somewhat frivolous.

As reflected in old sayings and stories, fiddling and banjo picking had long been condemned by those who could not or would not play the instruments. Lunsford referred to a cartoon character named Hambone who said, "De preacher, he object to de banjo, but he always pat he feets." He told a story to illustrate attitudes toward fiddlers:

> This man said to a man he'd sold a ham to, "Did that ham have any little black bugs in it?" "Yeah, it had some." "How many?" "Why that ham had more bugs in it than there are fiddlers in hell."

John Lair had a saying to the same point, "Anybody that plays the fiddle or parts his hair in the middle is on the skids to hell." Lunsford remarked that one fellow had reported that "his wife had got so hell-bent for heaven that she took and burnt my old fiddle" and another had said wistfully that when he was a boy he wanted a fiddle, but his father had said he'd better not. "I guess he was right," he concluded.[14]

Preachers blasted Lunsford from their pulpits as a corrupting influence with his picking, fiddling, dancing, singing worldly songs, and encouraging others to do likewise. Always strongly interested in the church, he once agreed to teach a Sunday school class, but when the preacher heard that he was a leader of square dancing, he wrote saying that Lunsford couldn't teach Sunday school if he continued dancing. Lunsford remembered. "I never put it to issue, because you lost if you ever put it to issue."

"I remember that many of the young people were not permitted to come to our house to square dance—it was considered so sinful," Jo Lunsford Herron stated.[15] Jim Miller, who lives at Leicester and who courted Lynn, on the other hand didn't feel that many church people stayed away from the Lunsford dance parties. He remembered strong church-goers being there and dancing. He did recall, however, that church people would sometimes talk about Bascom because of his dancing and singing. "But whenever they needed to raise money, Bascom would be the first one they'd go to, and he'd give more money than any of the rest."[16]

"While our family was a regular church-attending unit of the Methodist Church, Dad was involved spasmodically, you might say, as he saw a place," Nelle remembered. "Once when the minister was absent, he took over as the lay preacher for one service—and somehow he worked in that song he sang so much, "Drinking of the Wine." He could don the Santa Claus suit at the church's Christmas program and delight the children with such simple humorous remarks as he read their names to receive gifts."

Lunsford's church attendance may have been discouraged somewhat by the attitude of some ministers and fellow worshippers who looked down upon his folkloric pursuits. By all accounts, however, he was a religious man, as his father had been before him. Lunsford had a great number of hymns and spirituals in his repertory, many collected from Negro churches. Merton commented on his avid reading of the Bible and other religious material. "His faith in God and his knowledge of the Bible impressed me at an early age. He was one of the best resources for reference in teaching Sunday School. He didn't take an active part in church work himself, except for short intervals, although he was considered an excellent Bible teacher. I was never doubtful of his faith and deep belief in God. This, plus his knowledge of the Bible, was of great comfort to him during his confinement (after his stroke)."

A good judge of human nature, he was not averse to getting involved in church politics, as Jo's anecdote reports:

> I'll add one funny remembrance which has to do with a split in the church. One faction split off after a stormy session one Sunday morning when a new Sunday school superintendent was elected. I was just a little tad and went home from church with a friend—that afternoon (seems the friend's family was among the split-off group that had planned a secret meeting at the church to start a separate Sunday school). The group met in the afternoon and planned an afternoon Sunday School apart and separate from the regular one—elected separate officers, etc. None of the adults in that group realized that one of the little tads in the group might be paying very much attention. I remember the whole idea was most interesting and amazing to me, and I went home giving all of the details to Munchie (our mother). Dad asked me a few questions. Later that week a most glowing report appeared in the Asheville paper—Dad had written the thing tongue-in-cheek—and it sounded great to the outsider. Only the very people involved could have seen the humor of the thing. That was the beginning and the end of the effort to divide the Sunday School.

Kermit Duckett, a Republican who carried on a friendly political rivalry with Lunsford, said, "Bascom was a good man. He never had a bad thing to say about anybody. If he couldn't say anything good, he just wouldn't say anything." Then he added, "I've seen him stand in a crowd of men where somebody began to run somebody else down. Bascom would just walk off somewheres else."

Duckett related another story about Bascom that indicated what always came first in his life. In 1952, when Lunsford ran in the primary for the state legislature, Duckett saw him in Asheville on election day and asked him why he wasn't at the polls campaigning. Bascom replied that he had to go to Tennessee to set up a dance program. Duckett said, "You can't go out of the state today. You're running for the legislature." Bascom replied that if the people wanted him, they'd vote for him whether he was in town or not. Later Duckett saw Bascom's campaign manager, Ketron Worley, a local merchant, and asked him if he knew where his candidate was. "Why, he's out beating the bushes. He'll be bringing 'em in here in a little while to vote." "Beating the bushes, my eye," Duckett replied. "Why he's gone clean out of this country." Lunsford lost the election, but his dance program no doubt went off without a hitch.[17]

"You might know that, from all his interests and causes in life, he was definitely not like the average father," Nelle observed. "As a small child this worried me somewhat—because, although we lived on a farm, my father did not work the farm like my father's friends. But as I grew older, I realized my father was giving us other values."

Lynn said, "I quite vividly remember when some considered him lazy and shiftless because he picked the banjo and sang, neglecting his law practice to run all over the country collecting songs and square dancing. However, this never seemed to bother him. He continued, undaunted in his quest for what he believed in despite the criticism.

Even though he was away from home much of the time, Lunsford was a proud family man. His absences reflected his many interests rather than a lack of affection for his wife and family, although they doubtless indicated a restlessness of spirit, too. One thing is clear: he could not have chosen a more suitable mate than Nellie Sara Triplett. Merton Lunsford Brown rememberd her mother in those years as being "quite ingenious and certainly a Rock of Gibralter in managing the farm and doing what she had to do to keep the family fed and clothed. If my mother had not been the kind of women she was, Dad would never have been able to accomplish all he did in his work."

"Bascom's interests and projects were far from supplying good stove wood and hickory back logs" (in comparison with his industrious father-in-law), Nelle wrote. "However, Nellie Sara Triplett used all those basic Triplett qualities with which she had been endowed—and, together, she and Bascom gave those seven children a priceless heritage—hard work, education, and an appreciation of the arts and traditions of the mountain people of Western North Carolina." Merton adds, "Among the things Dad stressed most in my growing up, as well as in my adult life—were honesty, truthfulness, and dependability. Although he was away so much, and my mother stressed these same traits, I always felt that he did as much to mold my life in this way, as she."

Nellie Lunsford with her son, Lamar, and grandson, Frank, on the farm (courtesy of Jo Lunsford Herron)

George Stephens, who with his wife frequently visited the Lunsford home, was an admirer of Mrs. Lunsford as well as her husband. "I admired the part Mrs. Lunsford played. She knew how to do what was needed and yet not overdo it. She just helped him to accomplish what was needed, and she was responsible for a great deal of the children's very worthwhile rearing, not that he neglected them, but she had more time with them. All in all it was an admirable match. It just worked out beautifully." Stephens was a close observer of the relationship. "Mrs. Lunsford could never be persuaded to take part in dancing. Now that was probably very cagey on her part. She knew what her most useful role was. I believe that her never doing anything which diminished his dominance was perhaps her greatest achievement. I never saw her dance. I did my best to get her to dance, but she never would."

Nelle had a similar observation. "Mother was in the background of our family—a very down to earth person—capable of seeing to every need of the family as a whole and each individual child. It was this strength that allowed Dad time to pursue his dreams."

Artus Moser remembered her as a thrifty woman. "She knew how to manage a farm. She got labor to do what she couldn't do. She carried on while he was away, and I think she was a very fine helpmate."

Filming *Music Makers of the Blue Ridge* in the Lunsford home (courtesy of Berea College Southern Appalachian Archive)

To young people in the community, the Lunsford home was a place where they could have a lot of fun and where they were welcome. "They were the most hospitable folks you ever saw," recalled Jim Miller who courted one of the daughters. "They'd make you right at home. Mrs. Lunsford would make doughnuts, and we'd push all of the furniture back against the walls and have a square dance while Bascom played the fiddle or banjo. It was good clean wholesome fun."

Lunsford frequently invited people from Madison, Buncombe, Haywood and sometimes other counties to pick, sing and dance. Byard Ray recalls going on many occasions to these gatherings with his clog-dancing mother. On a good evening one might have found Ray, Obray Ramsey, Red Parham, Sam Queen and a host of other neighbors, musicians, and dancers. Some gatherings were special events for the benefit of outside visitors, such as State Department guests from Russia (who had heard Bascom's recordings back home), or writers and photographers for magazines. The over-sized living room Bascom had built into the house on South Turkey Creek was frequently overtaxed.

"His bringing in neighbors and others to dance, who did cherish and appreciate what he was doing, enabled him to carry on and hold together the people," observed George Stephens. "I believe it made a big difference." Of course, many of those who danced and played at the Lunsford house also performed at the festivals. Some of the younger dance groups were formed at the Lunsford home, according to Jo.

While the Lunsford children never showed the talent and determination of their father, some of them were involved in his work. "Lynn went to the National

Folk Festival with the Lovingood String Band," Jo recalls. "I organized a square dance team and competed in Asheville in 1939—the year of Dad's visit to the White House. Most of the team had never danced before and we had fun teaching the inexperienced ones."

The best musician among the children, Lamar, could play the guitar, banjo, and string bass. He often played with bands at the Lunsford home and at festivals. Because he had been involved in his father's work in the festivals since he was a small boy, he was well prepared to take over as principal emcee when his father could no longer do it.

Lynn was also much involved in music. "As a young girl I accompanied Daddy on many trips during the summer months when he entertained at the various summer camps around Asheville," she wrote.

> His ability to completely captivate the young people made quite an impression on me. I am sure that I must have disappointed him many times because of my timidity. Although I picked the guitar, sang, and danced, I was in such awe of his natural charisma that I always felt inhibited. He never knew how passionately I wanted to . He literally had to drag "Sailor on the Deep Blue Sea" out of me. Once he overheard me at home singing "King William" and immediately wanted to know where I learned it. I told him about how we played a game to it during recess at school. He asked me to sing it to him until he could sing it with me. Little did I realize that I had made a discovery for him. It was not until Kern sent me some cassettes she made from his Library of Congress recordings that I knew he recorded that song and the story of how he heard it the first time.
>
> During the summers I adored going to mountain homes with him and had the fun of meeting most of the people mentioned in *Bascom Lamar Lunsford: 'Minstrel of the Appalachians'* by George Stephens and Pete Gilpin. Samantha Bumgarner was one of the most interesting of all. She was so vibrant and her eyes just danced when she greeted us. As she and Daddy picked their banjos they fairly made the mountains ring with their music.

"We learned many of the songs," Nelle wrote. "We tried our 'talents' out on one another, but we never became public performers to any great extent. My brother played the guitar and traveled with Dad quite a bit in working the annual folk festivals at Asheville. Lynn and I and a neighbor boy filled an engagement with him at a nearby high school once to perform between the acts of a school play. That was at Alexander, N.C., about 1933. We received $5.00 for the evening's work. He gave the three of us $1.00 each and kept $2.00. I played the banjo. Lynn and the neighbor, L.C. Culberson, played guitars. Dad made the performance lively and interesting—and the audience responded enthusiastically—though I can't remember what we sang or what he said. I was age 14 and had stagefright."

During festival time, many of the performers would stay at the Lunsford house, especially during the Depression when most had very little to spend on lodging. Nelle recalls that they had visitors throughout the year as a result of festival connections. "All was not singing and dancing and banjo picking," Nelle wrote. "Dad's quick wit and sense of humor was always a delight. He loved

Three generations of Lunsfords: Bascom, Laurence, and Lamar courtesy of Berea College Southern Appalachian Archive)

good yarns—and ghost stories—and even though they would be repetitions for me, I would listen just as intently as the first time when he would be telling a tale to some visitor."

The Lunsford children have many recollections of the festivals and other activities in what their father had been involved. Kern had gone away from home for training in nursing about the time the Mountain Dance and Folk Festival was founded. The other children went away, one by one, for further schooling or training, but all were aware of their father's involvements. Nelle reminisces about the early festivals:

> We had moved to Turkey Creek when I was nine years old, and the Mountain Dance and Folk Festival was just in its infancy at the time or shortly after....Those were days to remember. The "Depression" had hardly allowed anyone to escape.
>
> The performers came for three days, some from over 100 miles, sometimes in trucks converted into living quarters. They cooked meals over open fires at the edge of the ball park, and endured many discomforts, but they held the riches that Dad had discovered. They could sing, fiddle, pick the banjos, and guitars, etc., with traditional "grace" and style found nowhere else but deep in the mountains. I can still hear those haunting melodies drifting out over the ball park. They were the "pure" performers who had been singing and dancing for generations back. I am sure their pay was very small for the efforts and discomforts it took to make the festival each year, but they had found a friend in Dad, for he loved them as people and as individuals. Each year found us discussing for weeks afterward the individual personalities of people who came to perform. Some of them stayed in our home and we have made some lifelong friends through these festival acquaintances.

If the Lunsford home was not typical, it was interesting and alive, and the children maintained a philosophical attitude about their father's untypical activities. After he had became quite famous, with frequent newspaper and magazine articles on him and his work appearing, one of the daughters said to another, "He's become so famous, we're going to have to stop saying he's wacky and start saying he's eccentric." It was a joke Bascom would have enjoyed, for he frequently told jokes on himself, concluding with "the joke was on Bascom." Regardless of the children's possible attitudes toward their father and the family situation while they were growing up, they now are aware that their father and their equally remarkable mother endowed them with qualities more valuable than money, personal property and comfort.

Even though money was scarce as the children were growing up, the Lunsfords made sure they had a chance to pursue their educational interests. They were encouraged in literary matters, and good grammar was stressed. One of the daughters reported that anyone caught using bad grammar had to do some onerous task, such as cranking the spring phonograph or carrying in fire wood. All of the children, with the exception of Kern (who attended West Buncombe High School), graduated from the Leicester High School, near the family home on South Turkey Creek.

Kern attended nursing schools in Washington, D.C. and Greensboro, N.C., and after graduate study, became a nurse-anesthetist, working in North and

South Carolina. She died in March of 1981. Lamar graduated from North Carolina State College and has taught vocational agriculture in various N.C. high schools. He has two sons by a former wife, and he and his present wife Edna have a son. Ellen attended Blanton's Business College in Asheville and has worked as a secretary in a stock brokerage firm and in governmental offices in Washington. She is married to Arthur Boza, and they have one son. Lynn graduated from the Carolina School of Commerce and is secretary to the principal of a high school. Her husband is Zebulon Hadley, Jr. They have one son and a daughter. Nelle studied at Boyd Business University in Washington, D.C. and is retired from the staff of Miami Presbytery in Dayton, Ohio. She and her husband Jack Greenawald, have two sons. Merton attended Berea College for a year but graduated from Blanton's Business College. After working as a medical secretary, she now assists her husband, Sherrill Brown, in running a farm on South Turkey Creek near the old Lunsford place. Jo also attended Boyd Business University in Washington and later American University. She has been a Girl Scout and March of Dimes executive. She is married to Lewis Herron, and they have two daughters and a son.

The family farm on South Turkey Creek has been divided among the children. This legacy, along with the Mountain Dance and Folk Festival and the Mars Hill Lunsford Collection and festival, will likely cement the children and their descendants to each other as well as to the past.

The children helped Lunsford with his amazing scrapbook, probably the most ambitious one ever undertaken, growing, no doubt, out of obese smaller ones. The plywood covers measure 28 x 30; when the family stopped working on it, the scrapbook was at least eight inches thick. Not just a record of his doings, it also reflected the times and events through which he had lived. Mostly, though, it contained newspaper clippings, letters, photographs and other memorabilia of his remarkable life. He obviously missed few instances when his name was in print.

Nellie Lunsford, Bascom's and the children's "Rock of Gibralter," suffered a stroke in 1956 and lay paralyzed for four years before she died. Both she and Bascom were 78, and they had been married for 54 years. "Dad didn't miss but a few days visiting her in the hospital and nursing home," Merton wrote.

In August of 1960, he married Freda Metcalf English, the widow of Berry English of the Puncheon Fork community in the Laurel section of Madison County. She came from a musical family in Flag Pond, Tennessee. She had sung in Bascom's festivals for several years where she was a popular performer who won several trophies. She had been featured in broadcasts from radio stations in the region and had taped a program for NBC which was never aired.

Her health was precarious in the years they were together, but Lunsford supported her as she cared for his needs. "She thoroughly enjoyed being Mrs. Bascom Lamar Lunsford," Merton wrote. "But on the other hand, Dad was not an easy person to live with. She tried her hardest to do all she could for him. She

Bascom with his second wife, Freda, and Obray Ramsey (courtesy of Berea College Southern Appalachian Archive)

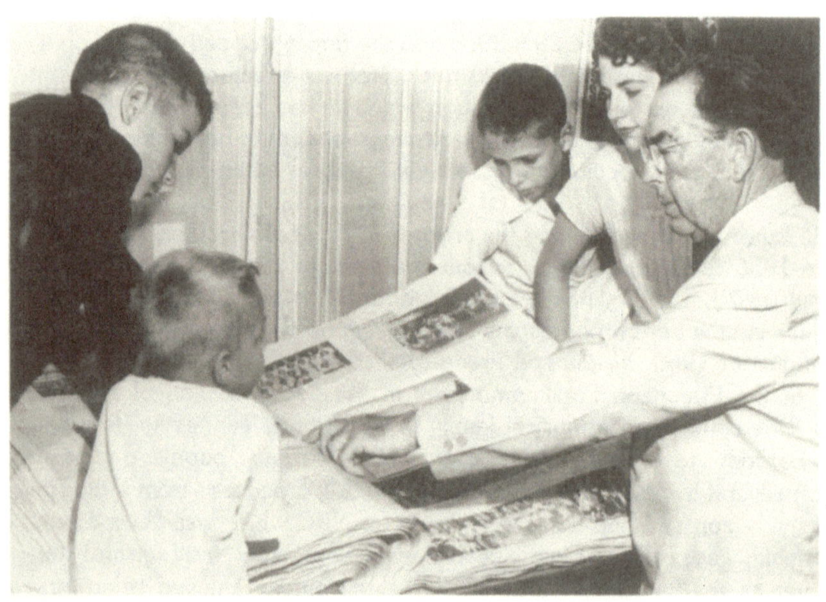

Bascom entertains his grandchildren with his big scrapbook (courtesy of Lunsford Collection, Mars Hill College)

loved Dad and we will always be grateful to her for all she did for him and for making it possible for him to remain 'on his own' until after age 91. This meant a lot to him and he sincerely tried to be as little trouble to her as he could be. He did numerous things to please her that amazed me for one his age."

"I would say that Freda was a great help to him," George Stephens commented. "She was a far humbler person in education, but she was a great satisfaction to him." Indeed, the second Mrs. Lunsford did care for Bascom in his declining years. After his stroke, they moved into an apartment in West Asheville to be near his doctors, drugstores and the hospital. She not only looked after his physical needs but also sang and played with him on various occasions, such as in the movie *Music Makers of the Blue Ridge* and on Lunsford's Riverside record.

Lunsford was beating the bushes for talent, traveling all over the country for lectures and concerts, recording, and assisting writers and film makers long after the age when most people have taken to their rocking chairs. Though in his 80s, he was also still running the Mountain Dance and Folk Festival. But then, in 1965, he suffered the first of two strokes. Jo described this first stroke:

> In June of 1965 Daddy was going over to Madison County to have a road built on some property he owned over there. He was to meet the road builder at the mill wheel over on Laurel River. When he got out of the car he faltered and could not speak. The folks in the resturant knew he was a friend of Obray Ramsey's and they called Obray. Obray told "I nussed your Daddy's head in my lap there until the ambulance came, and then I got the man to take him on over to Buncombe County to his doctor." This was the first stroke and was so severe it almost paralyzed his left side. He lost the use of that side temporarily, but regained most of the use of it. I am sure his determination to get well for the festival that August helped recovery. But he was hospitalized about six weeks and was unable to attend that festival. That is the only one he ever missed.

That year Lamar and his friends put the festival together and ran it. Bob Lindsey, director of travel and promotion of the Asheville Area Chamber of Commerce, did the most. "He almost single-handedly held it together," Jo wrote. "He truly idolized Daddy, and his unselfish efforts at keeping all the good parts intact during that crucial stage set a good pattern for continuity. Lamar served as the main master of ceremonies."

"If I were trying to describe Daddy," Merton wrote, "the first thing I would say is he was made of tough fiber. He had many hardships, reverses and disappointments throughout his life, some unavoidable and some from his own mistakes, since he was a dreamer, but he never let anything get him down. His endurance through all these things and the discomfort, during his illness, was amazing. The confinement alone was harder for him than the average person, as he had never been confined to anything long at a time."

Lynn told a story that illustrates the same characteristic:

> We built our summer cottage before "do-it-yourself" became popular and he was always anxious to see what we were working on. It was such rough going at first. I shall never forget some simple but very positive advice he gave us one day. We were digg-

ing the foundation when he came. It was one of those days when everything went wrong, the financial picture looked bleak and we were wondering if we had undertaken the impossible. When he realized how down in the mouth we were, he looked at us devilishly, but with gritty steel in his eyes and remarked, "Don't let NOTHIN' get you down. *I MEAN NOTHIN'*." He was very much concerned about our speaking correct grammar when we were growing up. However, he never lost the opportunity to coin his own phrase to suit the occasion to make his point hit the mark. The three of us laughed over this through the years and used it many times to encourage each other.

Even though he recovered satisfactorily from his stroke and the second, lighter one, Lunsford was never quite the same again. He gave up playing; "Timing is the key to music," he said. "And my timing is all gone." He gave his beloved banjo and fiddle to Mars Hill College, along with his collection of folk songs and other material. Up until the end, he would sing a little, and his foot would pat as he recited or sang verses, but he was unable to perform again. Pain was also constantly with him.

Jerry Israel, Freda, and Bascom at Lunsford's ninetieth birthday party (courtesy of Berea College Southern Appalachian Archive)

It was Thursday August 2, 1973, the opening night of the 46th Annual Mountain Dance and Folk Festival in Asheville, North Carolina. The audience—mountain natives, tourists, summer campers and long-haired young people from faraway places—waited noisily but with an eye always to the stage of the City Auditorium for the moment the festival would start. There was no printed program, but everyone knew that the festival would begin when the time was right.

The crowd quieted when Jerry Israel came on stage, flashing a grin that promised good things to come. He wasted no time in introducing the founder of the festival, Bascom Lamar Lunsford, whose 91 years rested heavily on him. But, leaning on Israel, he came to the microphone with burdened step, as his friends in the wings and in the audience remembered how he had been in earlier years at the festival when he had served as master of ceremonies, picked and sang, fiddled, called square dances and buck-danced with agility and joy.

The audience came to its feet with loud and sustained applause. Young and old eyes glittered with tears.

His frail body was bent and pained from strokes, but he stood with dignity and in command of the scene, in white suit and red carnation, until the applause tapered off and his friends took their seats. He blinked away tears, and his faded eyes began to dance as he greeted them in a surprisingly strong voice. Concerned friends could relax, for Lunsford's mind and memory were clear. Then he sang a verse of "Sourwood Mountain" to open officially the 46th Annual Festival. His singing voice was gone, barely reminiscent of the strong mountain tone of his prime years. Somehow, though, the tune came through the voice that could no longer cope with it, or perhaps it was just that sympathetic and knowing ears heard more than actually came forth. No matter, it was music to the ears of the audience, and it would have been a disappointment if any other voice had rendered this most traditional of mountain songs to open the festival.

Bascom Hall, who had helped with the festival, himself 95 years of age, came forward to stand with Lunsford. Looking toward the applauding audience, the two old men stood, seemingly satisfied with their work, before asking the fiddlers for "Gray Eagle" and making their way into the wings where Lunsford ensconced himself just behind a side curtain to receive his friends.

Presiding on stage was Lamar Lunsford, who had served as the festival's primary master of ceremonies since his father's stroke in 1965, and he had been involved since he was the age of his own son, Franklin Lamar, who was also present. Lunsford's second wife, Freda, and his six daughters critically appraised the proceedings. Lamar, tall, big-shouldered and handsome, adjusted the microphone and looked toward the wings.

"What're you going to do?" he asked of white-haired 74-year-old Virgil Sturgill, a Kentucky ballad singer.

As a tribute to Lunsford, Sturgill sang "Mountain Dew." Sturgill was followed by the Pisgah View Smooth Dancers, the defending champions from last year's festival, gliding through figures in the traditional step that had fascinated the Englishman Cecil Sharp more than half a century before. The program moved along as singers, musicians and dance groups got the casual nod from Lamar. There was no lack of talent: The Erwin High School Cloggers, who made the dust fly with their vigorous stomping; the Smooth Dancers from Elk Mountain; the Southern Appalachian Cloggers from Haywood County; the T.C. Robertson Cloggers from Limestone community; buck dancers such as Bill McElreath; bands including the Asheville Grass, the Glynn Lippert String Band, the Phipps Family Band; singers Quentin Ramsey, Betty Smith and others.

Lunsford was on stage to open the program on Friday and Saturday evenings. Afterwards, as he had done in years before, he sat in the wings listening to the music and greeting friends and admirers, but only for a little while. The previous year he had said to a reporter, "It's just terrible to be 90 years old." Speaking of his stroke, he allowed as how he could not fault the Lord for visiting this misfortune on him: "He's been mighty good to me."

When introduced to a man who had come all the way from Florida just to see him, Lunsford inquired with typical mountain humor, "Haven't you got anything more profitable to do? You're barkin' up a mighty lean tree."

Backstage at the festival, the musicians visited, joked, tuned up, exchanged songs and banjo styles. That year, perhaps sensing from his frail appearance that this might be his last festival, they made a point to visit with Bascom Lunsford. If this thought occurred to Lunsford, he did not reveal his feelings.

During the Saturday night's performance he surveyed the packed auditorium and asked for a 1974 calendar to determine the dates for the next festival. He expressed some irritation when family and friends could not come up with one quickly. But a calendar was produced, and he satisfied himself about 1974 dates.

Late on Saturday, the festival finally wound down officially, as many of the performers and others who had been in the audience took their instruments to the Westgate Shopping Center, where they played and sang into the dawn hours. But Bascom Lunsford, who in other years might have been there listening for new talent or material, was back on South Turkey Creek where he was staying with his daughter Merton.

Kern Lunsford, his oldest daughter, wrote, "Sunday morning, I stopped by to see Dad. It had been a big weekend, but Dad looked more alert than any of us! He had been at the auditorium for three nights in a row. But he talked about the value of our heritage of folklore and folk music, and even sang a few short songs."

Two weeks later, he grew ill and was taken to the hospital where his family drew around him. His 95-year-old brother, Blackwell, stroked his head, calling him "My little Bascom." On September 4 he died. It was fitting that he did not "go on," as he would have put it, until he had lived to see his work flourish, highlighted in the 46th Annual Mountain Dance and Folk Festival.

Walter "Red" Parham at the Mountain Dance and Folk Festival
(courtesy of Lunsford Collection, Mars Hill College)

Stories about his death and the accomplishments of his life appeared in major regional newspapers, *The Washington Post* and even *The China Post* published in Taiwan. *Newsweek* had covered the 46th Annual Dance and Folk Festival and praised Lunsford. Commentator Paul Harvey did a feature on him. U.S. Congressman (from N.C.) Roy Taylor wrote to Lamar to express his admiration for his father: "I do not know of any Western North Carolina citizen who has done more to put our area on the map and to preserve our music and folk heritage." He enclosed a copy of the *Washington Post* article and commented that it was a longer article than *The Post* would normally have on the death of a governor of a state. He ended with, "Your father was talented and he loved people."

The news stories and eulogies had strong opinions on Lunsford's accomplishments:

> ...one of the world's foremost authorities on American Folklore....
>
> Some of his recordings were the first to be included in the Archives of American Folksong.
>
> *Washington Post*
>
> His life's work was devoted to bringing the value of folklore to the public's attention. "I want to call attention for the good it may do the value of traditional culture as compared with the value of our artistic culture. The feller that knows the traditional background of his people has got the advantage over the feller that's go no idea 'cept something he's figured out on his own, purely from an artistic standpoint."
>
> ....the thing he loved so well flourishes after his passing. The arts of picking and fiddling, balladizing and buck-dancing were in his prime years thought no arts at all.
>
> *Charlotte Observer*
>
> It is the dream of most literate men to leave something permanent and constructive behind when they depart this world. Bascom Lamar Lunsford did.
>
> ...man of vision...singing troubadour...enriched the lives of those he met along life's way...going out among the people, he collected authentic ballads and instrumentals.
>
> Bascom Lunsford probably knew more about the mountains and mountain people than any other man...last of his breed...
>
> *Asheville Citizen*
>
> ...legendary minstrel of the Appalachians...
>
> *China Post*

Dr. Fred Bentley, president of Mars Hill College, gave the eulogy at the funeral. "Bascom Lunsford saw...values which to him were as sacred as life itself...his commitment to a cause, a principal, a way of life, preserved what so many were running from and others were seeking to change. He has seen the pendulum make a full swing. The ballads, tales and dances which were expressed by our grandparents, mostly abandoned by their children, are now reborn in their grandchildren. This rebirth could not have occurred had it not been for the man known as 'the Minstrel of the Appalachians.' "

The Sixth Annual Minstrel of Appalachia Festival, held at Mars Hill College on the 5th and 6th of the following October, was made into a memorial event. The festival had a double purpose: to commemorate the work of Lunsford and to promote Appalachian traditional culture. On Saturday evening of the Mars Hill festival, tributes were given to a packed auditorium.

Ed Howard from the Mars Hill community said, "He taught me that the true value of a human being is greater than any personal gain. He sacrificed for himself, his people and his music. Monetary gain he put aside."

As his tribute, Tommy Hunter of Mars Hill played fiddle tunes that were beloved by Lunsford.

Dr. Cratis Williams, dean of the Graduate School at Appalachian State University, spoke for the Appalachian Consortium of colleges and for the North Carolina Folklore Society:

> I want to go back almost 50 years to tell you what the situation was at the time Mr. Lunsford decided that we needed to do something to save the mountain culture. It was in the mid 1920s. The World War had stimulated quite a bit of economic growth and movement in the population. The Jazz Age had come along and had brought a new kind of music. The recording companies were meeting mountain singers in places like Charlotte, recording songs on 78 records and selling them to mountain people who had crank phonographs. But also the Tin Pan Alley people had taken up this country music and were adapting it to what was becoming known as hillbilly music. A whole tradition was likely to be corrupted on the one hand, and likely to be forced out of respectability on the other.
>
> Mr. Bascom Lamar Lunsford, who had grown up in this marvelous culture, who had learned intimately the mountain people of Western North Carolina, and who himself learned to play and to sing and to speak the language of the people and understand them, became very much concerned about what was happening. So, he originated the folk festival that was presented in Asheville first in 1928.
>
> He was particularly the man for this task, for he had the middle-class respectability of a lawyer, so that he could talk to the people at that social level. He was also a well-educated man with a great deal of self-confidence and assurance and knew what he was all about. He could talk with the people in the mountains, who were already beginning to be shy about their own culture and traditions, and make them proud of what they represented and what they could do. He could talk to the people of Asheville who were willing to support him with a festival....
>
> He was not only identified with the living tradition but also with the scholarly tradition. He gave the whole folk movement respectability at at time when it needed this support. He is the bridge between the folk revival and the folk tradition that our grandfathers knew intimately.
>
> I am honored to pay this tribute to the man who was at the right place at the right time with what it took.

Many letters came to the family from those who had known Lunsford and his work. One of the most appreciated ones was from a member of the family he had visited on his many trips through the mountains. "We knew he couldn't live forever, but for some reason we thought he could! And really he will! The great contribution he has made to our cultural heritage promised his lasting worth....Mother and her sisters recall happy experiences they shared as young girls gathered around the parlor piano when he came to town."

Alan Jabbour, head of the Archive of Folk Song at the Library of Congress, wrote, "We were saddened by the news of the death of your father, but the sadness was tempered by a warm appreciation for the splendid accomplishments of his long and full life. He made a lasting contribution to our understanding of Appalachian culture and life, and the Library of Congress may count itself fortunate to have been able to assist in the recording of his lifelong contribution."

And so Bascom Lamar Lunsford "went on over yonder," eulogized widely for his accomplishments.

Freda, who depended on him for emotional balance, survived him by scarcely a year. Home from the hospital for a weekend visit, she took her own life.

NOTES

1. Author's interview with Artus Moser, Swannanoa, N.C., 8-7-74.
2. Author's interview with Byard Ray, Asheville, N.C., 8-7-74.
3. Letter from Davis Lunsford to Kern Lunsford, 9-15-73.
4. Author's interview with George Stephens, 8-6-74.
5. *The Virginia Magazine of History and Biography*, vol. 17, no. 1 (Jan., 1909).
6. Author's interview with Bascom Lamar Lunsford, West Asheville, N.C., 7-27-71.
7. Author's interview with Jerry Israel, Asheville, N.C., 8-7-74.
8. Interview with Mr. and Mrs. C.P. Wells, South Turkey Creek, N.C., by Jim Wayne Miller, December, 1973.
9. Interview with Jerry Israel, 8-7-74.
10. Interviews with George Stephens, 8-6-74, and Jerry Israel, 8-7-74; letter from Bob Lindsey, 3-12-75.
11. Letter from Jim Wayne Miller, 1-3-74.
12. Author's interview with Buell Kazee, Berea, Ky., 3-2-75.
13. "He'll Have to Go," by Joe and Audrey Allison, c. 1959 by Central Songs, a division of Beechwood Corp.
14. Author's interview with John Lair, Renfro Valley, Ky., 4-30-74.

CHAPTER 6
Bouquets and Arrows

What purposes did Lunsford have in mind? The question is a hard one, for while he talked much about his work, he did not discuss the broader cultural and political implications of his activities. Most of us, except for eager academics, find it difficult to verbalize the wispy theories that motivate us to action. Lunsford often referred to old singers dying with their treasures of ballads, of the old ways dying out, of the progressive pushing out the traditional and of the failure of the young to appreciate the value of old ways. But he was clearly ambivalent in his attitudes toward the old and the new. He started a festival to showcase traditional musicians and dancers at a time when most of his peers were clamoring for the fruits of the industrial age, and in fact, used a largely phoney tourist-attracting promotional effort to present his "authentic" show. He invested in the real estate boom that was a major threat to the very traditional culture that he cherished. He was like most of us who must choose between the allure of new ways and things and devotion to the old. Lunsford learned that in the marketplace of values and aesthetics one had to wheel and deal, that everything had its price and that whenever you won you also lost.

Was Lunsford attempting more than just to preserve and promote the old songs and dances that he happened to love? Obviously he was, but it is hard to find evidence that he had any kind of plan that could be called culturally political, even with current interpretation when political motives are readily attributed to anyone who appears to be swimming against the tides of history. Lunsford had his calling which he followed with as much zeal as anyone ever did. But he was an anomaly. He was of the folk and yet he was also middlestream mountain gentry. True, this made him uniquely able at enlisting the participation of almost all types of people in the mountains because, in addition to his enthusiastic and engaging personality, he could converse with one and all within the framework of their interests and understanding. One has to remember, however, that in addition to his presenting authentic folk talent around the country, he also travelled for the Asheville Chamber of Commerce puffing the virtues of the Land of the Sky and giving a shameless argument as to why the well-to-do should spend their money in Western North Carolina. The politicians he promoted for public office were those who looked after the progressive business interests of his area.

Yet as David Whisnant has written in a perceptive article for the *Appalachian Journal,*[1] Lunsford found a way between the old and the new. He had an instinct for what he was doing. He liked progress, but even more he loved the traditional ways of his youth. He knew he could not "preserve" the latter against the tide of the former as a lone worker, but he hoped it was possible to create a climate in which the old ways would be respected, and he knew that if they had the prestige of respect then they would be more likely to survive, in some form, into a new age. His instincts told him that he could not do what he wanted to do in direct conflict with the economic and social movements of his time. So he joined these forces and used them and their momentum and money to promote what was dear to his heart. Perhaps this would not have worked elsewhere, but the Asheville Chamber of Commerce was in business to sell the main product of Western North Carolina—climate and scenery and to some extent a way of life that had passed from most places in the country but which was strong and vibrant in the Blue Ridge and Smokies, or could be made to appear so. Handicrafts, music and colorful dances were a major part of the charm of the region. The Chamber needed Bascom to bring out the musicians and dancers for the tourists to see. Bascom needed the money and the promotional apparatus that the Chamber could muster. With the help of the Chamber, Bascom created an atmosphere where the folk arts were cherished. Thus they continued to grow, in somewhat changed forms to be sure, but with a new vitality, not just as quaint survivals but as evidence of a culture that had retained a special integrity.

David Whisnant insists that Lunsford "understood the emerging politics of culture in the United States and consciously chose" to do the work he did in order to create a new cultural form.

> The importance of Lunsford's Mountain Dance and Folk Festival extends far beyond its local context in western North Carolina. As the earliest of the folk festivals, it was an important seed-bed for hundreds of other festivals spread across the United States....It contributed to substantial cultural revitalization inside the region and projected a new image of regional culture to a national and international audience through media coverage and guest appearances at the White House and elsewhere. It constituted an important transitional cultural form between "the old and the new"—between the old rural, traditional, community and family-based culture and the emerging urban, industrial, media-dominated mass culture that swept through the mountains as it did through the rest of the country. It furnishes a complex and instructive example of intentional intervention into traditional culture by a forceful entrepreneur....[2]

Lunsford's intervention was certainly intentional, and the results are as Whisnant reports. He created a new cultural form, and it has promoted an appreciation of traditional arts that continues to grow in the decades following his death. He instinctively knew what he was doing in one sense and yet in others he was no doubt mucking along feeling for a way that would accomplish his purposes.

In choosing the folk festival as his primary means of creating the accepting and respectful atmosphere that he wanted, Lunsford relied on previous happenings, such as household gatherings of musicians and dancers and the fiddle contests that went back to Colonial days, but he had to create a new form that would reach larger groups. Whisnant mentions two aspects of Lunsford's personality that made it possible for him to shape the festival, after the Rhododendron Festival gave it birth, into a product almost solely of his own consciousness. These aspects were "his status as a member of the mountain intellectual elite and his propensity for self-promotion."

> Thus, Lunsford—for all the colorful stories (which are also true) about his working as a beekeeper, itinerant fruit tree salesman and the like—was an educated and sophisticated man who knew and loved the traditional culture in which he had been raised, but who also viewed it in wider intellectual frames of reference supplied by his personal and family history....
>
> Thus, if it was Lunsford's knowledge of and love for mountain culture that provided his motive, it was his *doubleness of vision* that gave form to his work. He made a set of observations and judgments about the worth of authentic mountain culture vis-a-vis both the popular misconceptions of it and the mass culture that was rapidly supplanting it. He made some calculations about the "Your-culture-isn't-worth-anything/Yes-you're-right-our-culture-isn't-worth-anything" feedback loop that was so destructive to mountain people's dignity and consequently their desire to survive culturally. And like a Janus who could see both ways, he placed himself at the center of that cultural conflict.
>
> From that position he functioned for mountain people, apparently, as a mirror of—and a magnet for—their better, self-respecting selves; for the mass audience within and beyond the mountains he became a corrective symbol of mountain culture, a charismatic counter-example that did not fit their preconceptions, an item of data that forced a reconsideration of theory.
>
> The role Bascom chose for himself called upon him, however, to walk a fine line between projecting a new dignified image of a self-respecting mountain man, and merely self-interested self-promotion.[3]

As already iterated, Bascom used everything at his disposal to publicize himself as the Squire of South Turkey Creek, the Minstrel of the Appalachians and the like. He was not a modest man, in an area that prized modesty, because he knew that his crusade was largely dependent upon his personal skills and charisma. However, he rarely promoted himself apart from Appalachian traditions, and he said over and over that his business was "to draw attention to the fine cultural value of our traditional music and our dancing and the fine honor of our people." He talked always of the 'true cultural worth of the mountain people.' Thus he was not consumed, like many other musicians, by his own importance as a performer and the desire "to make it big" in the world of entertainment. His festival was a showcase for mountain talent. His role was to select and present that talent in a way that lent it dignity and importance.

He was criticized for his selections of talent and the way he ran the festival. Some objected to songs or tunes of questionable folk authenticity. Lunsford replied by saying that his purpose was to "get as much good in as you can and keep as much bad out as you can" but that he couldn't do this too exactly because he had to consider the feelings and aesthetic of each performer. "I'd ask them to do one song that I wanted," he said, "and then I'd let them do something that they wanted to do." It was a tradeoff that has troubled festival directors since Bascom. For example, Guy Logsdon, who produces festivals on Southwest life in Oklahoma, feels that traditional folks ought to be allowed to do what they do best, to make their own decisions about what they will present at festivals; however, Ralph Rinzler, director of the Festival of American Folklife at the Smithsonian Institution, feels that he should be a "cultural advocate," noting that Doc Watson played electric guitar in a VFW dance hall band when he first saw him, and that he (Rinzler) encouraged him to play what he played before this period in his life.[4] Lunsford was certainly a cultural advocate in that he encouraged his performers to play what suited his sense of what was their best traditional material, but he recognized the right of these musicians also to play what they treasured. He knew that traditional musicians did not discriminate between categories of music that they enjoyed playing. To an extent, the performers and their wishes were as important to Lunsford as was the overall effect of the festival.

The most distinguished musicologist to comment on Lunsford's festival was Charles Seeger. He visited the Mountain Dance and Folk Festival in August of 1936, as a part of his job with the Resettlement Administration Music Program. Seeger, by the way, believed that "proletarian music is an integral part of the question of social evolution." "Music," he commented, "is one of the cultural forms through which the work of humanizing and preparation operates. Thus, it becomes 'a weapon in the class struggle'...."[5] In a confidential memorandum[6] to his superior in the Resettlement Administration, Seeger commented on Lunsford's festival and compared it with the White Top Festival in Virginia and the Lewisburg, Pennsylvania Festival. One reason he liked Lunsford and his festival was because he saw Bascom as being "clearly of the same class as the contestants and as the average sitter on the bleachers...." He observed that Lunsford's "audience [was] mainly composed of friends and compatriots of the contestants, who were well versed in the accomplishments on exhibition and were quick to express approval or disapproval with unimpeachable authority."

> Very few notables came from outside....The rural element predominated to such an extent that even the hardened urban visitor felt partly absorbed by it. I should say that I think it is a very worthwhile affair. Although the playing was not phenomenal in any way, it was good and free. The singing was poor; I could not determine the reason. But the dancing was really fine; about 10 teams competed and all were better than the best seen elsewhere.

He called the Lewisburg festival "a kind of vaudeville show in which the traditional element was squeezed to the wall when it could not be made grotesque, sensational or ludicrous." He was most offended by what he called "the obvious patronizing of the humbler people," and the way "the old miners who sang some really fine stuff were patted on the back by the master of ceremonies and shooed around the stage and off it." He called the White Top Festival "a feast of paradox," where the "small coterie who manage the affair do not entirely agree, either in theory or practice" and are "self-contradictory to a degree...that possibly instead of furthering their aim they are destroying the possibility of its realization." Seeger went on to say that the Lewisburg and White Top Festivals "run the risk of being pernicious influences," and charged "I saw several examples of good old musicians who have been practically ruined, turned into detestable lapdogs, by these well-meaning, self-advertising city cultivators of the 'folk'."

Seeger concluded:

> The Asheville one is pretty healthy. A very little loosening up, freeing it from the Chamber of Commerce, allowing a bit more contemporary stuff, and letting the people themselves build it up—I should not say a word against it. But Lewisburg and White Top are both reactionary to the core-under the guise of antiquarianism the one destroys, even while it popularizes, while the other, under the smoke-screen of pseudo-scholarship, is really sinister.

It is important that a politically leftist scholar, who saw music as a vital element in social evolution, was basically impressed with Bascom's festival because he saw it *as of the people themselves*. He termed the other two festivals "reactionary" because he thought that they were trying to create a "folk" that did not exist. As an activist, he wished to encourage Lunsford and to fight those who ran the other festivals. Seeger's regard for Lunsford's work led him to hire Lunsford as a field worker for the Music Program of the Resettlement Administration.[7] In this role, apparently, Lunsford worked primarily with the Resettlement Administration's Skyline Farms in Alabama after an initial two-week training session, under Seeger, in Washington, but he also served as a troubleshooter at other resettlement communities.[8] It is unlikely that Lunsford and Seeger agreed on much politically and likely that each used the other to further their separate purposes. Yet in a fundamental sense, they shared the same politics of culture. Seeger's vision was no doubt more far-reaching in that he wanted to remake society and saw music as a tool in that cause. Lunsford also wanted to affect society, but he was satisfied to preserve traditional practices in a world that was already changing. However, both were prophetic in their belief in the value of folk traditions in strengthening the cultural fabric of the country.

Lunsford's tenure with the Music Program was short because of its demise under criticism by conservative preachers and by Republicans in the political campaign of 1936. It is doubtful if Lunsford and Seeger would have tolerated one another much longer anyhow. While they agreed on programs that equated folk music with high-culture music, it is certain that Lunsford was an uneasy ally in Seeger's quest for a "cultural democracy." He would have had problems with Seeger's two stated goals: the integraton of all the arts into a culture based on a community rather than personal values and the politicization of the folk so that music, rather than being an end in itself, would become instead "a means for achieving larger social and economic goals."[9] Lunsford believed that folk music was an end in itself, and he refused to sing at rallies against American policies in

Vietnam late in his life because he didn't think that folk music should be used in such a way.[10] He would have had qualms against undermining the traditional independence of mountain people, even though he saw the need for community organizations.

Seeger apparently never commented on Lunsford's politics. Neither did Lunsford comment publicly on Seeger's. Years later he was kind to Seeger's activist son, Pete, when he came south to collect songs. However, when Mike, another son approached him, he commented that he had done enough for the Seegers.[11] This remark most likely reflected his feelings for Pete's politics as well as those of his father.

Jim Wolfe, a New Yorker who is now a social worker in Chicago, visited with Lunsford in 1953 and remembered his being vocal against those who used folk music in their politics:

> At this time folk music was very strong in political movements, going back to Henry Wallace running for president in 1948. I had been involved in that campaign and knew a lot of the left-wing musicians who sang in Greenwich Village and other places in New York. So, we talked of political things, and I brought up Pete Seeger and Woody Guthrie. I remember Bascom becoming strongly indignant, or upset, or at least verbalizing a great deal about those, I believe he said, communists. My memory is that he was suspicious and concerned about left-wing people and folk music being misused. He felt that this was mountain music, maybe songs about life and issues in life, but it was not something (these are memories) that ought to be used for political reasons.

Wolfe was quick to give his positive impressions of Lunsford, remembering him as "crusty, tough, warm but reserved. He was very giving of himself. He absolutely loved what he was doing. I followed him around while he was doing farm and household chores. Mrs. Lunsford was hospitable, and I spent the night with them."[12]

Wolfe's recollections give evidence that Bascom's natural political conservatism was heightened by the anti-communist era in American life brought on by the McCarthy hearings.

During the 60s and early 70s, other liberal and radical activists criticized Lunsford for not taking a stand on various social issues. An age that melded politics and folk music together produced persons who assumed that the two had always been linked, and they seemed genuinely surprised when they discovered that Lunsford, whom they admired as a performer and festival promoter, was not a social activist just as they were. One example raises most of the criticisms that were levelled at Lunsford. In an article entitled "Bascom Lamar Lunsford: The Limits of a Folk Hero" (*Southern Exposure*, Spring/Summer, 1974), Bill Finger pays tribute to Lunsford for knowing the value of regional history and folk heritage long before there were university departments of folklore or *Foxfire* books, but he condemned his lack of social conscience and his failure to fight against the exploitive forces that emperiled the traditional culture.[13]

"Lunsford's work as a folklorist spanned a 50-year period of complex social change in the Southern Appalachian Highlands." Finger wrote, then listed the numerous federal projects and corporations that had come to the mountains and whose activities brought a threat to the old ways.

> He responded to the menace of assimilation with what he knew, the music and its impact on the mountain people. His fame and legend indicate his success in preserving the traditional music. But the threats to mountain society continue to grow stronger and more complex, revealing the limits of Lunsford's approach to cultural survival.

Finger goes on to say that while Lunsford was working to revive and preserve the music, the region was going through rapid change. His conclusion was that the region needed "dynamic leaders as well as static heroes." Stating his own preference, if not that of Lunsford's festival-goers, he wrote, "The long verses of the English ballads lacked the contemporary poignance of the protest songs from the textile or paper mills."

> The limits of Bascom Lamar Lunsford as a folk hero became clear in this cultural and political context. His was not a voice of political struggle; he did not involve himself in the labor struggles of the thirties and forties, nor did he often speak out against the potential dangers of land developers. In fact he disapproved of the political music of great balladeers like Woody Guthrie and Pete Seeger. Lunsford lived with integrity and purpose; he nurtured the natural bonds that an indigenous musical tradition creates between people. But his personal history, his times, and his narrow concern for music limited his perception of the complex forces eroding the social base of the very culture he wished to preserve.

When Finger's opinions were quoted to a long-time Lunsford associate in the festivals, the response was both emphatic and unprintable. Indeed Finger views Lunsford's work with an entirely different consciousness and a different perspective from that of Lunsford. He evaluates Lunsford in work that he never attempted and suggests courses of action that would have been out of character, considering Lunsford's time and place and his political and social learnings. He accuses Lunsford of not solving monumental problems which also have not been solved by the organizations and social activists that Finger suggests Lunsford's festival enthusiasts should join. This is not to say that the list of dangers that Finger presents are not real and threatening and that they should not be opposed. Folklorists, musicians and other mountain culturemongers should join forces with those who protest political, industrial and other exploitations of the region and its people. However, many of those who were influenced by Bascom will find it hard to use traditional music just as a means to foster togetherness at political meetings, and harder still to see traditional ballads abandoned altogether in favor of composed songs in protest of current regional problems. Lunsford thought the traditional songs and dances were ends in themselves and worthy of practice. Perhaps to many this is shortsighted or even frivolous, but to others Bascom's argument was sufficient.

Some serious questions were raised about Lunsford's integrity in terms of the festival, mostly from musicians who had performed at his festival and who were not willing to have quotations attributed to them. The main charge was that he controlled the judges and personally decided who should win the competitive events. One said, "His ways of doing things was crooked."

> He was biased toward Sam Queen and the Soco Gap Dance Team and would throw it to them. One musician told me that Bascom told him that if he would come play at the festival, he'd see that he won, and he did win year after year. He favored certain ones. They [the contests] were definitely rigged.

Another former festival participant said, "Some people got preferential treatment. Some people did win who didn't deserve it. He picked his own judges. I think he interfered with decisions." He went on:

> I was told that if you had enough money you could win anything. One man told me he lacked ten dollars having enough for his dance team to win one year. He [Lunsford] favored Sam Queen who usually won, but Sam was one of the best dancers that ever was. He favored Obray Ramsey, Manco Sneed, Byard Ray, George Pegram and Red Parham, and he would put his favorite people ahead of others on the program.

Another person, long associated with the festival, acknowledged that Lunsford did at times influence the judges to present prizes to those he preferred as performers, or to those whom he needed to accompany him to other events such as the State Fair Festival. Lunsford always had trouble getting musicians to lay down their regular work to go off with him for several days to entertain various groups. A prize at the Mountain Dance and Folk Festival could influence them to help him when he needed them. Another charge by this same person, who greatly appreciated Lunsford's work, was that he also slipped varying amounts of money to certain performers (who ostensibly were rewarded only if they won prizes) so as to keep them coming and also to make sure that they were favorably disposed toward him if he needed them to perform elsewhere.

It is hard to evaluate these charges since there is nothing on record to substantiate them, and some of them are hearsay. There is no doubt that these performers were sincere in the belief that Lunsford decided who should win at his festival, but others in a position to know, are doubtful that Lunsford tampered with the judging. Artus and Mabel Moser, who were judges for both dancing and music, defend him against these charges and say that he never tried to influence them in their decisions. Another dance judge, who did not wish to be identified, also defended Lunsford. He said that some judges might have been influenced by knowledge of Lunsford's favorite teams and would seek to please him. He denied that Lunsford had ever tried to influence him when he was a judge.

It is not surprising that there would be strong feelings and suspicion about the judging aspect of the festival, since the competition was strong, and there is evidence of frequent disputes over the decisions of the judges. It is hard to imagine that Lunsford could have gotten away with fixing the competitive events, since such a system could not have been kept a secret. However, Lunsford probably did make his own ideas known about dancers and musicians, and thus he no doubt influenced judges who were not secure in their own opinions.[14]

Tributes to Lunsford were abundant. Sarah Gertrude Knott, founder of the National Folk Festival, wrote, "He was what he was, strong and true, adding to these characteristics a dignity and truth of the inherited form in text and tune as he got them from other generations. He danced the Southern Appalachian dances with true fashion, yet he took liberties as he felt them, just naturally keeping the dances true to form. Bascom will be sadly missed, not only in his native state, but wherever the British legacies of folk songs and dances are carried on in the United States."[15]

Harold H. Martin wrote that "he is by no means merely a mountain troubadour, twanging and yodeling his way from frolic to frolic. He is a folklore scholar who has often appeared before learned groups to talk mountain music." But Martin also said that his greatest contribution was not his scholarly work such as recordings. "The best thing he has done has been to awaken the pride of his own people in their traditional music...."[16] *The Asheville Times* (1973) called him "the dean of American folklorists." Bob Terrell, in an *Asheville Citizen-Times* article (March 19, 1973) wrote that in collecting and preserving Appalachian folk music, "Bascom Lamar Lunsford stands at the head of his class."

Jerry Israel commented:

> As far as our area, Western North Carolina, is concerned, it will be years before we learn the significance of his contribution, purely because he did it when he did. That is the thing. If he had done it in the late 50s it wouldn't have been anything...The fact that he did it when he did and that it worked puts it really beyond our comprehension, when you try to think of the far-reaching ramifications of what this festival caused. As I've told today's dancers, if it hadn't been for the festival—and the festival and Bascom were synonymous back then—you wouldn't be dancing.

Ballad singer Betty Smith made a similar statement: "Well, I think he just got out and spread the music around, when not too many people were really doing that."

"In my opinion these traditions wouldn't have been here without him," stated Earl Ward, a member of the Watauga County family that gave Jack tales to Richard Chase. John Parris, columnist for *The Asheville Citizen-Times* (June 26, 1970) wrote, "He has done more to preserve the old ballads and the old folk songs than any man in all the country." Raymond Lowery, in a *Raleigh News and Observer* article (October 20,1963) said, "North Carolina's real big daddy of traditional folk music is Bascom Lamar Lunsford, 'the Minstrel of the Appalachians and folk balladeer extraordinaire'...,[he] probably knows more authentic ballads than any man in America....The prodigious feat of singing in Washington [Library of Congress] alone lasted seven days and represents the largest single contribution of any performer."

Pete Gilpin and George M. Stephens wrote in their book that "Bascom Lamar Lunsford has reopened a reservoir of folk music for all the world. But he would have done it anyway, whether the rest of the world stopped to listen or not." In assessing Lunsford's gifts, George Stephens and Richard Wynne, publisher of *The Asheville Citizen-Times*, agreed that he "enjoyed the respect of scholars. Beyond that, though, he knew how to reach out and touch every one of us, from the humblest to the highest. This is the special meaning of this man who has brought such riches to our time....Ever so dedicated to his high aims, he has literally become a leader in bringing back our proud folk heritage of native poetry borne on inspired song. Likewise in lively dance he rescued a rare pleasure which was dying out."

Jesse James Bailey, former sheriff of both Madison and Buncombe Counties, said, "He was a typical mountain man. He was an asset to his community, he didn't accomplish—like myself—a great deal except in this mountain folk music. [But] I think it was worthwhile for him because he loved it and he preserved it. I think that if he hadn't done it we wouldn't have the old traditions we love now. I've seen him build this thing [the festival] from the ground floor, and he did a marvelous job. He built it all these years alone. And he had the know-how."

"Mr. Lunsford was a man of many trades and good at all of them." Artus Moser said, "Lunsford came along, and he educated the people of this region. His great contribution was that he revived the musical traditions, and he kept going in the face of criticism. His main contribution, in my opinion, was to revive the folklore and to take the gaff, as it were—to stand the criticism—to sponsor all of this and to keep it going." Joseph Haas wrote in *The Chicago Daily News* (August 17, 1963) "Lunsford has done more than anyone except, perhaps the famed English folk song collector, Cecil Sharp, to preserve the rich heritage of folk song in the Appalachian region." Haas also quoted Barry Vogel, a 20-year-old musical pilgrim from California: "Anyone interested in folk music has heard of Mr. Lunsford. That's why I'm here."

Some of the praise is adulatory, to be sure, for people tend to feel strongly about Bascom Lunsford. As Moser and others have indicated, some of the criticism was so strong and doubtless deserved, but much of it was brought on by a failure to understand what Lunsford was doing, a disagreement over what was or was not worth saving and promoting, and how one should go about the task.

Aside from the religious critics, the most persistent critics were those who were strict in their definitions of folklore—the purists—who were involved in similar work and who had doubts about Lunsford's style and methods, and indeed about some of the content of his repertory and programs.

Ray M. Lawless (*Folksingers and Folksongs in America*, 1960) pointed out the basic critical problem in Lunsford's festivals, "the problem of presenting genuinely traditional material, and at the same time making it acceptable entertainment. Many are interested merely in entertainment, in the popular sense, and have wanted to bring in current popular music—country and western....Lunsford, like many other festival directors, has been obliged to make compromises with his 'new culture' to the extent that some serious students question whether his festivals are in authentic tradition."

Others, feeling that tradition constantly changes, accused certain purists of trying to "freeze" traditions at a certain point, permitting no more changes. Sarah Gertrude Knott felt that traditions do change and that Lunsford was perfectly justified in allowing "new" expressions into his festival. "Time changed certain things," she wrote, "and Bascom was not hide-bound. He made his own songs, made them so well because he was so steeped in tradition, that no one could tell it. Who cares in one way? That has always been done." "Old Mountain Dew" supports Miss Knott's point about Bascom's songs. However, his other compositions have not been passed on in the oral tradition.

As to the festival, Miss Knott says, "I went to Bascom's festival a few years ago, and I heard a few say, 'Why does Bascom allow the newer songs or music on the festival program?' 'It is changing,' I said, 'Bascom did not change this festival. Time and a new way of life, a force stronger than Bascom is at work on all folk activities. Bascom is struggling to find the way between the old and the new.' " Miss Knott also pointed out that Lunsford fought hard to maintain the traditional styles and material. "Several years ago I was there but could not see him. He was too ill. I talked with him over the phone. He was strong in his plea for me to keep up the effort to hold to the traditional."

George Stephens and Jerry Israel felt that Lunsford made some wise changes. Stephens noted that the younger people weren't interested in the straight traditional square dancing any longer, but were looking for something new. When the clog-step became popular, Lunsford "had the breadth and wisdom to allow it to come in. Actually the younger generation likes the clogging much better than it likes the smooth dancing, in general. Mainly it's a tribute to his breadth and understanding." However, Stephens conceded, "Lunsford resisted clogging mildly, but he resisted it. It would certainly be a surprise to me if he had *any* part in encouraging it." On the subject of Bascom's giving in to modern ways, Israel said, "He gave in to a certain degree, but I don't think it was against his better judgement. I think it was *because* of his better judgment."

Israel made another point, which conflicts with Charles Seeger's analysis: "The White Top Festival [in Virginia] was authentic, but it was boring as hell. It was just for the pure in heart. You can't sit for six hours and listen to people sing 30-verse ballads." Israel's point raises the basic question of whether a folk festival should educate by presenting only authentic traditional materials or whether it should also strive to entertain with some material that reflects changing generations and tastes. Comparing his festivals to a buffet table, Bascom said he tried to have something for everyone. He also made it plain that he felt "it is entertainment when I am endeavoring to present the finest of our traditional culture."

To be fair to Lunsford, one should recognize that he accepted some new things and rejected others. He felt that the clog dance was traditional in the mountains, even if it had not been the traditional step in a set dance. Therefore, he felt the dance was not harmed by the dancers' using this step in place of the smooth running step. But many disagreed with him. When asked how he felt about cadenced clog dancing, Jerry Israel replied, "Why I think it's terrible, but the crowd likes it. I don't know what could be done, if anything, to reverse the trend." Certainly the clog has become a much-loved part of the square dance, by both dance groups and audiences. (It should be remembered that the Mountain Dance and Folk Festival has two categories of dancing: clog and smooth.)

Some unknowing people suspected that Lunsford had invented the clog, or had borrowed it from some other setting and introduced it to square dancing. One person waited one night at the festival to ask Lunsford where he got the clog step. His reply was , "It was here before you were born." Marguerite Bidstrup, past director of the John C. Campbell Folk School, who had observed the running set dance at Pine Mountain, Kentucky, before Cecil Sharp had collected it there, was shocked to see the clog step in the set dances at the Mountain Dance and Folk Festival and explained her dismay with, "I had a high standard for the dance." Because of the young dancers' growing enthusiasm for the clog, many of the more staid institutions that promoted folk dancing had a great deal of trouble getting them to stick to the running step. To many dance teachers, the clog step was anathema, and Lunsford was accused of being the cause of the new craze. There is little doubt that Lunsford's festival had indeed presented the exciting clog step to large audiences and thus created the desire of some dancers to adopt it.

Lunsford was guilty as charged of promoting, even reluctantly, the clog step. But the charge that the clog was in no way traditional is false. The clog dance was a traditional dance in England and an American adaptation was known throughout the Appalachian region as an individual dance. It is strange that critics of the clog have overlooked Cecil Sharp's mention of it as a sometimes spontaneous part of the promenade in the running set. The question is not whether the clog was a traditional step in mountain dancing; it certainly was. Instead, the question is whether it was ever a standard step in set dancing. By most accounts it was not.

Many who were willing to accept the clog step in dance sets were not ready to accept steel toe and heel taps, which were added to accentuate the rhythm of the step. Few, aside from the dancers, supported toe and heel taps. Dr. W. Amos ("Doc") Abrams, formerly president of the North Carolina Folklore Society and English professor at Appalachian State University, made a partial defense. "I have had and still have some misgivings about supporting the use of steel toe and heel plates, but I must say that in dancing, too, perhaps, for all things there is a season....I would not wish cloggers to use steel plates while dancing in my living room or on my brick patio, but on an open platform above the crowd...or even on a stout plywood platform beneath a tent....these steel plates attract, stir the blood, and add to the effectiveness (yes, the spectacularity) of the entertainment. I have seen their power on the spectators on many occasions. They somehow belong to the rock and roll rhythms, the split-the-ear volume, etc. of this present time." Abrams also said that he "*cannot* accept....their use in smooth dancing where the appeal comes from the swaying of the bodies and the muted shuffles of the feet and the coordinated gestures of the dancers."

The "smooth dance" as it was known at Lunsford's festival was obviously as much influenced by this descriptive adjective as the Kentucky square dance was influenced at Berea College and elsewhere by Cecil Sharp's descriptive title of "running set." Some of the smooth dance sets accentuate their smoothness to the extent that they look unnatural and uncomfortable. The ladies' costumes, often with crinoline underskirts, encourage a mincing, swishing gait. The competition among dance teams enhanced showiness and took away from the naturalness of the dancing. It also produced a competitive spirit in Western North Carolina that is rivaled only by basketball and created a standard dancing style and aesthetic that are identifiable from that in other parts of the region.

Clogging is obviously related to the clog dance in northern England which came from the type of shoe—the wooden clog—worn by workers. Numerous dance groups in the northwest of England still wear such shoes. In this country the buck dance, or clog, was done long ago in rough boots with hobnails in the heels and soles, as described by Byard Ray and others. In both England and America the main point of the clog step is to beat a ringing rhythm with the feet. Whether or not this noise, energetic motion, and showmanship is desirable depends on one's taste, but it is clear that all of it has a traditional base.

Ethel Capps, former recreation teacher and director of the Country Dancers at Berea College, gave her opinions about the influence of the Mountain Dance and Folk Festival, and similar festivals, on traditional styles.

> When you put it on as a show or as a contest where you win money—what happens is that the people who take part and try to win the prize, they just go to all kinds of lengths to get attention. They try to be as exotic and interesting as they can be, far and above what they would be if they were doing it in a natural kind of way. It will change it. It's like putting hormones on a plant. It makes them too big and too important. Sometimes the effect of tourists on an audience is bad. Out West, for example, when you see Indian dances put on for tourists, some are traditional, but some have costumes and all that aren't traditional. This would not have happened if it were done in a natural way. [17]

The late Frank Smith, Miss Capps' predecessor at Berea College, and founder of the Berea College Country Dancers, stressed the same point in his *The Appalachian Square Dance.*

> When you dance for the public a lot of things are likely to happen... the public likes dressing up in costumes and appreciates special little spectacular touches. So you put on a ten-gallon hat and wear special dancing pants; a girl has a dress made to swish like a wheat field in the wind. Then you bow elaborately... When you promenade a girl, at the end you end with twirling her a couple of times. Then you fix up the calls....and mannerisms that had little to do with...the Appalachian Square Dance...This is not to say that these changes are in themselves undesirable. Freedom to experiment with dance forms could be important even for the survival of traditional dance.[18]

Smith also claimed that a number of factors, such as easy travel and communicaton, commercial incentives, festivals and other gatherings "at which the variety of traditions used is astonishingly wide," may all tend to break down traditions. Smith does not offer any hard and fast suggestions for promoting traditions without changing them into something else. In fact, he was not against change, but he did feel that leaders should be aware of corrupting influences and should hold some reverence for past traditions.

Ethel Capps offered some reasons why other folklorists and promoters criticized Lunsford. "He promoted clogging. The way they did it was offensive to some people, and the fact that it was just a big show, and some would go to any length to create attention for their group. Some of the groups were kind of mechanical, with everybody on the same foot at the same time." This criticism is valid. If the singer, instrumentalist, or dance group is more interested in winning or in pleasing the crowd than in sticking to traditional styles, then styles may follow current tastes and trends. The bluegrass phenomenon is a case in point. When Scruggs-style, three-finger banjo picking became the rage, most banjo pickers who could adopted that style. At most festivals now, frailing banjo pickers in the string bands are rare. The same can be said for fiddle and guitar styles. Bluegrass, for better or worse (and many traditional musicians, including Lunsford, insisted that it is nothing new), is currently the dominant string and band style. There is no doubt that audience wishes entered into the growth of bluegrass. Lunsford nevertheless would have appreciated the comment of the late Frank Proffitt in regard to Earl Scruggs' style of banjo picking, "I wish I knew how to do that—and then not do it."

Some feel that festivals, with consequent audience pressures, have brought about a better quality of musicianship and dancing. Jerry Israel believes that musicans today are better than they ever were before. "My great-grandmother played the fiddle, but she may have played it only three or four times a year. That's the way it was with some of the festival musicians back years ago. They may not have played for a month or two before the festival. The musicians today, all they do is make music. They are a breed apart." Israel also mentioned another factor, the outside musician, that contributed to the better quality of the music. "In the 50s we began to get what we referred to as the 'New York unwashed.' In quite a few cases they played music better than we did, because to us, it was an important part of our lives, but it was only a *part* of our lives. They were professionals, or would like to have been, and they spent all of their time at it. But I don't resent the outsiders, not in the least. They're here because they are genuinely interested."

Israel's comments indicate that the kinds of musicians who play at festivals have changed, to a great extent. In the beginning they were the natural singers, like the ones Cecil Sharp described as the true folk singers—self-effacing, modest folks who did not need or care about an audience. Today there is a definite group of festival followers who appear wherever there is a musical get-together, and they invite themselves onto programs. Since many are fine musicians, they build a following which also puts pressure on festival directors. Israel feels that modern musicians, both mountaineers and outsiders, are becoming a group apart from the common folk. They play to win, or at least to please the audience. There is little question that Bascom's festivals and those that have followed have promoted musicians who like to "perform" for others rather than musicians who just love to share music.

Perhaps the very success of Bascom's festival and the ever-larger facilities needed for it dictate a new kind of musical activity. Folk music grew up among small groups—the family, sometimes a few neighbors and friends, or at most a few dozen people in an intimate setting. The Mountain Dance and Folk Festival is now held in the huge Asheville Civic Center. The modest and shy mountain singer is not at home in such a setting, and his qualities may be mostly lost on an audience. The professional musician who knows how to work an audience has the advantage over the modest traditional artist in such a setting. Yet with all of the shortcomings of the Mountain Dance and Folk Festival many believe that it has revived and created interest in the traditional arts, and that without it some might not be practiced at all, especially with the many amusements available to most people. "They sit home now and watch TV, or get in a car and go to the Asheville Mall," Jerry Israel affirms. "There are a very few close community ties. If you didn't have the festival influence where would you be? One thing I know, that Bascom's festival is responsible, totally responsible, for 99 percent of the dancing that's going on in Western North Carolina right now. If the festivals hadn't replaced the community gatherings, where would we be?" It is a good question. Israel exaggerates but he is partially right. Without the popular revival interest in traditional things, doubtlessly by large festivals and commercial concerts, many traditions would not be so vigorously alive today. These traditions most assuredly are not practiced as they were in our great-grandparents' days, but at least they are practiced.

A basic problem exists between native practitioners of Appalachian traditions such as Lunsford, and the "outsiders" who direct recreation, music, and dance programs at private schools, colleges, and other such institutions. Many of the latter are intrigued by the songs, dances, and tales brought from the British Isles and preserved by mountain people. They have been told by such collectors as Francis James Child, Cecil Sharp, and Richard Chase of the value of this material. But there was and still is a tendency on the part of some outsiders to accept only those traditions that were so legitimized—the English and Scottish ballads and folk songs, the tales about Jack, and the dances assumed to be derived from the English country dance. The other fiddle and banjo tunes, the rough humor, the frontier ditties, the sad old hymns, and the buck dance were questionable, however, to those who had been schooled on genteel folklore. In fact, the mountaineer himself was sometimes viewed as a questionable character, especially by those at the educational institutions, who conspired to change him into a more desirable person. Lunsford was different from practically all of the other folklore practitioners in that he was a native who loved and practiced almost all of the mountain traditions. For example, he sang the mountain versions of ballads, rather than versions that were perhaps more delicate and closer to the British Isles.

George Stephens spoke of the folk school and settlement school people who were involved in the folk arts and their skeptical view of Lunsford's work.

> They were strictly authentic British Isles source people, and they actually did not recognize the perfectly genuine filtering and transition in the 200 years since the British Isles. They wanted to go back to the Morris dances in England. That's all right. That's a worthwhile approach, but it doesn't have the meaning for today's mountain people. Now the folk schools are loyal to that approach. Fine. But this is the irreplaceable contribution of Mr. Lunsford. He was not against change. He realized that change was in the nature of traditional music from generation to generation. I don't believe that, except for trying to rule out the unnatural or spurious or the commercially motivated parts, I don't believe he opposed change.

Although not all of the settlement school and college people were guilty of harking back to England for their standards (it should be remembered that it was at Pine Mountain Settlement School that Sharp first saw the running set), some did use the English dances and the ballads as printed in English literature survey books or in Child's collection to measure Appalachian traditions. Many with specialized training in the dance or in music imposed this training on collected materials. For example, Gladys Jameson of Berea College collected hymns in mountain churches (where the tradition was to "line out" the songs to be sung in unison) and then arranged them in four-part harmony. The result, when delivered by a trained choir, was beautiful, but it was far removed from the manner in which they were traditionally sung. Cecil Sharp substituted jig tunes for the traditional fiddle tunes he had heard in Eastern Kentucky when he presented the running set. As Ethel Capps has pointed out, this definitely changed the dance because it then had a different feel. Many singers with trained voices used traditional folk music, with fine results, but such a presentation was quite different from that of a truly traditional singer.

Lunsford believed in presenting music or the dance as it was performed in its native setting. For example, when he sang the old hymn "Balm in Gilead," he usually pronounced the words as he had heard them in a mountain church, "There is a Ba'm in Gilled." The Child Ballad "Sweet William and Lady Margaret" he sang as "Little Marget," because that is how is was pronounced by Loretta Payne who taught it to him, and he sang "Lord Daniel's Wife" as "Lord Dan'l's Wife." Perhaps this was going further than he needed to, but it shows that he was never ashamed of mountain people and their ways of pronouncing words or performing their music, as long as they were genuine and sincere.

Although Lunsford cooperated with many people, some accused him of being a loner and said that he would not cooperate with others doing similar work. An example of this independence is a visit Lunsford once made to a meeting of the group that sponsored the Spring Dance Festival at Berea College. Looking around, he said, "Well, I see that you work as a group. I work alone." Another time he was asked to participate in presenting some square dancing at the annual Craftman's Fair in Asheville, sponsored by the Southern Highland Handicraft Guild. Instead of responding to the question of whether or not he would participate, he responded, it is charged, "I'm glad you see what we have been doing all these years." That ended that. The invitation was not pressed.[19]

In spite of the reports that Bascom did not cooperate with other promoters of the folk arts, he told Harold H. Martin that his interest was nourished by the continuing "interest of such fellow devotees as Mrs. Olive Dame Campbell of the John C. Campbell Folk School, where not only singing and dancing but all the ancient folkways were encouraged." In his square dance book Lunsford listed other centers in the mountains where square dancing was taught.

Another criticism of Lunsford was that his personal showmanship offended some other folklorists. They thought his "Minstrel of the Appalachians" title was going a little too far. They felt that it didn't fit the basic modesty for which mountain people are noted. "Doc" Abrams was one who accepted Lunsford as he was and saw the positive results of his personality. "Being first and foremost a showman," he wrote, "and yet, withal, a dedicated lover of the lore and traditions of the folk, Bascom Lunsford had no choice but to present himself in spectacular fashion. In my judgment, this aspect of his contributions was in fact the ice-breaker, the stimulus, which encouraged others to join him, literally, on the platform. I was never aware of any dearth of participants when he was around."

In his inimitable way, Abrams stressed the value of Lunsford's personality and style:

> I have been and consider myself an academic professor, having served as a chairman of an English Department for 17 years. Thus do I have the interest of an academician in folklore, research, research, research, scholarly papers reporting to others who make scholarly reports. But, Brother, my experience has shown that if you want to take folklore away from the folks, the best way to do so is to turn your folklore programs over to *us*, the professorial segment of our contemporary society! We desperately need a few Bascom Lamar Lunsfords to come along and save us from ourselves![20]

Other scholars appreciated Lunsford's contributions and his special qualities. Dr. Daniel Patterson, director of the Folklore Curriculum at the University of North Carolina at Chapel Hill, commented that Lunsford "could always delight audiences as a performer of the old songs." He stated further:

> Both his mountain people and outsiders appreciated his work in fostering the annual folk festivals to give recognition to traditional performers and encourage them to value their own lore. Mr Lunsford is also respected by folklorists for his work as a collector. He was one of the earliest to pay attention to Appalachian song. Twenty years before the English collector Cecil Sharp visited the area and published his remarkable findings, Mr. Lunsford had already begun to collect. At the time when most collectors were interested only in the Child ballads, he was open to an amazing range of traditional music. He gathered love songs, children's songs, banjo and fiddle tunes, work songs, spirituals, and a wide range of ballads. His recordings, publications, and manuscripts give us a valuable profile of the music known to the traditional performer in the North Carolina mountains at the beginning of this century. All of us are in his debt. [21]

Patterson's last point is an important one. Lunsford indeed was one of the first persons to collect, perform, and record such a wide variety of material. More than most other collectors, he viewed music and the traditions of his people as a natural phenomenon to be accepted, understood, and utilized without trying to strain it through current societal or individual tastes and biases. It was all legitimate in his view, if it had been honestly performed in the oral tradition.

While Patterson spoke mainly of Lunsford as a North Carolinian, Sarah Gertrude Knott tried to put his overall contribution into perspective by talking of his place in the history of British Isles folk songs. "I don't think any other person's name should go higher than that of Bascom Lamar Lunsford," she wrote after his death, "because of the long list of folk songs (ballads and folk songs) that he passed on through his books, his recordings and in the living form—as he influenced others at festivals and as he lived day by day among his neighbors. No other person has had more influence on me."

There was some variance of opinion on Lunsford as a performer—as a picker and singer. Pete Seeger said, "He was a good banjo picker with a deep love of mountain music. I only met him a couple of times but I will always feel deeply grateful to him." In his foreword to Bascom's Folkways record, Seeger wrote a tribute to the five-string banjo as well as to Lunsford. "Someday the music schools of the nation will recognize the worth of the banjo as Mr. Lunsford plays it, though at present it is largely unwritten and unrecognized....A few Yankee youth, fallen in love with American folk music, owe Mr. Lunsford a considerable debt; they have learned the banjo from his records, patiently transcribing them, note by note."

Lunsford, and also Samantha Bumgarner, did indeed have a profound effect on Seeger. After he heard them at the 1935 Mountain Dance and Folk Festival, he abandoned his four-string tenor banjo forever and made the five-string his basic instrument. From Seeger, in person and through his instructional book which features Lunsford and his picking style along with those of other great mountain banjo players, hundreds if not thousands of other young Americans have learned to play the banjo to some degree of effectiveness.

Scott Wiseman, who was also a banjo picker, had less praise for his picking style.

In my opinion he was not a very good banjo player, but he was never backward about picking up an instrument on any occasion and plunking a few chords as he sang in his twangy, Turkey Creek mountain style. It was a distinctive ancient backwoods style... He was never interested in the latest commercial hillbilly records or songs that were currently popular but always had something to say about tracing folk songs, their many versions, complicated relationships, and histories. He never changed his style in spite of the influence of crooners, yodelers and all of the commercial country million-seller artists.

"He was just fair as a musician," said John Lair, putting Lunsford's worth into perspective. "His value was in his recollection of the songs and not in the way he presented them. But he had an authenticity about him." This is a theme that many persons touched on when commenting on Bascom. They felt that he was genuine and sincere in what he did.

Artus Moser, who had recorded him for the Library of Congress, also commented on his performing style. "His voice was not too good for ballad singing. He had a good voice, but I don't think he ever tried to improve it. There was a certain twang to it that was always the same." But, Moser added, "Oh, he was authentic." Moser was somewhat critical of Lunsford's ballad repertory. "He didn't have the feeling for texture of the ballad. He was willing to bring in modern expressions. He added a touch of dare-deviltry, and there was a little touch of making them into comedy. The ballads that he and Stringfield edited for *30 and 1 Folksongs* are not a good collection in my estimation. They did not select the finest ballads. Some were fragments."

Moser's judgement is stern. He himself is a well-known collector and ballad singer with three albums to his credit. His approach is scholarly; he usually sings the classical British ballads and his own taste is obviously different from Bascom's. For many years Bascom would not invite Moser to sing; he thought Moser's style was too professional and remote from the traditional mountain singer, though Moser is a native of the region.

Perhaps the important thing about Bascom's playing and singing is that it was honest and genuine, completely traditional to the region. He played and sang the music primarily as he had learned it. He probably learned few tunes from books or from records. He did not read music, although he could probably pick out a melody from the musical notation. It would, however, have been against his principles to do so. To him, folk music was oral music, and he learned almost all of his songs from other musicians.

As noted earlier, Bascom played the banjo in the styles traditional to Western North Carolina. He could frail the banjo, but his basic lick was the two-finger (thumb and forefinger) picking style common in Western North Carolina. He played mostly just to accompany his voice. Although he would play the melody between verses, he rarely played purely instrumental tunes on the banjo. He was an authority on fiddle tunes and had little patience with musicians who could not distinguish between similar fiddle tunes. He played for square dances, but he knew that his skill on the fiddle did not approach that of a dozen other good fiddlers whom he knew. Therefore, he had a first-rate band to play for his dancers, but he would join in occasionally on the banjo.

He had definite feelings about how songs should be presented. As Raymond Lowery stated in a *Raleigh News and Observer* article (October 20, 1963), "As a folk music scholar, composer, and performer, Bascom has a tendency to look with disdain upon a number of current ballad singers and city billies who've never been 'on top of old Smoky'."

Lunsford stated, according to Lowery, "I can excuse them for not knowing the difference between 'Boogerman' and 'Buckin' Mule,' but when the performers subject the ballad to caricature, mockery, or ridicule, they exceed the bounds of good taste."

Lowery further stated that Lunsford "thinks the great folk ballads should be presented at their 'traditional, unspoiled best with a special emphasis on accuracy.' " Lunsford's adherence to this latter point is illustrated in his singing of "The Death of Queen Jane," a ballad about the third wife of Henry VIII. Lunsford called Henry "Prince Henry," as he had learned it, even though he knew Henry was the king. Also, the version he had collected and used was only a fragment. It would have been easy for him to piece a complete version together from the Child or other collections, but he sang just what had been given to him.

"He does not sing a song in the usual sense," Stephens and Gilpin wrote. "He tells the story and this is the key to his love for the mountain songs."

A ballad is a plain story simply told, he would say. He felt that the story in the ballad was the important thing, and that the tune was merely an aid for telling that story. Perhaps this accounts for some of the rather plain and ordinary ballad tunes he sometimes employed when more refined tunes were also traditionally sung in the region. He accepted the scholarly notion of the time (which reflected Child's influence) that a ballad is almost always in third, rather than in the first, person, and that the singer, or narrator, is not connected to the story. The ballad is about another time and another set of people; therefore, the singer stays remote from and uninvolved in the story. He commented:

> Acting out the part is offensive to one who knows. A fellow came by trying to learn a certain ballad. He put more into it than there was. He put unnecessary expressions to show his feelings of misfortune. Folks want to exaggerate what they know about something to impress you, when they know only certain outstanding features.
>
> Here's the idea. A song tells a story—tells something. The poetry is the message, and the music is the aid. A fellow ought to believe his own story, so to speak, no matter what it is . A man ought to sing it like it was a fact. Now for example:
>
> John Henry was a little baby,
> Sittin' on his Papa's knee,
> He looked up to his Papa and he said,
> The hammer'll be the death of me, Lord, Lord.
> The hammer'll be the death of me.
>
> John Henry's a wonderful piece of music. It's a wonderful thing. So you sing it like you believe it was a fact.

He preached naturalness in both dress and musicianship. He felt that others sometimes tried too hard, as in presenting a ballad, or sometimes in trying to copy superficially the styles of folk musicians.

> Let me tell you about that. Had a fellow who played at the festival who learned to play a violin before he did the fiddle. But he took a notion that it was all right to have this mountain music. So he'd stick the fiddle down here on his chest as he's seen mountain fiddlers do it, and he'd bear down on it so that he broke the hair out of a bow or two. Bascom Hall, who helped me with the festivals, borrowed a bow or two, about two I believe, and he broke the hair out of both of them. Hall said, "What's the matter with that fellow? He broke the hair out of two fiddle bows I borrowed for him," I said, "Why nothing, only that he just learned to play the violin before the fiddle, and now he's just trying to imitate a fiddler."

While Artus Moser felt that Bascom did indeed act out some of the ballads to put more life into them and that he also liked some of the racy ballads, Bascom's playing for effect would have been against his own teaching, and indeed his recordings do not support Moser's criticism. He was against showiness in the presentation of a ballad and spoke often of the need for being natural and for allowing the ballad to sell itself without an unseemly projection of the musician into the music and story.

John Lair talked admiringly of the skill with which Bascom taught square dancing to various clubs in the Cincinnati area. Byard Ray and Walter Parham also remembered how he could take a group of people who had never danced before and have them dancing before the evening was done. Nothing on record questions Bascom's skill in dancing and in teaching the Appalachian square dance, except for criticisms by those who disagreed about the clog step. Lunsford personally did not do the clog step in a dance, for he preferred the old smooth style. He could do a buck and wing as a solo dance, though, and he liked to do so at the festival or at any other gathering, especially when he was quite old, in order to show that he still had a lot of life in him.

Bascom Lamar Lunsford was highly praised and roundly criticized, but his positive influence is strong. Pete Seeger put him into perspective:

> Marc Antony was wrong. The good in people lives after them. The worst doesn't last so long. Architects' best buildings stand up. The bad ones fall down. Bascom's work will stand for a long time.[22]

"I feared that, as the old folks passed on, they would take with them to their graves all memory of the tunes and lyrics which once the mountain people had sung with such joy and gusto," Lunsford once said, explaining his motivation. As a fellow Madison Countian Lee Wallin said of a great old ballad singer who had passed on, "It's hard to think that a voice like that is silent now."[23] There was wonder, puzzlement, and a hurting loss in his voice as he said it. It is well nigh impossible for us today, who never heard more than one or two of the truly natural traditional singers, to comprehend what it really means to lose one or all of them. For many of us—not all, for some of the common people instinctively know the importance of tradition—there was a time when we might have lost much of our traditional legacy so thoroughly that we would not have known we suffered a loss. And this is the worst kind of poverty—not knowing that one lacks something vital. But we did not lose it, thanks to Lunsford and those others who knew its value.

Many of the revered old-timers have passed on: Aunt Samantha Bumgarner, Uncle Nat Marler, Marcus Martin, Manco Sneed, Fiddling Bill Hensley, George Pegram, Bill McElreath—and Bascom Lamar Lunsford. Yet they are still with us through electronic recordings, photography, the printed word, and more importantly, through the large number of young people who, as a result of festivals and other get-togethers, know at least some of their repertories and styles. These particular old-timers were recorded and imitated primarily because of the Mountain Dance and Folk Festival. Even Bascom himself was best known for his festival, from which his other contributions grew. But for Bascom's festival and the opportunities growing out of it, the names and music of many mountain musicians would have remained unknown, except in their immediate locality.

In 1974, the year after Bascom's death, the 47th Mountain Dance and Folk Festival was forced into new quarters—the new Asheville Civic Center. A huge place, larger than the cornfields of some of the performers, it was more suited to the talents of Bob Hope, Johnny Cash, and the Lipizzan Stallions, who were in fact among the first to do shows there. But the Mountain Dance and Folk Festival outdrew them all. There were 5,800 the final night, and at least 10,000 admissions for the three nights. Because of the seemingly endless stream of talent, most of the audience remained until the end on Saturday night, which came at 1:30. They enthusiastically cheered the dancers and applauded the singers and musicians, in spite of a less than perfect sound system and acres of space between them and their favorite performers.

Each evening 10 fiddlers in a line on stage played "Gray Eagle," as an opener and as a tribute to Lunsford. Memorial statements came from his old friends George M. Stephens, George Tisdale, (manager of Southern Bell Telephone Company and a long-time chairman of the Folk Heritage Committee) and ex-sheriff Jesse James Bailey.

The festival itself was a tribute to Bascom: hundreds of musicians and dancers doing what they liked to do, and thousands of people coming from heaven-knows-where to listen to traditional music and to see the dancers whirl. Lamar Lunsford manned the microphones for a good part of each evening, inquiring, "What are you going to do?" as the performers came on stage. Jo Lunsford Herron managed the square dance competition. Two other daughters, Kern and Merton, were in the audience.

"I think the festival was better this year, in terms of authentic performers, than it has been in the recent past," Artus Moser stated. "There always has been great interest in receiving an invitation to perform in Bascom Lunsford's festival," Jerry Israel said. "This year the degree of interest is exceptional. Part of it is the

Virgil Sturgill, Kentucky ballad singer, at the Festival (courtesy of Berea College Southern Appalachian Archives)

Musicians on stage at the Mountain Dance and Folk Festival (courtesy of Berea College Southern Appalachian Archive)

new building, I think. Then Mr. Lunsford's passing seems to have increased people's interest in the work he had done and in his festival."

As Artus Moser suggests, the 1974 festival may have been better than it had been in recent years, but it was also harder to find and present truly authentic performers. Mrs. Jackie Ward, now primarily responsible for rounding up new talent commented, "Not many years ago the playing of old-time mountain music here was like a strong stream. Now it is more like a mountain spring. Those who play the real thing are getting fewer and fewer." Yet, with those who have played at the festival through the years, with the talent that comes through the Shindig on the Green, which Mr. and Mrs. Ward manage, with the help of Joe Bly, and with the talent they locate elsewhere, there were more good performers than could be presented in a normal evening's performance, and many aspirants were turned away. The performers ranged from the real old-timers—Cas Wallin and Inez Chandler, ballad singers, and Morris Norton, tune-bow player, all from Madison County—to Roger Sprung and his string band from back East. In between were such superb singers and instrumentalists as Byard Ray, who teamed up with Lou Therrell, Betty Smith, Vivian Hartsoe, and Betty Sue Johnson to form a group called the Appalachian Folks; the Quay Smathers Family Dutch Cove Band; Mack Snodderly and Tommy Hunter and their Hornpipers; Red Parham and George Pegram; the Uptown Grass from Asheville; Jim Trantham, ballad singer from Canton, North Carolina, the Bear Wallow Band from Madison County; Tex Burleson, mouth harp player from Johnson City, Tennessee; musical saw player Ken Harrison from Raleigh; the Stoney Creek Boys; and Virgil Sturgill, white-maned Kentucky ballad singer.

So there it was, proof that the old traditions were still strong, the old-timers still hanging in there, proudly presenting their beloved music, and the new generations coming on, like 18-year-old Liz Smathers of the Dutch Cove Band, a fourth-generation fiddler. It was a different and more elaborate setting from the first festivals, but the flavor seemed the same, except that now—all over Asheville, Western North Carolina, and the wider region—people are enormously proud of the festival and the quality of the performers. Some of the young generation have come to mountain musical traditions through the instruction of their parents and grandparents, while others have come to them from the disillusionment with midstream society, with its unsure images, commercial trafficking even in music, fleeting styles and spurious tastes. The 47th Annual Mountain Dance and Folk Festival drew a variety of mountain people and folks from elsewhere because the traditions were old, lasting, and genuine. It was Bascom's gift beyond the grave, to a nation that was becoming unsure of its history and destiny. Permeating the festival was a sense of strength and abiding values.

Unfortunately, the most traditional elements of Appalachian music have become scarcer at the Mountain Dance and Folk Festival in the years since Bascom's death. At the 1981 Festival no unaccompanied ballad singers were on the program, the bands ran mostly to bluegrass and many of the singers and musicians would have to be classified as revivalist rather than traditional. The Shindig on the Green held on the courthouse lawn on summer Saturday evenings and managed by Jackie and Earl Ward and Joe Bly, long-time members of the Festival Committee, serves the purpose of attracting talent and channeling it into the festival, but it is not a substitute for the kind of field work that Bascom once did. Without constant scouting for talent, the festival producers are under pressure to use the most aggressive and most technically impressive musicians rather than those who may best represent the traditions of Appalachian people.

Lunsford lived to see folklore departments flourish in the universities and to see colleges add courses dealing with various aspects of Appalachian life and culture. The Appalachian Consortium, to which he became an advisor, is made up of southern Appalachian colleges and other organizations. The purpose of the Consortium is to encourage courses relating to the region and to make courses at a given college or university available to students at other member institutions. Appalachian studies courses have been started at several other regional colleges and universities, and in 1977, an annual Appalachian Studies Conference was formed.

"I'm glad to see colleges taking an interest in traditional culture," Lunsford said in 1971. "They ought to teach it right along with art culture. Traditional culture is most lasting and more powerful than art culture and a person ought to know something about traditional culture." He saw a need for counter streams of information about mountain people. That was what his festival and his other activities were all about. But he saw the need for more than that. He had hoped for a time when prestigious mountain people and institutions would speak proudly about mountain culture and promote the mountain traditional arts.

"The fellow who knows the traditional background of his people has the advantage over someone that has no idea about it," he said. "The folk side is bigger than the other side, the artistic side. It's more important than the other side." Jean Earnhardt in *The Greensboro Daily News* (June 7, 1964) explained Bascom's reasons for pushing the ballads: "To him the old songs are wonderful for they speak of the things that unite people—love and sadness, growing up and marrying, and death." But it wasn't just the ballads. It was the meaning behind the traditions, the essence of the common people, that he thought all young people ought to know about. And he especially thought that those who wanted to sing the folk songs ought to have a feel for the tradition. The art of a thing alone was not enough. He felt that some of the popular folk singers had more art than feeling for the material. Someone asked him what he thought of a certain popular folk singer. "I said he is pretty good, pretty good. He used to be better than he is now. He knows art music, and that hurts some. If you are tied down to the precision of a thing it's like a preacher reading his sermon." He didn't feel, though, that there was necessarily a conflict between artistry and authenticity. He encouraged people to improve their artistry, although when it came to a choice between artistry and a feel for the value of the traditional material, he chose the latter.

Lunsford lived to see the folk revival and hundreds of folk festivals stemming from his own festival. He had problems with some of the practitioners of the new folk styles, but he was genuinely pleased with the awakened interest in the arts of the common people. He went his way, gently remonstrating with those who departed from his example, but never bitter against them because they did not see things his way. In his last years he seemed to cherish the many people who had taken on the task of promoting mountain traditions. Satisfied with his own work, he was ready to leave it in the many new hands, even though he might not agree with everyone's methods and style.

Indeed, with the number of persons and institutions promoting, teaching, or performing folk materials, their future is secure. However, one cannot escape the fact that as the old-timers die, there are fewer and fewer of the truly authentic practitioners of the old arts. Yet Lunsford could have expected no more than that the young people would learn to appreciate and to participate in the old traditions. Through his festivals and other work he showed new generations the beauty of mountain traditions and made them see that these gifts from the past could meet both their own artistic needs and their need to be glued in some way to the past. It is a tribute to Lunsford and to others who worked in similar causes that the rich mountain cultural heritage lives through succeeding generations.

"I'll tell you that I've had a lot of fun. I've had more fun than anybody." Lunsford said when he was 89. That seems to be the best note on which to end this account of his life and work. He changed folks' attitudes about mountain

"I camped and slept on the road."
(Courtesy of Lunsford Collection, Mars Hill College)

traditions; many who had turned away from these traditions came back, while new generations grew to love them. In helping them to understand and love their traditions, he helped mountaineers to regain respect for themselves, and he helped countless outsiders, who had seen only the negative side of Appalachian life through the media's treatment of the region, to see that there was a great deal more to Appalachian culture than they had realized. His accomplishments over three-quarters of a century required hard and imaginative work. In his success, though, he wanted everyone to know that he "had more fun than anybody."

Lunsford crossed hell on that rotten rail, with a scant look downward, and he grabbed for and got a strong hold on the essence of Appalachian culture. He happily presented and interpreted that culture wherever he went in a life of constant motion. It was his calling, his special job of work, and his delight.

Bascom and Nellie Lunsford with their children in 1954. From left to right, top row: Ellen Weir, Lamar Lunsford, Jo Herron, Kern Lunsford. Bottom row: Nelle Greenawald, Lynn Hadley, Bascom Lamar Lunsford, Nellie Lunsford, Merton Brown (courtesy of Lunsford Collection, Mars Hill College)

NOTES

1. David Whisnant, "Finding the Way Between the Old and the New: The Mountain Dance and Folk Festival and Bascom Lamar Lunsford's work as a Citizen," *Appalachian Journal*, Vol 7, No. 1-2 (Autumn-Winter, 1979-80), pp. 135-154.

2. Whisnant, *op. cit.*, p. 136.

3. *Ibid.*, pp. 140-41.

4. David Whisnant, *Folk Festival Issues* (Los Angeles: John Edwards Memorial Foundation), 1978, p. 10.

5. Jannelle Warren-Findley, "Musicians and Mountaineers: The Resettlement Administration's Music Program in Appalachia, 1935-37," *Appalachian Journal*, Vol. 7, No. 1-2 (Autumn-Winter, 1979-80), p. 105.

6. Charles Seeger, confidential memorandum to Adrian Dornbush, 8-21-36; Library of Congress, U.S. Farm Security Administration, Miscellaneous Matter, X-ML 379.5 .F309.

7. Warren-Findley, *op cit.*, p. 112.

8. *Ibid.*, p. 117.

9. *Ibid.*, p. 113.

10. Pete Gilpen and George Stephens, *Minstrel of the Appalachians* (Asheville: Stephens Printing Co.), 1966, p. 20.

11. Author's interview with Mike Seeger, Renfro Valley, Ky., 7-12-74.

12. Author's interview with Jim Wolfe, Berea, Ky., 6-26-81.

13. Bill Finger, "Bascom Lamar Lunsford: The Limits of a Folk Hero" *Southern Exposure*, Spring/Summer, 1974.

14. A friend, who read an earlier version of this book, told the author of musicians who were critical of Lunsford's running of the festival. Two such musicians were subsequently interviewed, but they declined to have their names used in connection with their charges. Since they were people who are well thought of and obviously sincere in their beliefs, their views were included but were balanced with the opinions of Artus and Mabel Moser and another judge who also declined to be identified because of his current associations.

15. Letter from Sarah Gertrude Knott, 1-12-74.

16. Harold H. Martin, "Minstrel Man of the Appalachians," *Saturday Evening Post*, Vol. 220, No. 47 (May 22, 1948).

17. Author's interview with Ethel Capps, Berea, Ky., 1974.

18. Frank H. Smith, *The Appalachian Square Dance* (Berea, Kentucky: The Berea College Press), 1955, pp. 17-18.

19. Letter from Marguerite Bidstrup, December, 1973.

20. Letter from W. Amos Abrams, undated, cir. 1974.

21. Statement from Daniel Patterson, cir. 1974.

22. Letter from Peter Seeger, 1-10-74.

23. In *Music Makers of the Blue Ridge*, a film by Jonathan Gordon and David Hoffman, National Educational Television, 1967.

BIBLIOGRAPHY

Asheville Citizen and Times, Numerous unsigned articles through the years on the Mountain Dance and Folk Festival.

Beard, Anne Winsmore,*The Personal Folk Song Collection of Bascom Lamar Lunsford*, Master's Thesis, Miami University, 1959.

Bledsoe, Jerry, "The Minstrel of the Appalachians," *Greensboro Daily News* (March 19, 1972).

Botkin, B.A., *A Treasury of Southern Folklore* (New York: Crown Publishers), 1949.

Campbell, John C., *The Southern Highlander and His Homeland* (New York: Russell Sage Foundation), 1921; rpt. University Press of Kentucky, 1969.

Charlotte Observer, "Mountain Music's Grand Old Man," (September 5, 1973).

Chujoy, Anotole, and Manchester, P.W., *The Dance Encyclopedia* (New York: Simon and Schuster), 1967

Combs, Josiah H., *The Kentucky Highlands from a Native Mountaineer's Viewpoint* (Lexington, Kentucky; J.L. Richardson Co.), 1913.

__________________*Folk Songs of the Southern United States*, ed. D.K. Wilgus (Austin: University of Texas Press), 1967.

Cowles, Mary, "43rd Dance and Folk Festival Opens," *Asheville Citizen* (July 31, 1970).

Earnhardt, Jean A., "Even the Royal Foot Will Pat to Strains of Lunsford's Music," *Greensboro Daily News* (June 7, 1964).

Ervin, Sam J., Jr., *Humor of a Country Lawyer* (Chapel Hill: University of North Carolina Press, 1983).

Finger, Bill, "Bascom Lamar Lunsford: The Limits of a Folk Hero," *Southern Exposure*, Vol. 2, No. 1 (1974).

Gilpen, Pete, and Stephens, George, *Bascom Lamar Lunsford: Minstrel of the Appalachians* (Asheville: Stephens Press), 1966.

Gordon, Jonathan, "Bascom," *Diplomat* (August, 1966).

Green, Lewis W., "The Folk Festival is Audience, Too," *Asheville Citizen* (August 2, 1969).

Haas, Joseph, "The Ballad Singer from Banjo Branch," *Chicago Daily News* (August 17, 1963).

Hailey, Jean R., "Bascom Lamar Lunsford Dies," *The Washington Post* (September 6, 1973).

Heaton, C.P., "The 5-string Banjo in North Carolina," *Southern Folklore Quarterly*, Vol. XXXV, No. 1 (March, 1971).

"Hudson Tells What Ails the Folk Festival," *The Chapel Hill Weekly* (June 17, 1955).

Jackson, Dot, "He Picked His way Through Life," *Charlotte Observer* (October 4, 1973).

Johnson, Sid S. (ed.), *Texans Who Wore the Gray* (No publisher noted), 1907.

Kephart, Horace, *Our Southern Highlanders* (New York: The McMillan Company), 1913.

Lowery, Raymond, "Folk: A New Musical Kick," *Raleigh News and Observer* (October 20, 1963).

Lunsford, Bascom Lamar, "Annual Mountain Dance and Folk Festival," *Disc Collector* No. 18) 1961).

__________________ and Lamar Stringfield, *30 and 1 Folk Songs from the Southern Mountains* (New York: Carl Fischer, Inc.), 1929.

__________________ *Reminiscences*, unpublished paper in the Lunsford Collection at Mars Hill College.

Lunsford, James Bassett, *History of the Newfound Baptist Association*, mimeographed undated.

McLeod, John Angus, *From These Stones* (Mars Hill, North Carolina: Mars Hill College), 1955.

____________________ *Minstrel of the Appalachians*, unpublished biography of Lunsford in the Mars Hill Library, 1973.

Martin, Harold H., "Minstrel Man of the Appalachians," *Saturday Evening Post*, Vol. 220, No. 47 (May 22, 1948).

Malone, Bill, *Country Music, U.S.A.* (Austin: University of Texas Press), 1968.

Miller, Jim Wayne, *The More Things Change the More They Stay the Same* (Frankfort, Kentucky: The Whippoorwill Press), 1971.

Parris, John, "The King Smiled and the Queen Patted Her Foot," *Asheville Citizen and Times* (July 26, 1970).

____________________ "Bascom Lunsford - A Living Legend," *Asheville Citizen and Times* (July 26, 1970).

Potts, J. Manning (ed.), *The Journals and Letters of Francis Asbury*, Vol. II (Nashville: Abingdon Press), 1958.

Raffe, W.G., *Dictionary of the Dance* (New York: A.S. Barnes and Company), 1964.

Scarborough, Dorothy,*A Song Catcher in the Southern Mountains* (New York: Columbia University Press), 1937.

Sharp, Cecil, *English Folk Songs from the Southern Appalachians*, Maud Karpeles (ed.), 2 Vols. (London: Oxford University Press), 1932.

Smith, Frank H., *The Appalachian Square Dance* (Berea, Kentucky: The Berea College Press), 1955.

"Tar Heel of the Week, Bascom Lamar Lunsford," *Raleigh News and Observer* (June 5, 1955), Sec. IV, P.3.

Terrill, Bob, "Festival Opens at Auditorium," *Asheville Citizen* (August 4, 1972).

____________________ "No Wrinkles on Their Hearts," *Asheville Citizen* (August 5, 1972).

____________________ "Nearing 90, But He's Still Quite a Toe-Tapper," *Asheville Citizen and Times* (March 19, 1973).

____________________ "The Heart of a Friend," *Asheville Citizen* (September 5, 1983).

The Virginia Magazine of History and Biography, Vol. 17, No. 1 (January, 1909).

Warren-Findley, Jannelle, "Musicians and Mountaineers: The Resettlement Administration's Music Program in Appalachia, 1935-37," *Appalachian Journal*, Vol. 7, No. 1-2 (Autumn-Winter, 1979-80).

Wellman, Manly Wade, *The Kingdom of Madison* (Chapel Hill: University of North Carolina Press), 1973.

Whisnant, David, "Finding the Way Between the Old and the New: The Mountain Dance and Folk Festival and Bascom Lamar Lunsford's Work as a Citizen," *Appalachian Journal*, Vol. 7, No. 1-2 (Autumn-Winter, 1979-80).

____________________ (ed.), *Folk Festival Issues* (Los Angeles: John Edwards Memorial Foundation), 1978.

White, Newman Ivey (gen. ed.), *The Frank C. Brown Collection of North Carolina Folklore*, 7 vol. (Durham: Duke University Press), 1952-57.

Wolfe, Thomas, *The Hills Beyond* (New York: Harper Brothers), 1941.

____________________ *Look Homeward, Angel* (New York: Charles Scribner's Sons), 1929.

____________________ *You Can't Go Home Again* (New York: Harper Brothers), 1940.

INTERVIEWS

Asch, Moses, New York City by telephone, 1981.

Bailey, Jesse James, Asheville, North Carolina, in Asheville, August 3, 1974.

Ball, Helen, Oxford, Ohio, by telephone, December 7, 1983.

Bannerman, Glenn, Richmond, Virginia, in Berea, Kentucky, 1974.

Bronson, Bertrand, Berkeley, California, by telephone, November 17, 1983.

Capps, Ethel, Berea, Kentucky, in Berea, 1974.

Emmett, Louis, Greensboro, North Carolina, at Rock Hill, South Carolina, November 19, 1983.

Goldstein, Kenneth, Philadelphia, Pennsylvania, in Washington, D.C., November 16, 1978, by telephone, November 16, 1983.

Greenawald, Nelle Lunsford, Florida City, Florida, in Berea, Kentucky, October 13, 1974; by telephone, July 8, 1981.

Herron, Jo Lunsford, Carrollton, Texas, in Lake Junaluska, North Carolina, March 4, 1974.

Israel, Jerry, Asheville, North Carolina, in Asheville, August 6, 1974.

Kazee, Buell, Winchester, Kentucky, in Winchester, March 2, 1975.

Knott, Sarah Gertrude, Princeton, Kentucky, in Berea, Kentucky, December, 1973.

Lair, John, Renfro Valley, Kentucky, in Renfro Valley, April 30, 1974.

Ledford, Lily May, Lexington, Kentucky, in Berea, Kentucky, June 25, 1975.

Lindsey, Bob, Asheville, by telephone, July, 1974, February and March, 1975.

Lunsford, Bascom, Asheville, North Carolina, in Asheville, July 27, 1971.

Lunsford, Kern, Jonas Ridge, North Carolina, in Mars Hill, North Carolina, 1972 1973; Asheville, North Carolina, 1974.

McLain, Beatrice, Tuscaloosa, Alabama, in Berea, Kentucky, December, 1973.

McLain, Raymond K., Berea, Kentucky, in Berea, 1973, 1974, 1975.

McWhiney, Grady, Ft. Worth, Texas, at Rock Hill, South Carolina, November 16, 1983.

Miller, Edith, Oxford, Ohio, by telephone, November 23 & 29, 1983.

Miller, Jim Wayne, Bowling Green, Kentucky, in Berea, Kentucky, 1973, 1974, 1975.

Moser, Artus, Swannanoa, North Carolina, in Swannanoa, August 7, 1974.

Moser, Joan, Swannanoa, North Carolina, with Bascom Lamar Lunsford, South Turkey Creek, North Carolina, December 29, 1959.

O'Carroll, Tom, Newbury Port, Massachusettes, at Rock Hill, South Carolina, November 19, 1983.

Pegram, George, Asheboro, North Carolina, in Berea, Kentucky, July 2, 1974.

Ramsay, John, Berea, Kentucky, in Berea, 1974, 1975.

Ray, Byard, Marshall, North Carolina, in Asheville, North Carolina, August 7, 1974.

Seeger, Mike, Garrett Park, Maryland, in Renfro Valley, Kentucky, July 12, 1974.

Sprung, Roger, New York City, by telephone, July 1974.

Stephens, George M., Asheville, North Carolina, in Asheville, August 2, 1974; in Berea, Kentucky, November 9, 1974.

Ward, Earl, Asheville, North Carolina, in Asheville, July 3, 1974.

Ward, Jackie, Asheville, North Carolina, by telephone, July 5, 1974.

Wolfe, Jim, Chicago, Illinois, in Berea, Kentucky, June 6, 1981.

CORRESPONDENCE

W. Amos Abrams, Raleigh, North Carolina.
Marguerite Bidstrup, Brasstown, North Carolina.
Merton Lunsford Brown, Leicester, North Carolina.
Nelle Lunsford Greenawald, Florida City, Florida.
Lynn Lunsford Hadley, Wilson, North Carolina.
Jo Lunsford Herron, Carrollton, Texas.
Sarah Gertrude Knott, Princeton, Kentucky.
Debora Kodish, Austin, Texas.
Bob Lindsey, Asheville, North Carolina.
Kern Lunsford, Jonas Ridge, North Carolina.
Jim Wayne Miller, Bowling Green, Kentucky.
Daniel Patterson, Chapel Hill, North Carolina
Pete Seeger, Beacon, New York.
George M. Stephens, Asheville, North Carolina.
Scott Wiseman, Spruce Pine, North Carolina.

Appendices

APPENDIX I

Bascom Lamar Lunsford's Memory Collection of Ballads, Songs, Hymns, Singing Games, Fiddle Tunes, Stories, Verse, etc.

The ballads, songs, hymns and singing games are identified where possible with references to Francis James Child's *English and Scottish Popular Ballads,* Cecil Sharp's *English Folk Songs from the Southern Mountains*, G. Malcolm Laws' *American Balladry from the British Broadsides* and *Native American Balladry, The Frank C. Brown Collection of North Carolina Folklore,* Leonard Roberts' *The Sang Branch Settlers* (containing the oral traditions of the Couch family of eastern Kentucky), George Pullen Jackson's *White Spirituals of the Southern Uplands* (U), *White and Negro Spirituals* (W) and *Another Sheaf of White Spirituals* (A) and Vance Randolph's *Ozark Folksongs*(4 vols.).

Also, the name and location of Lunsford's source of the item, dates, occasional comments from Lunsford, and other such information is included for most of the material.

The grouping is as suggested by Lunsford's classifications.

Group A—Variants of English and Scottish ballads in the Child Collection.

Barbara Allen (Bonny Barbara Allen). Child 84.

Black Jack Davie (The Gypsy Laddie). Child 200. Selma Clubb, South Turkey Creek, Buncombe County, North Carolina

Bonnie George Campbell. Child 210.

The Death of Queen Jane. Child 170. "Known since childhood. It is traditionally sung in the Southern Appalachian Region."

The False Wife (James Harris or the Demon Lover). Child 243.

The Gallow's Tree (The Maid Freed from the Gallows). Child 95. Mrs. Dill, Henderson County, North Carolina.

George Collins (Lady Alice). Child 85. Miss Lois Whitted, Leicester High School, North Carolina.

Little Marget (Fair Margaret and Sweet William). Child 74. Miss Loretta Payne, Roaring Fork, Madison County, North Carolina.

Lord Daniel's Wife (Little Musgrave and Lady Barnard). Child 81. T.L. Sigmond Alexander County, North Carolina.

Lord Lovel. Child 75. Mrs. Charles Parker, Raleigh, North Carolina.

Lord Thomas (Lord Thomas and Fair Anett). Child 73. Mrs. Wycaster, Raven's Ford, Oconalufty River, North Carolina.

The Mermaid. Child 289.

Merry Golden Tree (The Golden Vanity). Child 286. Ada Moss, Cullowhee, North Carolina.

The Old Man of the North Country (The Two Sisters). Child 10. "Sung in the Great Smokies."

The Old Man Who Lived Under the Hill (The Farmer's Curst Wife). Child 278. Hettie Lane, Rabbit Ham Creek, Buncombe County, North Carolina.

The Proud Irish Lady (The Brown Girl). Child 295. Miss Etta McKinney, "Dark Corners Section" between North and South Carolina, 1925.

The Three Little Babes (The Wife of Usher's Well). Child 79. Bonnie Meadows, Madison County, North Carolina.

The Three Night's Experience (Our Goodman). Child 274.

Group B—Other ballads, including those from British broadsides, American ballads about murders, and disasters, comic ballads, ballads of author origin and some that in a more technical classification might well be in a folk song category, but all of which tell stories.

Awake, O, Awake (The Drowsy Sleeper). Laws M 4. Mrs. Lennie Green, Meat Camp Creek, Watauga County, North Carolina.

Barney McCoy. Brown II 113. Charlie Weatherman, Iredell County, North Carolina.

Bill Ormand. 'This is based on a tragedy taking place in eastern North Carolina several years ago.'

Booth (Booth Killed Lincoln). "I've known the tune Wilkes Booth since a boy. I secured a text from W. J. Morgan, Transylvania County, North Carolina, some several years ago."

Brady. Laws I 9. Miss Cooper Martin, Briar Creek, Wilkes County, North Carolina (1903).

The Broken Engagement. Brown II 115 B.

Bryan's Last Battle (About William Jennings Bryan in the Scopes Trial). Composed by Lunsford in 1925.

Bury Me Not on the Lone Prairie. Laws B l. Miss Edwina Bryson, Cowee School, Macon County, North Carolina.

The Butcher Boy. Laws P 24. Lois Witted, Liecester, North Carolina.

Captain, Captain Tell Me True. Bown II 104 B,C, and D. Mrs. Minyard Miller Bluff, Madison County, North Carolina.

Casey Jones. Laws G 1.

Charles Guiteau (About the assassin of President Garfield). Laws E 11.

Courtin' the Widow. Ms. Cinderella Kenard, West Plains Missouri.

Czolgotz (or Buffalo, about the assassin of President McKinley).

Darby's Ram (The Ram of Derby). Brown II 176.

The Dishonest Miller (The Miller's Will). Laws Q 21.

Edward (Edwin in the Lowlands Low). Laws M 34. Mrs. D.W. Townsend, Bat Cave, North Carolina.

Ellen Smith (About a murder in Forsythe County, North Carolina in 1893). Laws F 11. Lulu Browning, Nebo, North Carolina (1925). "This is sung to the tune of How Firm a Foundation."

The Farmer's Boy. Laws Q 30. "Learned this as a boy."

The Fate of Santa Barbara. Laws G 45(?) (About the 1924 earthquake). Composed by Lunsford in 1925.

Floyd Collins (tune of Charles Guiteau). Laws G 22. Learned from phonograph record (1925).

Frankie and Albert. Laws I 3. "I've heard it all my life."

Frankie Silver (or Hanged, about a Burke County, North Carolina murder in 1881). Laws E 13. "This text is said to have been written by Frankie Silver before she was hanged at Morganton, North Carolina, on July 12, 1883 for murdering her husband."

Froggie Went A-Courting. Sharp 220 B. Mrs Ruth Caldwell, Campabello, South Carolina.

Good-bye My Darling, I Must Leave You.

Jack and Joe. (Popular song in oral tradition). Brown II 274. Miss Edwina Bryson, Cowee School, Macon County, North Carolina.

Jesse James. Laws E1. Sam Sumner, Bear Wallow, near Bat Cave, Henderson County North Carolina (1903).

John Hardy. Laws I 2.

John Henry. Laws I 1.

John Kirby (About a 'Dark Corners' Killing). Mrs. Etta McKinney, Tigerville in Dark Corners (between North and South Carolina) (1927).

Judge Henry (parody on John Henry relating to Ku Klux Klan. Written by Lunsford).

Little Mary Phagan. Laws F 20. "Written (presumably the text) in 1920 by Dinah ________(no last name). Clay County, North Carolina."

Lost John Dean. "That's a tune the boys often play on the french harp."

Lula Wall. Listed by Laws, NAB, in ballad-like pieces, p. 278. Miss Ada Green, Sweetwater Creek, Clay County, North Carolina.

Martha Penix (About a Randolph County, North Carolina murder around 1884). "I received this text from Miss Ava Chammes, Randolph County, North Carolina. This tragedy occurred near Guilford County (around 1884). This text is written on a ticket possibly used before 1850."

Mr. Garfield (A somewhat light treatment of the assassination of President Garfield in 1881). Anderson Williams, Henderson County, North Carolina (1903).

Newfound Song (About a local happening). Jake Brooks, Brooks Branch, Buncombe County, who wrote it.

No Ku Klux Out Tonight (About the Deaver Family of Madison County, North Carolina). "This was sung to me by Doc Sams, Madison County, North Carolina who said he knew these characters. This is possibly a parody on the tune Gettin' up Stairs."

Nol Pros Nellie, "A parody on Nellie Gray which I am guilty of having composed and sung."

Old Fate (About a local thief, to the tune of the Crawdad Song). Doc Tallant, Asheville, North Carolina (1931).

Old Ninety-Seven. Laws G 2. "This text is from a student at Fruitland Institute, Henderson County, North Carolina."

On a Bright and Summer's Morning (A hunting song). Similar to Sharp 159. "Eugene Sutton of Cataloochee Creek in the Great Smoky Mountain Park area, is the only person I've ever heard sing this song."

On Robert's Farm. Claud Reeves (who said he made the song), head of Little River, Transylvania County, North Carolina.

On the Banks of the Ohio. Laws F 5. "I learned this from individuals who were raised in the Ohio Valley."

Pearl Bryan (About a Fort Thomas, Kentucky, murder in 1896). Laws F 2. Doc Tallant, Asheville, North Carolina.

Poor Naomi Wise. Laws F 4. "Miss Ava Chammes of Randolph County, North Carolina, the scene of this tragedy in 1803*, wrote this text on April 22, 1818, and she furnished me with a copy. I've seen Adams' Spring and the grave of Naomi Wise at Providence Church."

*Other sources place the date at 1808.

Pretty Fair Miss (Soldier's Return). Laws H 42. Doc (Gilbert) Tallant, Madison County and Asheville, North Carolina.

Pretty Mohee. Laws H 8. Pearl Wiggins, Bryson City, North Carolina.

Railroad Bill. Laws I 13.

Roanoke River (The Homesick Boy). Brown II 170. Bertie Stack, Olin Township, Iredell County, North Carolina (1903).

The Romish Lady (religious ballad in shape-note tradition). Laws Q 32, Jackson S 27. Mrs. R.L. Masters, head of East Fork, Transylvania County, North Carolina.

Roving Gambler. Laws H 4.

The Ruined Cobbler (Peg and Awl).

Springfield Mountain. Laws G 16.

The Ship That Never Returned. Brown II 215. (Composed by Henry C. Work).

Swannanoa Tunnel. Brown II 270 H and I. "This is a song brought by Negroes."

That Good Ole Mountain Dew. Composed by Lunsford in 1920.

Three Brave Men (To the tune of Frankie and Johnny). Jake Brooks, Brooks' Branch, Buncombe County, North Carolina, (who was said to have written the song).

Tom Dooley (or Laura Foster, about a Wilkes County, North Carolina, murder in 1866). Laws F 36. T. L. Sigmond, Alexander County, North Carolina.

Tumble Di I Dye Ding Dye Aye (Katy Morey). Laws H 24. Miss Ethel Bishop, Cane Creek, Henderson County, North Carolina.

The War is Now Raging. Laws 033. Learned from daughter Lynn Lunsford who learned it from Hettie Lane, South Turkey Creek, North Carolina.

Wild Bill Jones. Laws E 10.

Young Man and A Maid. (Related to Laws M 3 and other ballads of opposition to lovers). Doc Tallant, Asheville, North Carolina.

Group C—Folk Songs

Alice Moore. Mrs. Ed Litterell, Swain County, N.C. (1925). "No doubt this is based on a local happening."

Alphabet Song. (As an aid to learning). Randolph, IV, 400-3.

Bye, Bye My Darling. Andy McGee, Big Sandymush, North Carolina (1902).

Captain With His Whiskers. Randolph II, 287-9. "I heard my mother sing this."

Careless Love. Mrs. Annis Boyd, Big Sandymush, North Carolina.

Charming Betsy. Brown III 256. "A type of mountain banjo tune."

Cindy. Brown III 404. "Known since a boy. Heard it at parties."

Come in, said the Barber. Jimmy Cole, Newfound Creek, Buncombe County (1856).

Corina.

Cumberland Gap. Brown III 329. "Has been played throughout the Southern Appalachian territory. It is a great party tune."

Darling Cora (Moonshining Song). Roberts 59. Mrs. Ocie Bailey, Chandler, North Carolina, Also version from Pleaz Mobley, Manchester, Kentucky.

The Dewdrops are falling on Me. Bruce Slaughter, Cheoa River, Graham County, North Carolina. "Heard Letch Reynolds sing it in 1901."

Dogget's Gap (parody on Cumberland Gap). Brown III 329. "This song is related to a love story that is said to have its beginning at Dogget's Gap in the outlying spurs of the Great Smoky Mountains."

Down in the Valley. Brown III 281. Miss Jeanette Lydie, Sugarloaf Mountain, Henderson County, North Carolina.

Down in Union County. "Sung in the upper part of South Carolina."

Down the Road. Brown III 441. Hardy Haney (1898). "I've played this since I was 15 years old." Similar to Roberts 69. Some lines from Ida Red.

Dummy Line. Brown III 435.

Fly Around Little Red Bird. (Tune of Roving Gambler).

Free Little Bird. Brown III 255 H. Tom Boyd. Rabbit Ham, Buncombe County, North Carolina.

Georgia Buck. Brown III 500 B. "I've known this song since about 1895."

Go and Leave Me if You Wish To (Fond Affection). Lela Ammons, Graham County, North Carolina.

Goin' Across the Sea.

Goin' Down Town. Brown III 415. "Known since I was 10 years old."

Green Grow the Laurels. Brown III 280. "Known since a child." Miss Ruth Hutcheson, Columbus (Polk County), North Carolina (furnished text).

Ground Hog. Brown III 221. Mrs. Clark, Clark's Creek, Watauga County, North Carolina.

High Top Shoes. Brown III 301 B. "This is possibly the foundation of John Henry."

Hunh-A-Wunh. "Mitchell Shook (Buncombe County, North Carolina) said the Indians sang this. I do not give this as authentic, but I remember it from childhood."

Hull-A-Ma-Gullama. Maude Huntington Meade.

I Have No One to Love Me. Mrs. Annis Boyd, Big Sandymush Creek.

I Love Little Willie. Brown III 307. Ruth Hutcheson, Columbus (Polk County), North Carolina.

I Love Somebody, Yes I do. (Tune of Soldier's Joy).

I Wish I was A Mole in the Ground. Brown III 173. Fred Moody, Haywood County, North Carolina.

I Wish I was a Single Girl Again. Brown III 28.

I Wish I was Single Again. Brown III 19. Miss Reba Masters, East Fork, Transylvania County, North Carolina.

I Wish I were a Swallow. Brown III 254.

I'll be Glad when You're Dead, You Rascal, You.

I'm Goin' Back to Georgia. Brown III 250 and 248 B and C.

I'm Going Down the Road Feeling Bad. Brown III 441.

Italy (or Going to Italy). Brown III E. "Many of the mountain songs are named after places. This one is named after a mountain community. I heard this at a square dance on Sugarloaf Mountain, Henderson County, North Carolina."

It's My Little Bonnie Blue Eyes. Brown III 284. "Known all my life."

Jack O' Diamonds. Brown III 50.

Jenny Jenkins. Brown III 69. Charles Edwards, Rabbit Ham Creek, Buncombe County, North Carolina.

Johnson Boys. Brown III 338.

Kind Miss (Kind Sir, or The Courting Cage). Brown III 3. Ruth Caldwell, Campobello, South Carolina.

Kitty Clyde (Kitty Kline). Brown III 255.

The Last Gold Dollar. Samantha Bumgarner, Little Savanna Creek, Jackson County, North Carolina.

Laurel Valley (parody on Red River Valley). Brown III 260.

Little Birdie. Roberts 62. "Possibly related to 'They Cut Down the Old Pine Tree'."

Little Turtle Dove. Brown III 249. Letch Reynolds, Buncombe County, North Carolina (1901).

Little Willie. Brown III 307.

Lonesome Dove. Related to Child 76.

Meet Me in the Moonlight (Prisoner's song). Brown III 350. "I have a text of this dated 1905."

Multiplication Song (As an aid to learning).

My Dearest Friend 'Tis Fare Thee Well. W.B. Love, Burke County, North Carolina (1901).

My Dear Old Innocent Boy (Buffalo Boy or Dear Old Reckless Boy). Melvin Medford, Pigeon River, Haywood County, N.C. "This text was written down for me by Mrs. Ocie Bailey."

My Home's Across the Smoky Mountains. Brown III 278. Lou Greer, Valley of the Catawba River.

Oh Lawsy Me. Miss Etta Shook, Pinnacle Mountain, Buncombe County, North Carolina (1898).

Oh, To Me the Time Rolls Nigh When You and I Must Part. Related to Brown III 258 B and Sharp 77. Mrs. Noah Lovingood, Marble, North Carolina.

Old Jimmy Sutton. "Played in Piedmont of North Carolina." (tune of Walking in the Parlor).

Old Joe Clark. Brown III 86. "A mountain fiddle tune."

Old Nieper. Brown III 123 B and C.

Old Rosin the Beau. Brown III 32.

Old Smoky. Mrs. Noah Lovingood, Marble (Cherokee County), North Carolina.

Old Woman All Dressed in White (Skin and Bones Woman) Brown III 142. Mrs. Rankin, Guilford, North Carolina.

One Dark and Stormy Night. Marvin Bowman, Iredell County, North Carolina.

Paper of Pins. Brown III 253. "Learned from my mother when I was just a boy."

Pretty Little Pink. Brown III 78 C. Miss Maude Sanders, Graham County, N.C.

Pretty Saro, Brown III 252. "I heard my mother sing this song. This text is from W.J. Morgan, Transylvania County, North Carolina.

Rabbit a Rabbit. Brown III 167 I. "I heard this when I was five years old."

Reuben. Brown III 236 B. "Heard about 1898. It gives something about the origin of blues."

Sam Hunnicut's Plantation Song. "Sam Hunnicut is a famous bear hunter in the Great Smoky Mountains, having killed 64 bears."

She Gave Me Kisses One. Miss Youngblood, Johnson County, North Carolina.

Short Life and Trouble. Roberts 57.

Shout Lula. Brown III 183.

Sky Yai Yipper Come A Yea Yea Yea. "Known since a boy. It is based on a local happening."

Some Will Come On Saturday Night (Single Life). Brown III 18. "Learned in 1890."

Sourwood Mountain. Brown III 251. "It was said when I was a boy that you could start fiddling Sourwood Mountain on Shelton Laurel (Madison County) and they'd all go to fighting."

Sundown.

That Blue-Eyed Girl. Brown III 286. "Similar in tune to Black Jack Davy."

There are Nine Blue Bottles on the Wall. Brown III 190.

To the Pines. Brown III 283. "First heard this around Table Rock and Hawks' bill secton, close to Linville Falls."

Waggoner Lad. Brown III 250. Mr. Bud Lydie, Henderson County, North Carolina.

Weeping Willow Tree. Brown III 267. "Heard sung in the Valley of the French Broad in 1902."

When the Last Old Shovel's Laid Down. (Sung by Bascom and Freda Lunsford in the film, *The Vanishing Frontier*.)

The Whole Hog. Similar to Brown III 177. O.K. Bennett, Fines Creek, Haywood County, North Carolina.

A Woman's Tongue Will Never Take a Rest. Willard Randall, Rutherford County, North Carolina.

Group D—Popular Songs in the Oral Tradition.

As I Go Out on Sunday (I'll Never Get Drunk Anymore). Brown III 36A.

Buffalo Gals. Brown III 81.

The Cat Came Back. Randolph III 198-200.

Coonshine "I heard it when just a boy."

Diner Iner.

Don't Forget Me, Little Darling. Greer and Cook Sisters, Catawba County, North Carolina. Randolph IV 207-9.

Down At Widow Johnson's. "I heard this song from Miss Lola Grant when I was teaching about a mile below Dogget's Gap in 1902." (Madison County, North Carolina)

Down Where the Watermelon Grows. "Composed by Grady Reagon, Buncombe County, North Carolina."

The Dying Girl's Message. Randolph IV 168-9. Miss Ada Green, Clay County, North Carolina (1904).

The Eastbound Train.

Ella's Grave. "Heard in Piedmont of North Carolina."

Essie, Dear. Lela Ammons, Mountain Creek, Graham County, North Carolina (1904). "Songs like this are of author origin, but it is interesting how they are transmitted orally."

Good-bye, My Darling, I Must Leave You. "When the young people meet at mountain parties, they sing songs of this kind—the author type of song. Mix them with folk songs."

Hand Me Down My Walking Cane. Brown III 363.

I'll Remember You Love in My Prayers. (Composed by Will S. Hayes) "Marvin Bowman sang this for me in Iredell Township (N.C.) in 1903."

I'm Goin' to Live Anyhow Until I Die. Cleve Lunsford, Hunting Creek, Wilkes County, North Carolina (1903).

In the Shadow of the Pines. "Of author origin, but it has been transmitted orally."

I'se Gwine Back to Dixie.

Kidder Cole. Felix Eugene Alley of Cartoogachaye Creek, Macon County, North Carolina, composed this song about his girl friend, Kidder Cole of Cashiers Valley. Alley became a prominent North Carolina judge. The song is in the western North Carolina oral tradition.

Kitty Wells. Brown III 411. "Learned from my mother." Also versions from Evelyn Whitt, Glennie Rogers, Viva Parker, Geneva Evritt, Bessie Littrell, Edna Thompson, and Vance Ledford.

Little Brown Jug. Brown III 33. Miss Nora Morgan, Horseshoe, North Carolina (1902).

Little Old Log Cabin in the Lane. (by Will S. Hayes) "Learned from my mother when I was a child."

The Little Rosewood Casket. Randolph IV 269-72. "Undoubtedly of author origin, but it has a variety of different stanzas."

Lorena (by J.P. Webster and H.D.L. Webster) Randolph IV 257-9 Lela Ammons, Macon County, North Carolina (1904).

Maple on the Hill. "A song of author origin."

May I Sleep in Your Barn Tonight, Mister? Brown 356. "This is sung to the tune of Red River Valley."

Nellie Gray.

Nine Blue Bottles. Related to Brown III 190. "This is sung in the Piedmont of North Carolina."

The Old Gray Mare. Not the same as Brown III 174 or 175. "I used to like to go up on Hanlon Mountain and play this song."

Old Stepstone. Lela Ammons, Graham County, North Carolina (1904). "These types of songs are transmitted orally from community to community."

Old Uncle Ned. (To tune of Little Margaret). Brown III 420.

The Picture That is Turned to the Wall. (By Charles Graham) Miss Bradley, Reems Creek, Buncombe County, North Carolina.

Put My Little Shoes Away. Randolph IV 178-80.

The Railroad Flagman (Verses from a Dear Companion). Randolph IV 235. "Sung around Bryson City, North Carolina."

Row Us Over the Tide. Miss Ada Green, Clay County, North Carolina (1904).

Shortenin' Bread. Brown III 461 D. "I saw a printed text of this as a boy, but these are the stanzas I've picked up through the years."

Sunny Tennessee. Marvin Bowman, Mitchell County, North Carolina (1903).

Susanna. Brown 408. "I saw a printed text as a boy."

That Little Logwood Cabin. Miss Ada Lunsford, Hunting Creek, Wilkes County, North Carolina (1903).

Them Golden Slippers. Jimmy Cole, Newfound Creek, Buncombe County, (1896).

They Cut Down the Old Pine Tree.

Thompson's Old Gray Mule. Brown III 512 and 513.

When the Roses Bloom Again Beside the River. Miss Maude Burleson, Spruce Pine, North Carolina.

Won't You Spread the Flocks of Flowers O'er My Grave. Lovingood sisters, Cherokee County, North Carolina.

You May Say I'm Vicious.

Group E—Religious Songs.

Amazing Grace. (By John Newton). Jackson A 142,S 163.

Blessed Be the Name. (By Charles Wesley).

The Devil is Defeated. Miss Queen Justice, Clear Creek Valley, Henderson County North Carolina (1902).

Drinking of the Wine. Fragment mistakenly listed in Brown III 48 as a drinking song. "I heard this in 1903 at a Children's Day Program in a Negro congregation in the Yadkin Valley, Wilkes County, N.C."

Dry Bones (Negro Spiritual). "Heard in the French Broad Valley." Also from Fletch Rhymer, Buncombe County, N.C.

Go Wash in that Beautiful Pool. Brown III 575. "Heard at Round Hill Church (South Turkey Creek) when a boy."

Heaven Bells. "Known since 1895."

Hide Thou Me (Negro spiritual). "Sung to me by a Negro boyhood friend Mitchell Shook."

How Firm a Foundation. (By George Keith). Jackson A99, A 109, A 158, A 168.

How Tedious and Tasteless the Hour. (Text by John Newton). Tune attributed to J.T. White in *Sacred Harp*. Jackson A 110, A 137, A 149, S 92.

I Am Bound for the Promised Land. Brown III 581. (by Samuel Stennet). Jackson S 238, W 208. "When I was 10 years old, I would help sing this at Western Chapel on South Turkey Creek, Buncombe County, North Carolina."

I Shall Not Be Moved. Brown III 596 B.

I Want to be An Angel. "The first tune I ever learned."

I Will Arise. Jackson S 232, W 204.

I'm A-Goin' to Tell my Good Lord Howdy (Negro Spiritual). Learned from a boyhood friend, Fred Boring.

I'm Not A-Goin' to Lay My 'Ligion Down (Negro spiritual). "Often heard in my home community."

In That Morning (by W.C. Stanley and William Walker). "When six years old, I heard Rev. T.N. Hunnicut at Forks of Ivy (Madison County), at a protracted meeting, sing this song." Jackson S 197, U 260, U 254.

It's A Long Time Talking About the Serving of the Lord.

Jesus Loves Even Me. (By P. P. Bliss). "Heard as a child."

Jordan Am A Hard Road to Travel (Negro spiritual). "Built upon an old fiddle tune."

Little David. Brown III 608 and 609. "This is a Negro spiritual. I first heard it at Snow Hill School between Tater Hill and Hanlon Mountain.

The Lone Pilgrim. Brown III 542. (Text by B.F. White.) "This is one I like very much."

My Old Father's Gone Along.

Oh, Mary Don't You Weep. Brown III 545. "Heard at a Negro Camp meeting in Leicester Township, Buncombe County, North Carolina."

Old Time Religion. "This tune is sometimes speeded up and played for square dances." Jackson S 218.

One Day As I Was Walking Along. Learned from Negro preacher Rev. H.L. Davis, Landrum, South Carolina. "The Negroes have furnished a wonderful contribution to folk singing of America. They have built upon the religious singing of the white people and have put in their own contribution."

Orphan Children Have A Hard Time. "The Society for the Preservation of Negro Spirituals at Charlotte sing this."

The Prettiest Thing I Ever Done (Was serve the Lord). "Known from my youth." Jackson A 9.

The Same Train (This Train). Clinton Sisters, Head of Flat Creek, Buncombe County, North Carolina. "It is often sung by Negroes."

The Ship That is Sailing High. Mrs. Ocie Bailey, Hominy Valley, Buncombe County, North Carolina.

Standing in the Need of Prayer. Brown III 637. "The Negroes often have a repetition of father, mother, brother, sister and so on in their spirituals."

Swing-a-Low. Willard Randolph, Rutherford County, North Carolina. "Some of these songs are the basis, I feel, for the Negro Spirituals."

There is a Balm in Gilead. "This song is somewhat changed due to incorrect memories of those who sang it. I learned it from my mother."

Trot Us On the Other Side of Jordan.

The Uncloudy Day (Composed by J.K. Alwood).

What Wondrous Love is This. Jackson S 114-115.

When the First Trumpet Sounds. "When I was a boy of 15, I heard Will Tinsley, Alexandria, North Carolina, sing this Negro spiritual." Jackson A 17.

Who Will Be a Witness (Negro spiritual). Charlie Weatherman, New Hope Township, Iredell County, North Carolina (1903).

Group F—Play-Party Games.

Dr. Jones. Brown III 90. "Learned on Paw Paw Creek in Madison County, North Carolina, at the home of Doc Payne, as a boy before a big fireplace."

Four Little Prisoners. "In the earlier days people did not endorse square dancing. So play-party games like this became common."

Johnny Brown. "A game we used to play."

King William. Randolph III 344-9. "My daughter Miss Lynn Huntington Lunsford learned this at Leicester High School."

Skip to My Lou. Randolph III 287-91. "Sometimes they call this Steal a Partner."

The Twelve Apostles. Randolph IV 34-8. "I sang this when a boy along with the Waldroup and Stevens children on Rabbit Ham in Buncombe County, North Carolina."

We're Marching Around the Love Ring. Brown III 76. "I've known this from childhood."

Group G—Fiddle Tunes.

Arkansas Traveler. Brown III 330 I. See story in Appendix.

Billy in the Low Ground. John Carver (?) of Carvers Fork (?).

Black-Eyed Susie. Brown III 311.

Love my wife, love my baby,
Love my biscuits sopped in gravy.

Bonaparte's Retreat. "I learned this tune from my mother. She told me how to tune the fiddle...The G string is suppose to represent the drum in the retreat."

Buffalo Gals. Brown III 81.

Cackling Hen. "It's interesting to go high up in the mountains to a mountain home where the boys and girls gather on Saturday evening and have an old-time square dance in the regular mountain style.. This is a fiddle tune that we often hear in that section... This is true to form with the exception that a sure-enough old-time fiddler can make a hen cackle when he plays the Cackling Hen."

Cluck Old Hen. "I'll call attention again to the way the folk musician tunes his fiddle [for this tune]. He either lowers the A and the E, or raises the G and D one note...The folk fiddler plays with the open strings as much as possible."

Columbia.

Columbia, Columbia, glory arise,
The queen of the world and the child of the skies.

Cripple Creek. Brown III 299. "Named for Cripple Creek in Buncombe County, North Carolina, that was named for Cripple Creek, a mining town in the West.

The Downfall of Paris (related to both the Rakes of Mallow and Mississippi Sawyer).

Green March. "I heard this from Bob Rogers when I was about twelve years old."

Heights of Alabama. "Which Frank Ember used to play when I was a boy about eight years old and also my Uncle Os Deaver [played it]."

Hell Broke Loose in Georgia. "Man down in our state named Dave Vance, who used to rock his baby to sleep and sing, 'Ain't no Hell in Georgia [repeat three times].' Possibly he raised a sturdy race with that kind of a lullaby."

Jenny Lind. "This fiddle tune I've heard in my home section for forty years. It is called Jenny Lind Forever."

Kitty Puss. "I've known this since I was a child,

Can't dance with Kitty Puss
You can't dance with nothin'
Can't dance with Kitty Puss
You can't dance with nothin'."

Laurel Lonesome. "My great-uncle Os Deaver, who lived on the Forks of Ivy, at Big Ivy and Little Ivy in Madison County, when a young man, lost a valuable horse, and he trailed it to the Shelton Laurel. He failed to find it on Laurel. He spent that night at a mountain home, and while he was playing Laurel Lonesome a drunken woman raised up and said 'Os, I want you to play that old lonesome tune one time more.' So he always said he got a name for his fiddle tune which he had made Laurel Lonesome."

Liza Jane. Brown III 437.

March to the Tune of Captain With His Whiskers. (See Group C.)

The Methodist Preacher. "This is played with a raised bass [G string] like they used to play Arkansas Traveler."

Nancy Rollin.

Newt's Dream. "You know, I would like to go over here on the valley of the North Toe River in Mitchell County in my own state and hear Miss Maude Burleson, a pretty little blonde girl, play that fiddle tune called Newt's Dream. It's nice to hear a tune like that and then hear the caller say, 'four hands around circle to the left...."

Old Granny Rattletrap.

Old Granny Rattletrap, what's you doin' there?
Runnin' through the cotton patch hard as I can tear.

Old Sally Good'in. Brown III 89. "It's fine to go to an old-time party in the mountains. Get a large bunch of boys and girls, move the furniture out, and start up a dance, while the fellow plays Old Sally Good'in."

Racking Pony.

Roaring River. "Frank Ember played this for me in 1895."

Rye Straw. "This is Rye Straw, a party tune. There are some words to it, but they cannot be sung in this collection."

Sally Ann. "Many of the mountain songs have numbers of unrelated stanzas. Often those tunes are speeded up and used for party pieces, such as this one."

Sally Johnson. "A fiddle tune I've heard all my life."

The Scolding Wife. "The Scolding Wife is a fiddle tune played in the mountains. The folk fiddler often runs the E string down—does not use the standard tuning in playing this tune [elsewhere he refers to the Scolding Wife key]."

Sifting Sands. Brown III 479 and 480. "This is one tune to Sifting Sands, a tune that is very old. There is some provincial history connected to this tune that is embarrassing yet to some of the citizens of my own state."

The little bee make the honey comb
The big bee eat the honey
The niggers hoe the cotton and corn
And the white folks take the money.

"It is a fact that at Raleigh, North Carolina, a Carpetbagger, Ned (?) Fletcher made and would sing "Sifting Sands."

Snow Bird. "Possibly named for Snowbird Creek in Graham County where some of the Cherokees live."

Soldier's Joy.

Ten Steps. "This is an old fiddle tune....which I have known since a child. This is played by my great-uncle Os Deaver, who lived on Little Ivy in Madison County, North Carolina."

Tucker's Barn.

Turkey Buzzard. Brown III 105 A.

Shoot that turkey buzzard
Flyin' o'er the hollow.
Shoot that turkey buzzard
Flyin' o'er the hollow.

When Walking in the Parlor. Brown III 341 E and F.

When I Die, Bury Me Deep. Brown III 38. "I've known this since I was 10 years old."

Group H—Stories, Tales, Verse, etc.

Arkansas Traveler (story).

The Big Toe (scary story). "I've known this since I was a child."

The Big Turnip (story).

Calling Sim (Story about preacher, delivered in preaching chant). "Heard from a Negro preacher."

The Crazy Woman Story. Brown I P. 681. "Heard since a youth."

Damage Suit (recited verses, perhaps from a song). Tom Chrisman, Madison County, North Carolina.

Eli Webb and John Webb (Story about Marshall, North Carolina).

The Girl at the Gate (poem). "I learned this from my father."

I Feel Like Hell (play on hymn lines). "Known since a child."

Is that Your Paw? (story).

The Light is Bad, My Eyes are Dim (story on preacher "lining out" hymns as the congregation mistakes his words). "Known since a child."

Mountain Sermon (Variation on a piece of Southwest humor by William P. Brannan that is in the folk tradition).

Now, Brethern, Be Mighty Careful (story).

Oh How I Long to be There. "When I was a barefoot boy, I heard the late Hon. Locke Craig, former governor of North Carolina tell this story in Leicester, North Carolina."

Seventy Degrees (story).

A Stump Speech in the Tenth District (humorous political speech).

Tongue Twisters.

The Ugliest Man (story).

Well, Said the Blackbird (recited as a verse). "I've known this for a number of years."

We'll Take A Mortgage on the Hogs (story).

We Will Try to Catch the Flea (play on a hymn line). "Known since a child."

Who is your Pa? (story).

The Young Rat (story).

APPENDIX II

Bascom Lamar Lunsford Columbia University Library Recordings, 1935 On Aluminum Discs

1

1. Dedication
2. Expression of Thanks
3. Black Jack Davy
4. George Campbell
5. The Hangman's Tree
6. Billy Boy
7. Billy Boy
8. The Old Man of the North Country
9. George Collins
10. The Three Nights Experience
11. The Old Man Who Lived Under A Hill
12. Barbara Allen
13. Little Marget
14. Lonesome Dove
15. The Hangman's Tree
16. The Hangman's Tree

2

1. The Proud Irish Lady
2. The Three Little Babes
3. The False Wife
4. The Mermaid
5. Hell Broke Loose in Georgia
6. Lord Lovel
7. Ten Steps
8. Lord Daniel's Wife
9. Merry Golden Tree
10. Jenny Lind
11. It's My Little Bonnie Blue Eyes
12. Sally Ann
13. Awake, O, Wake
14. My Home's Across The Smoky Mountains

3

1. Frankie
2. Frankie (Continued)
3. I'm Riding on That New River Train
4. I'm Going Back to Georgia
5. The Scolding Wife
6. The Dishonest Miller
7. Laurel Lonesome
8. To The Pines
9. Jack-O-Diamonds
10. The Dew Drops Are Falling on Me
11. Kitty Puss
12. Turkey Buzzard
13. The Death of Queen Jane
14. A Bright and Summer's Morning

4

1. Short Life and Trouble
2. I Love Somebody, Yes, I Do
3. Old Smoky
4. Pretty Fair Miss or Soldier's Return
5. Shout Lula
6. Edward
7. Newt's Dream
8. Little Turtle Dove
9. Little Turtle Dove
10. Black-Eyed Susie
11. Froggie Went A-Courtin'
12. Reuben
13. The Wagoner's Lad
14. Liza Jane
15. The Butcher's Boy
16. Rye Straw
17. Tumble Di I Dye Ding Dye Aye
18. The Farmer's Boy

5

1. Young Man and Maid
2. Captain, Captain
3. The Roving Gambler and Fly Roun' Little Red Bird
4. The War is Now Raging
5. I Love Little Willie
6. The Downfall of Paris
7. I Wish I Was A Single Girl Again
8. The Dummy Line and Variants
9. The Dummy Line and Variants
10. Oh To Me The Time Rolls Nigh
11. Courtin' The Widow and Speech about meaningless syllables
12. I'm Going Down the Road Feeling Bad
13. I'll Be Glad When You're Dead, You Rascal, You
14. Free A Little Bird
15. Go and Leave Me If You Wish To
16. Swannanoa Tunnel

6

1. Cackling Hen and Dance Calls
2. Black-Eyed Susan
3. Laurel Valley
4. Corina
5. My Dearest Friend 'Tis Fare Thee Well
6. Tucker's Barn
7. The Ruined Cobbler
8. On A Bright and Summer's Morning
9. Georgia Buck
10. Kidder Cole
11. Maple On The Hill
12. Maple On The Hill
13. Meet Me In The Moonlight or The Prisoner's Song
14. Good-by Darling, I Must Leave You
15. Kind Miss
16. The Old Woman All Dressed in White
17. My Dear Old Innocent Boy
18. Bonaparte's Retreat

7

1. I Wish I Was Single Again
2. The Whole Hog
3. Roaring River
4. Pretty Mohee
5. Sam Hunnicut's Plantation Song
6. Darling Cora
7. Billy In The Low Ground
8. That Blue-Eyed Girl
9. Little Birdie
10. Diner Iner
11. Charming Betsy
12. Snow Bird
13. Red Apple Juice
14. Johnson Boys
15. Lost John Dean
16. Railroad Bill
17. Goin' Across the Sea
18. I Wish I Was A Mole in the Ground

8

1. Pretty Little Pink
2. The Broken Engagement
3. When I Die, Bury Me Deep
4. I Have No One To Love Me
5. Song of the Sea
6. Walking in the Parlor
7. Frankie
8. Careless Love
9. Careless Love (Continued)
10. Some Will Come On Saturday Night
11. Cripple Creek
12. Shortenin' Bread
13. Sifting Sands
14. Green March
15. Mountain Dew
16. The Cat Came Back
17. Down Where The Watermelon Grows
18. I'm Going Away
19. Heights of Alabama
20. Casey Jones
21. Suzanna

9

1. Little Brown Jug
2. Rosin The Bow
3. A Woman's Tongue Will Never Take A Rest
4. Old Nipper, followed by a tongue twister
5. The Arkansas Traveler
6. Bye Bye My Darling
7. The Last Gold Dollar
8. Sally Johnson
9. Italy
10. Buffalo Gals
11. Old Joe Clark
12. Cluck Old Hen
13. Nol Pros Nellie
14. Oh Lawsy Me
15. There Are Nine Blue Bottles on The Wall
16. She Gave Kisses One

10

1. The Weeping Willow Tree
2. Old Granny Rattletrap
3. Cindy
4. The Dying Girl's Message
5. Essie, Dear
6. Kitty Clyde or (Kline)
7. The Little Rosewood Casket
8. In the Shadow of the Pines
9. Barney McCoy
10. Lula Wall
11. As I Go Out On Sunday or I'll Never Get Drunk Anymore
12. When The Roses Are In Bloom
13. Down In The Valley
14. Down In The Valley (Continued)
15. Don't Forget Me Little Darling

11

1. Old Stepstone
2. Nancy Rolling
3. The Eastbound Train
4. Little Old Log Cabin In the Lane
5. Roanoke River (The Homesick Boy)
6. Row Us Over the Tide
7. Kitty Wells
8. Old Sally Good'in
9. Put My Little Shoes Away
10. The Ship That Never Returned
11. The Ship That Never Returned (Continued)
12. Won't You Spread the Flocks of Flowers O'er My Grave
13. Ella's Grave
14. Can I Sleep In Your Barn Tonight, Mister?
15. They Cut Down That Old Pine Tree
16. Jack and Joe

12

1. Green Grow the Laurels
2. The Ship that Is Sailing High
3. The Railroad Flagman
4. Oh Bury Me Not
5. The Romish Lady
6. Pretty Saro
7. Little Willie
8. Columbia
9. The Picture That Is Turned to the Wall
10. The Picture That is Turned to the Wall (Continued)
11. Lorena
12. Nellie Gray
13. Nellie Gray (Continued)
14. Old Uncle Ned
15. Sunny Tennessee
16. Captain With His Whiskers
17. A March On the Same Tune
18. I'll Remember You Love In My Prayers

13

1. That Little Logwood Cabin
2. I'm Goin' To Live Anyhow Until I Die
3. Down at Widow Johnson's
4. I'se Gwine Back to Dixie
5. The Old Gray Mare
6. The Ground Hog
7. Rabbit a Rabbit
8. Brady
9. Goin' Down Town
10. Sourwood Mountain
11. Sourwood Mountain (Continued)
12. Down the Road
13. Old Jimmy Sutton
14. Thompson's Old Gray Mule
15. Down In Union County
16. Coonshine
17. Hand Me Down My Walking Cane
18. Come In Said the Barber
19. Them Golden Slippers
20. Eli Webb and John Webb

14

1. The Prettiest Thing I Ever Done
2. The Lone Pilgrim
3. It's a Long Time Talking About the Serving of the Lord
4. What Wondrous Love Is This
5. What Wondrous Love Is This (Continued)
6. There is a Balm In Gilead
7. My Eyes Are Dim
8. This Light Is Bad, My Eyes Are Dim
9. We Will Try to Catch A Flea
10. I Feel Like Hell
11. In That Morning
12. Heaven Bells
13. Oh How I Long To Be There
14. Orphan Children Have A Hard Time In This World
15. I Will Arise
16. Old Time Religion
17. Go Wash In That Beautiful Pool
18. Jesus Loves Me
19. The Same Train
20. The Devil Is Defeated

15

1. Little David
2. Dry Bones
3. I'm A-goin' To Tell My Good Lord Howdy
4. Hide Thou Me
5. Swing-a-low
6. One Day I Was Walking Along
7. Jordan Am A Hard Road To Travel
8. I'm Not A-gonna Lay My 'Ligion Down
9. Who Will Be A Witness?
10. ABC's, Multiplication Tables
11. Hunh A Woh
12. Johnny Brown
13. The Twelve Apostles
14. Dr. Jones
15. Callin' Sim
16. We're Marching Round The Love Ring
17. King William
18. Square Dance Calls

16

1. Four Little Prisoners
2. Skip To My Lou
3. Jolly Is The Miller
4. Dance Calls
5. Drinking Of The Wine
6. Oh Mary Don't You Weep
7. When The First Trumpet Sounds
8. Standing In The Need of Prayer
9. Mountain Sermon
10. The Girl At The Gate
11. The Girl At The Gate (Continued)
12. The Story of the Big Toe
13. The Story of the Big Toe (Continued)
14. Well, Said The Blackbird
15. The Crazy Woman's Story

17

1. The Young Rat
2. Poor Naomi Wise
3. Pearl Bryan
4. Ellen Smith
5. Jessie James
6. Alice Moore
7. John Hardy
8. Old Ninety Seven
9. Damage Suit
10. Bill Ormand
11. Wild Bill Jones
12. Doggett's Gap

18

1. No Ku Klux Out Tonight
2. John Kirby
3. Three Brave Men
4. The New Found Song
5. Old Fate
6. On Robert's Farm
7. Floyd Collins
8. Little Mary Phagan
9. Kidder Cole
10. John Henry
11. John Henry (continued)
12. High Top Shoes
13. John Hardy
14. On The Banks of the Ohio
15. Tom Dooley or Laura Foster

19

1. Fate of Santa Barbara
2. Bryan's Last Battle
3. Booth
4. Booth
5. Charles Guiteau
6. Sky Yai Yipper Coma A Yea Yea Yea
7. Cumberland Gap
8. Cindy
9. I Want To Be An Angel
10. Mr. Garfield
11. Mr. Garfield (Continued)

20

1. Czolgotz or Buffalo
2. Martha Penix
3. Martha Penix (Continued)
4. Hanged or Frankie Silvers
5. Hanged or Frankie Silvers (Continued)

APPENDIX III

Bascom Lamar Lunsford
Library of Congress Recording Project, 1949
(45 Double faced 16' originals)

9474A1	Black Jack Davie
9474A2	Bonnie George Campbell (Cumberland Gap)
9474A3	The Hangmans Tree (Two versions)
9474B1	Billy Boy
9474B2	The Old Man in the North Country
9474B3	George Collins (or Coggins)
9475A1	The Three Good Nights (Our Good Man)
9475A2	The Farmer's Curst Wife (The Old Man Lived Under the Hill)
9475A3	Sweet William and Lady Margaret
9475B1	Barbara Allen
9475B2	Little Betty Ann (Lady Margaret)
9475B3	The Lass of Roch Royal
9476A1	Lord Thomas
9476A2	The Death of Queen Jane
9476A3	The Brown Girl
9476B1	The Wife of Ushers Well
9476B2	The False Wife—The House Carpenter (Fiddle tune is Old Joe Clark)
9476B3	The Mermaid Song
9477A1	Hell Broke Loose in Georgia
9477A2	Lord Lovel
9477A3	Ten Steps
9477B1	Lord Daniel's Wife (Little Mathy Grew)
9477B2	The Golden Vanity (Merry Golden Tree) (Low Lands)
9478A1	Jenny Lind (Short Fiddle tune)
9478A2	Sally Ann (Short Fiddle tune)
9478A3	Bonnie Blue Eyes
9478A4	Awake, Awake (The Drowsy Sleeper)
9478B1	Frankie Baker
9478B2	My Home Across the Smoky Mountains
9479A1	I'm Going Back to Georgia
9479A2	The Scolding Wife (Fiddle)
9478A3	Laurel Lonesome (Lonesome Laurie) (Short fiddle tune)
9479B1	To the Pines, To the Pines

9479B2	Jack of Diamonds
9479B3	Dishonest Miller (The Miller's Will)
9479B4	The Dew-Drops Are Falling on Me
9480A1	Turkey Buzzard (Fiddle) Fragment of "You Can't Dance Kitty"
9480A2	Paper of Pins
9480A3	Jenny Jenkins
9480A4	Darby's Ram
9480B1	Methodist Preacher
9480B2	Short Life of Trouble
9480B3	Love Somebody
9480B4	Springfield Mountain (The Big Serpent)
9481A1	I Wish I Were a Swallow
9481A2	Must I Go Bound (Spiritual)
9481A3	Old Smoky
9481B1	Pretty Fair Maid
9481B2	Shout Little Lulu
9481B3	Shout Little Lulu (Added stanza and comment)
9481B4	Edmond (Young Edwin in the Lowlands Low)
9482A1	Little Turtle Dove
9482A2	Newt's Dream with Dance Calls (Fiddle)
9482A3	Black-Eyed Susie
9482B1	Froggie Went A' Courtin'
9482B2	Reuben (Banjo tune)
9482B3	A Wagoner (The Wagoner Lad)
9483A1	Lisa Jane
9483A2	Tumble Di I Dye Ding Dye Aye (Katie Morey)
9483A3	Farmers Boy
9483A4	The Butchers Boy
9483B1	Rye Straw (Fiddle tune) (no title given on record)
9483B2	Rye Straw (Added title with additional comment)
9483B3	Young Man and Maid
9483B4	Captain, Captain (with Butcher Boy version)
9484A1	The Roving Gambler
9484A2	Little Willie
9484A3	Trot Us On the Other Side of Jordan
9484A4	I Wish I Was a Single Girl Again (Use A5)
9484A5	I Wish I Was a Single Girl Again
9484A6	Dummy Line
9484B1	The Lonesome Road Blues
9484B2	I'll Be Glad When You're Dead You Rascal, You
9484B3	Free A Little Bird
9485A1	Fond Affection
9485A2	The Swannanoa Tunnel (Version of the Water Boy)
9485A3	Laurel Valley (or name of local valley, Red River, etc)
9485B1	Cackling Hen with fiddle and square dance calls

9485B3 Tune to 'Black-Eyed Susie' - Imitative words
9485B4 The War Is Now Raging
9485B5 Courtin' the Widder

9486A1 New River Train
9486A2 Oh to Me the Time Draws Nigh
9486A3 Corina
9486A4 On a Bright and Summer's Morning
9486B1 Georgia Buck
9486B2 My Dearest Friend
9486B3 Tucker's Barn
9486B4 Ruint Cobbler (White Spiritual) (Cue: Take the second one for copying)

9487A1 Kidder Cole
9487A2 Maple on the Hill
9487A3 Meet Me in the Moonlight
9487B1 Kind Miss
9487B2 Good Night My Darling, I Must Leave You
9487B3 The Old Woman Dressed in White
9487B4 My Dear Old Innocent Boy

9488A1 Bonaparte's Retreat (Fiddle)
9488A2 I Wish I was Single Again
9488A3 Whole Hog
9488A4 Roarin' River
9488A5 Sam Hunnicutt's Plantation Yodel
9488B1 Little Mohee
9488B2 Darling Cora
9488B3 Billy in the Low Ground (Fiddle)
9488B4 Blue-Eyed Girl

9489A2 Charming Betsy
9489A3 Snowbird
9489A4 Red Apple Juice
9489A5 Johnson Boys
9489B1 I Wish I Were a Mole in the Ground
9489B2 Lost John Dean
9489B3 Railroad Bill
9489B4 Going Cross the Sea

9490A1 Pretty Little Pink
9490A2 Bury Me Deep
9409A3 No One to Love Me (The Sailor on the Deep Blue Sea)
9490A4 The Song of the Sea
9490A5 Walking in the Parlor
9490B1 Frankie and Albert (Additional stanzas)
9490B2 Careless Love
9490B3 Some Will Come on Saturday Night
9490B4 Cripple Creek

9491A1	Shortening Bread
9491A2	Sifting Sand (Fragment)
9491A3	Old Mountain Dew
9491A4	Down Where the Watermelon Grows
9491B1	Rosin the Beau
9491B2	Rosin the Beau
9491B3	The Cackling Hen Song (Fiddle)
9491B4	A Woman's Tongue Will Never Take a Rest
9491B5	Old Neiper
9492A1	Heights of Alabama (Fiddle)
9492A2	Casey Jones
9492A3	Susanna
9492A4	Little Brown Jug
9492B1	Arkansas Traveler
9492B2	Bye, Bye, My Darling
9492B3	Italy (Mountain Banjo Song)
9493A1	Buffalo Girl
9493A2	Old Joe Clark
9493A3	Nol Pros Nellie
9493B1	Oh! Lawzey Me
9493B2	Nine Blue Bottles on the Wall
9493B3	She Gave Kisses One
9493B4	The Weeping Willow Tree
9494A1	Sally Johnson (Fiddle Tune)
9494A2	Old Granny Rattle Trap (Fiddle and 1 verse)
9494A3	Cluck Old Hen (Fiddle Tune)
9494A4	The Dying Girl's Message
9494B1	The Last Gold Dollar
9494B2	Cindy
9494B3	Essie Dear
9494B4	The Little Rosewood Casket
9495A1	Kitty Clyde
9495A2	Roll in My Sweet Baby's Arms
9495A3	In the Shadow of the Pines
9495B1	Barney McCoy (4 lines only)
9495B2	Lulu Wall
9495B3	I'll Never Get Drunk Anymore
9495B4	When the Roses Bloom Again
9496A1	Down in the Valley
9496A2	Down in the Valley
9496A3	Don't Forget Me Little Darling
9496B1	Old Stepstone
9496B2	East Bound Train
9496B3	Little Log Cabin in the Lane

9497A1	Roanoke River
9497A2	Row Us Over the Tide
9497A3	Kitty Wells
9497B1	Put My Little Shoes Away
9497B2	Ship That Never Returned
9497B3	Won't You Spread the Flock of Flowers
9498A1	May I Sleep in Your Barn, Mister (incomplete)
9498A2	They Cut Down the Ol' Pine Tree
9498A3	Green Grows the Laurel
9498B1	The Ship That Is Sailing High
9498B2	Railroad Flagman
9498B3	Bury Me Not On the Prairie
9498B4	The Romish Lady (Protestant religious; short)
9499A1	Little Willie
9499A2	The Picture That Is Turned to the Wall
9499A3	Lorena
9499B1	Nellie Gray
9499B2	Old Uncle Ned
9499B3	Sunny Tennessee
9500A1	I'll Remember You Love, in My Prayers
9500A2	Once I Had an Old Gray Mare
9500B1	Rabbit Rabbit
9500B2	Brady
9500B3	Goin' Down to Town
9500B4	Sourwood Mountain
9501A1	Down the Road
9501A2	Down in Union County
9501A3	Hand Me Down My Walking Cane
9501A4	Golden Slippers
9501B1	What Wondrous Love or Sinking Down
9501B2	My Eyes Are Dim (Story)
9501B3	In That Morning
9502A1	Heaven Bells
9502A2	Oh, How I Long to Be There (Short Talk)
9502A3	Orphan Children Have a Hard Time
9502A4	I Am Bound For the Promised Land
9502B1	Old Time Religion
9502B2	Go Wash in That Beautiful Pool
9502B3	Jesus Loves Me
9502B4	The Devil is Defeated
9503A1	Train
9503A2	Dry Bones
9503A3	Hard Shell Preachin' (Sermon)
9503B1	Mr. Garfield's Assassination

9504A1	Little David
9504A2	I'm Goin' To Tell the Good Lord Howdy
9504A3	Swing Low
9504B1	One Day As I Was Walkin' Along (Short Negro Spiritual)
9504B2	Lie Down Me (Hide, Thou, Me)
9504B3	I'm Not Goin' to Lay My Religion Down
9504B4	Who Will Be a Witness
9505A1	Alphabet Song
9505A2	Hulla-A-Gullum
9505A3	Hu-hunch-a hunh
9505A4	Johnny Brown
9505A5	Johnny Brown
9505B1	Twelve Apostles
9505B2	Calling Sim
9505B3	Calling Sim
9505B4	Doctor Jones (Game)
9506A1	Four Little Prisoners (Game)
9506A2	Skip to My Lou, My Darling
9506A3	We Are Marching Around the Love Ring
9506A4	King William (Game)
9506B1	Square Dance Calls
9507A1	Jolly Is the Miller (Game)
9507A2	Drinkin' of the Wine (Negro Spiritual)
9507A3	When the First Trumpets Shall Sound (Negro Spiritual)
9507A4	Oh, Mary Don't You Weep or Moan
9507B1	Standing in the Need of Prayer
9507B2	Naomi Wise
9507B3	Pearl Bryant
9508A1	Ellen Smith
9508A2	Jesse James
9508B1	Jesse James
9509A1	John Hardy
9509A2	Ol' 97
9509A3	Damage Suit
9509A4	Wild Bill Jones
9509B1	Doggett's Gap
9509B2	No Ku Klux Out Tonight
9509B3	Bill Ormand
9510A1	John Kirby
9510A2	John Henry
	John Henry (Continued for copy)
9510B1	On the Banks of the Ohio (Do over for B2)
9510B2	On the Banks of the Ohio

9511A1	Bill Ormand
9511A2	Down on Robert's Farm
9511A3	Laura Foster
9511B1	Fate of Santa Barbara (Defect in Material on record)
9511B2	Fate of Santa Barbara (Use this only)
9512A1	Bryan's Last Battle
9512A2	Booth Killed Lincoln: or J. Wilkes Booth
9512A3	Booth Killed Lincoln; or J. Wilkes Booth
9512B1	Booth Killed Lincoln (Use this for copy)
9512B2	Booth Killed Lincoln (Different version than above) with fiddle
9512B3	Charles Guiteau
9513A1	Old Billy Shook
9513A2	Cumberland Gap
9513A3	Czolgotz
9513A4	The Girl at the Gate
9513B1	Where's My Big Toe
9513B2	The Lily of the West
9514A1	Birds in the Tree Tops
9514A2	Sundown
9514A3	The Boston Burglar
9514B1	Bonny Doon
9514B2	The Uncloudy Day
9514B3	Blessed Be the Name
9514B4	Baa, Baa, Black Sheep
9515A1	Amazing Grace
9515A2	The Prettiest Thing I Ever Done
9515A3	Down at Widow Johnson's
9515B1	The Captain and His Whiskers
9515B2	Sally Goodin (Fiddle)
9515B3	Jenny Lind (Fiddle)
9515B4	Watermelon Smilin' on the Vine
9516A1	I'se Goin' Back to Dixie
9516A2	I'm Goin' to Live 'till I Die
9516B1	"Come In", Said the Barber
9516B2	Little Birdie
9516B3	Judge Henry - Parodies of
9516B4	My Old Father's Gone Along
9517A1	There is a Balm in Gilead
	Go Wash in That Beautiful Pool
9517A2	The Lone Pilgrim
	How Tedious the Hour
	Ella's Grave
9517A3	My Hightop Shoes
	Old Time Religion
9517B1	Thompson's Old Gray Mule

	The Cat Came Back
9517B2,3	Old Jimmy Sutton (Spiral is to miss defect in record)
	Coonshine
9517B4,5	I Had a Pious Father (Spiral is to miss defect)
	Columbia
9518A1	Racking Pony - Fiddle Tune
	Sally Ann - Fiddle Tune
9518A2	One Dark and Stormy Night
9518A3	You May Say I'm Vicious
9518A4	How Firm a Foundation
9518B1	Dedication

APPENDIX IV

Bascom Lamar Lunsford Discography

by Norm Cohen

The following discography lists all commercial recordings made by Bascom Lunsford to the present. Of his recordings for the Library of Congress Archive of American Folk Song, only those commercially available are included.

In the following listing the first column gives master number and issued take (if known); the second, the title; the third gives labels and release numbers. Record label names are abbreviated as follows: Br = Brunswick, Co = Columbia, Cor = Coral (Japanese release), Cty = County, OK = Okeh, Vo = Vocation, Folk = Folkways.

15 March 1924, Atlanta, Ga. General Phonograph Corp.

Bascom Lamar Lunsford, vocal and banjo.

8578-a	Jesse James	OK 40155
8579-a	I Wish I Was a Mole In the Ground	OK 40155

ca. 27 Aug 1925, Asheville, No. Car. General Phono Co.

Bascom Lamar Lunsford, vocal and Banjo; Blackwell Lunsford, fiddle.

9292-a	Fate of Santa Barbara	OK 45008
9293-a	Sherman Valley	OK 45008

ca. Feb 1928, Ashland, KY. Brunswick-Balke-Collender Co.

Bascom Lamar Lunsford, vocal and banjo. (Issued master number is underlined).

AL 117-**118**	Lost John Dean	Br 227, Vo 5246
AL **119**-120	Get Along Home Cindy	Br 228
AL 121-**122**	Mountain Dew	Br 219
AL **123**-124	"Nol Pros" Nellie	Br 230
AL **125**-126	Lulu Wall	Br 229, Vo 5252
AL **127**-128	Darby's Ram	Br 228, Br 80089, Br BL 59001, Cor MH 174
AL 129-**130**	Stepstones	Br 231, Br 314
AL 131-**132**	I Wish I Was a Mole In the Ground	Br 219, Folk FA 2953 (FP 243
AL 133-**134**	Kidder Cole	Br 230
AL 135-**136**	Italy	Br 227, Vo 5246
AL 137-**138**	Little Turtle Dove	Br 229, Vo 5252, Cty 515
AL 139-**140**	Dry Bones	Br 231, Br 314, Folk FA 2952 (FP 252)

NOTE: When Masters 118, 125, 136, and 138 were transferred to Vocalion, they were assigned new master numbers: E-7414, 7416, 7415, and 7419, respectively.

15 or 16 April 1930, Atlanta,Ga. Columbia Phono Corp
Bascom Lamar Lunsford, speech.

150228-2	Speaking the Truth	Co15595-D
150229-1	A Stump Speech In the Tenth District	Co 15595-D

Feb-Mar 1935, New York, N.Y. Library of Congress.
Bascom Lamar Lunsford, vocal and fiddle

1788-Al,	A2 Barbara Allen	AFS L54

Sept 1946, Leicester, N.C. Library of Congress.
Bascom Lamar Lunsford, vocal; and banjo, -1.
Master numbers not available for this or any of the following sessions.

Jesse James	-1	AFS 97; AFS L20
Baa, Baa, Black Sheep		AFS 97; AFS L20
I Wish I Was A Mole In The Ground	-1	AFS 102; AFS L21
On a Bright and Summer's Morning	-1	AFS 104; AFS L21
Death of Queen Jane		AFS 104, AFS L21

1949, Washington, D.C. Library of Congress.
Bascom Lamar Lunsford, vocal; with banjo, -1; unaccompanied fiddle,-2

Zolgotz (or White House Blues)	-1	AFS L29
Mr. Garfield	-1	AFS L29
Charles Guiteau		AFS L29
Booth Killed Lincoln		AFS L29
Booth Killed Lincoln		AFS L29

April 14, 1947, Los Angeles, Cal., by Ralph Auf der Heide and Frances Lynne (?) for Eagle Records but released in 1953 by Folkways Corp.
Smoky Mountain Ballads: Bascom Lamar Lunsford, vocal with banjo.

Swannanoa Tunnel		Folk FP 40
Mr. Garfield		Folk FP 40
Jennie Jenkins		Folk FP 40
Little Marget		Folk FP 40
On the Banks of the Ohio		Folk FP 40
Springfield Mountain		Folk FP 40
The Death of Queen Jane		Folk FP 40
Mole in the Ground	Subsequently Folk FE 4530,	Folk FP 40

Sept. 1956, Asheville, No. Carolina. By Paul Clayton. Riverside Records.
Bascom Lamar Lunsford, vocal and banjo; Freda English, vocal -1; guitar -2.

Poor Jesse James		Riverside RLP 12-645
Go To Italy		Riverside RLP 12-645
The Merry Golden Tree		Riverside RLP 12-645
I Shall Not Be Moved	-1, 2	Riverside RLP 12-645
The Derby Ram		Riverside RLP 12-645

The Old Man From the North Country	-2	Riverside RLP 12-645
The Miller's Will		Riverside RLP 12-645
Sundown		Riverside RLP 12-645
Fly Around, My Blue-Eyed Girl		Riverside RLP 12-645
Black Jack Davy		Riverside RLP 12-645
Weeping Willow Tree	-1, 2	Riverside RLP 12-645
Swing Low, Chariot		Riverside RLP 12-645
The Sailor on the Deep Blue Sea		Riverside RLP 12-645
John Henry		Riverside RLP 12-645

Sept. 1956, Asheville, No. Carolina by Kenneth Goldstein. Rounder Records Corp.
Music from South Turkey Creek: Bascom Lamar Lunsford, George Pegram and Red Parham, vocals, banjo, guitar and harmonica

Side one, Bascom Lamar Lunsford	
Free Little Bird	Rounder 0065
Old Mountain Dew	Rounder 0065
Lily of the West	Rounder 0065
Lord Joshuay	Rounder 0065
Drinking of the Wine	Rounder 0065
Essie Dear	Rounder 0065
On a Bright and Summer's Morning	Rounder 0065
Goodbye Dear Old Stepstone	
Poor Ellen Smith	Rounder 0065
Georgia Buck	Rounder 0065
Side two, George Pegram and Red Parham	
Lost John	Rounder 0065
Pig in a Pen	Rounder 0065
Red and George Breakdown	Rounder 0065
Charlie Lawson	Rounder 0065
A Leaf from the Sea	Rounder 0065
Old Joe Clark	Rounder 0065
T Model Ford and Train	Rounder 0065
Mama Blues	Rounder 0065
Roll on, Buddy	Rounder 0065
Keep My Skillet Good and Greasy	Rounder 0065
Cindy	Rounder 0065
Poor Ellen Smith	Rounder 0065
Old Rattler	Rounder 0065

1989, The American Experience, PBS Video
Ballad of a Mountain Man [video].
Available from Varied Directions, Inc. 69 Elm Street, Camden, ME 04843.

1996, Smithsonian/Folkways
Bascom Lamar Lunsford: Ballads, Banjo Tunes, and Sacred Songs of Western North Carolina [compact disc].

Swannanoa Tunnel	Smithsonian Folkways	40082
The Mermaid Song	Smithsonian Folkways	40082
Ten Steps	Smithsonian Folkways	40082
Little Turtle Dove	Smithsonian Folkways	40082
In the Shadow of the Pines	Smithsonian Folkways	40082
Swing Low	Smithsonian Folkways	40082
Bonny George Campbell	Smithsonian Folkways	40082
I Wish I Was a Mole in the Ground	Smithsonian Folkways	40082
On a Bright and Summer's Morning	Smithsonian Folkways	40082
To the Pines, To the Pines	Smithsonian Folkways	40082
Dry Bones	Smithsonian Folkways	40082
The Last Gold Dollar	Smithsonian Folkways	40082
Rye Straw	Smithsonian Folkways	40082
Old Mountain Dew	Smithsonian Folkways	40082
Italy	Smithsonian Folkways	40082
Death of Queen Jane	Smithsonian Folkways	40082
Old Stepstone	Smithsonian Folkways	40082
Drinking of the Wine	Smithsonian Folkways	40082
Dedication	Smithsonian Folkways	40082

Synopsis of Bascom Lamar Lunsford's non-commercial recordings.
Lunsford's earliest recordings were made in ca. 1922 in No. Carolina by Frank C. Brown on cylinders. Approximately 32 items were recorded. In Oct-Dec 1925 Robert W. Gordon recorded some 39 cylinders in No. Carolina. In Feb-March 1935, George W. Hibbitt and William Cabell Greet recorded approximately 303 masters in New York. Sidney Robertson (Cowell) recorded 11 items in Leicester, No. Carolina, in Nov 1936, 4 more in Washington, D.C., in March 1937, and 5 more in Chicago in May 1937. 317 items were recorded in Washington, D.C., in 1949. Other scattered items were recorded in Los Angeles (1947), Asheville (1941), Leicester (1946), and elsewhere in No. Carolina (1949, 1966).

Reprinted through the courtesy of Norm Cohen, Executive Secretary, The John Edwards Memorial Foundation, Folklore and Mythology Center, University of California at Los Angeles. Information regarding 1989 and 1996 recordings added by Loyal Jones, 2002.

APPENDIX V

A Preliminary List of Recordings of Bascom Lamar Lunsford in the Archive of Folk Song, Library of Congress July, 1971

Gordon cylinders A13-A46, A104, A199-202
Recorded by Robert Winslow Gordon, 1925

AFS 1778 AL—1841 B2
Recorded in New York, New York, February-March, 1935, by George W. Hibbitt and William Cabell Greet.

AFS 3155 B1-B2, 3166 Al-3168 B2
Recorded in Leicester, N.C., November, 1936, by Sidney Robertson (Cowell).

AFS 3241 A1-B2
Recorded in Washington, D.C., March, 1937, by Sidney Robertson (Cowell)

AFS 3244 A2, B1; 3251 A2; 3256 B2; 3257 A2; 3257 B1
Recorded at National Folk Festival, Chicago, Ill., May, 1937, by Sidney Robertson (Cowell).

AFS 9124-9125
Recorded in Los Angeles, Cal., 1947?, by Ralph Auf der Heide.

AFS 4788-4808 (scattered announcements and songs by BLL)
Recorded at Asheville Folk Festival, Asheville, N.C., 1941, by Alan Lomax, Jerome Wiesner, and Joseph Liss.

AFS 7959-I—7964 B (and scattered elsewhere)
Recorded by Artus Moser at Leicester, N.C., Sept., 1946. (Scattered items from Asheville, Renfro Valley, etc.)

AFS 8772-8851 (Scattered)
Recorded by Frank C. Brown, no place or date given, probably Buncombe Co., N.C., ca. 1922. (About 32 items originally recorded on cylinders, duplicated onto discs by Archive of Folk Song in later 1940s.)

AFS 9474-9518
Recorded at Library of Congress, 1949. (317 items.)

AFS 9901
Recorded at Library of Congress, 1949. (Interview of BLL by Duncan Emrich.)

AFS 14, 088 B
Recorded at South Turkey Creek, N.C., Feb., 1966, by James Scancerelli. (14 items.)

AFS 14,083-14,086

Recorded by Benjamin A. Botkin, North Carolina, Jan., 1949. (Includes scattered Lunsford items, part at least from Artus Moser's collection.)

AFS 14,220-14,221

Recorded by Benjamin A. Botkin, North Carolina, Jan., 1949. (Also includes scattered BLL items, partly at least from Moser.)

APPENDIX VI

A SAMPLING OF LUNSFORD'S TALES, ANECDOTES, ETC.

The Big Toe

Once there was a little crooked man and a little crooked woman, who lived together in a little crooked house. And they had a little crooked Irish potato patch. So one day they took the little crooked hoe and went out to the little crooked Irish potoato patch and dug some Irish potatoes.

They brought the potatoes in the house late at night. They put them in the fire, and when looking for the potatoes to place in the little crooked fireplace, they found a big toe. So they put the big toe in with the potatoes and roasted the big toe.

After a while they had a good meal with potatoes, and then they ate the big toe and went to bed in a little crooked bed.

In a little while, they heard a strange noise on the outside of the house, saying, "Where's my big toe? Where is my big toe? Where's my big toe?" So the little crooked man got up and went out and around the little cabin and back into the house and said he could see nothing. So he went to bed.

Then they heard the noise again. "Where's my big toe? Where's my big toe? Where's my big toe?" Then the little crooked woman went out and around the house and looked and came back and said she could find nothing. So she went to bed.

In a little while they heard the same noise. "Where's my big toe?" So they both got up immediately and went out and walked around the house clear to the chimney, and they looked up on the chimney and they saw a big black thing up there, with fierce looking eyes, with long claws and a big long bushy tail and long teeth.

And they said, "What's them big eyes for?"

He said, "To look you through."

They said, "What's them big claws for?"

"To dig your grave"

"What's that long bushy tail for?"

"To sweep your grave."

"What's them big teeth for?"

"To chomp your bones." (This is in a shout).

Mountain Sermon

Imagine a country audience with the minister ready to start his sermon.

Brethern and sistern, I do not come before you this evening to engage in any grammar talk or college highfalutin. But I come to prepare a per varse generation for the day of wrath, and my text when you find it you'll find tis somewhere a'twixt the lids of this old Bible from the first chapter of Second Chronicles to the last chapter of Timothy-Titus and when you find it you'll find it in these words: "And they shall gnaw a file and flee into the mountains of Hespudam where the lions roareth and the whang-doodle mourneth for its first-born."

Now my brethern there's different kinds of files. There's the rattail file, and there's the handsaw file, and there's a cross-cut file, and there's the profile and the defile, but the text says that they shall gnaw a file and flee into the mountains of the Hespudam where the lions roareth and the whang-doodle mourneth for its first-born.

And my brethern there's different kind of dams. There's Amsterdam, and then there's Rotterdam, and there's Beaverdam, but the last of all and the worst of all my brethern is I don't give a damn! But the text says that they shall gnaw a file and flee into the mountains of Hespudam where the lions roareth and the whang-doodle mourneth for its first-born.

Now my brethern, this reminds me of the man who lived up on the north fork of Little Pine Creek in Madison County, North Carolina. He had a little mill but it ground a heap of corn. But one night the fountain of the great deep was broken up and the windows of heaven were opened and the rains descended and the winds came and it washed that man's mill dam to kingdom come. And he got up the next morning, and he told the good old wife of his bosom that he wasn't worth a damn. But the text says that they shall gnaw a file and flee into the mountains of Hespudam where the lions roareth and the whang-doodle mourneth for its first-born.

My brethern, this doesn't mean the howling wilderness where John the Hard-shell Baptist fed on locusts and wild asses, but it means the city of New Orleans, the mother of harlots and hard lots where corn is six bits a bushel one day and nary a red the next. And where thieves and pickpockets go skittering about like weasels in a barnyard, and where honest men are sca'ser ner hen's teeth, and where a woman once took up your beloved teacher and bam-boozled him out of 127 plunks, in three jerks of the eye, or a twinkling of the sheep's tail, but she can't do it again, Hallelujah!

(This piece was written by William P. Brannan and appeared as "Where the Lion Roareth and the Whang-Doodle Mourneth," in *Tall Tales of the Southwest*, An Anthology of Southern and Southwestern Humor, 1830-1860, Franklin J. Meine (ed.), New York, Alfred A. Knopf, 1930, but learned by Lunsford in the oral tradition.

A Stump Speech in the Tenth District

Gentleman and fellow citizens of the good old county of Buncombe. The first thing I say is that I want to thank the ladies for bringing me these pretty flowers. The next is that I want to compliment the boys for that splendid fiddling and say that we'll have some more out'n them before we leave. And thirdly permit me to again remind you that I am an independent candidate for the Lower House and at our next election I expect to represent this district in Congress.

I'm glad to see so many of you farmers out here today. You come, some of you, with your feet on the ground and your hair stickin' out 'n the top of your hat a-fightin' for farm relief, when you don't know what you're fightin' for. Looks to me like you've already been relieved of about everything you ever had, but you better leave that to me after I get there.

My platform is like one of your hillside plows. When I gets to one end, I just turn the wing over and plow back t' other way, a simple twist of the wrist. That's all.

Fellow citizens, the Old Tenth is the grandest district in North Carolina. It stretches from the crest of Mt. Mitchell on the east to Hanging Dog Township in Cherokee County on the west, from the Great Smoky Mountain Park on the north to Spicer's Cove in the Dark Corners to the south. It stretches from the headwaters of the Nantahala to the mouth of South Turkey Creek.

Yes, some of you say that the women are agin' me in this campaign, and I'll tell you fer why. They know they can't brow-beat me around and have me to do things that I han't orter.

But I have stumped every township in this district and here's how I stand. I break even with them in Willyshot. I'll walk away with them in Sugar Loaf. I'm neck and neck with them in Bear Waller, and when it comes to Lower Fork, you boys know I've always stayed with them there.

I want to tell the dear people that this is a momentous campaign and getting more momentous as the day approaches, and let me tell you fer why. You can't beat Hoover on one hand, nor Max Gardner (a former North Carolina governor), on t'other, but I beg of you don't let 'em beat me.

My opponent claims he's got his preparation for office between college walls. I don't deny it of him, but I got my schoolin' a plowin' a bull in the meadow where the sun don't shine 'til 10 o'clock of a mornin' and sets before the shank of the evenin' and yet just watch me take my graduatin' exercises a -ridin' that jackass into the Capitol!

Now boys, all of you that are willin' to help me out in this fight and help me put this rotten ring out of business, just come forward and while the boys play a lively tune get one of these fruit jars. You'll find a two-dollar bill in the bottom of it. Take it out the back way up 'cross the fence into the pasture to the mouth of the Stillhouse Branch, and you boys will know the rest.

Calling Sim

A Negro preacher was asked to stay on in a community across the ridge and preach. So he says (in a preaching chant) "I'll tell you what I'll do. I'll go on top of the hill and cal ah." And he went up on top of the hill and he called.

He said "Hey, Sim - Whoo. Hey, Sim - Whoo."

Sim don't answer.

"Hey Sim, Whooee you go home and tell your a wife to tell my wife, that I'm a -goin' a preach over Sunday and I won't be home 'til Mondeeeee."

The Light is Bad, My Eyes Are Dim

Visualize a country church, where the minister is trying to line out his hymn for his congregation, and where the congregation mistakes his explanation for lining out the hymn.

The Minister: "This light is bad, my eyes are dim,
I sca'se can see to read my hymn"

The Congregation (to the tune of Amazing Grace): "This light is bad, my eyes are dim,
I sca'se can see to read my hymn."

Minister: "I did not mean sing a hymn
I only meant my eyes are dim."

Congregation sings minister's lines.

Minister: "Upon the honor of my hat,
I didn't mean for you to sing that."

Congregation sings minister's lines

Minister: "I didn't mean to sing at all.
I believe the Devil's in you all."

Congregation sings minister's lines.

Humorous Play on Hymn Lines

We will try to catch the flee -
We will try to catch the flee -
We will try to catch the fleeting hour.

I feel like hel -
I feel like hel -
I feel like helping some poor soul.

Now, Brethren, Be Mighty Careful

It seemed that a man's wife had gotten sick and she died. The neighbors came into help, and they provided for the casket. They came in and made the arrangements, and a lot of the neighbors were pallbearers. When they had the service, they called on the pallbearers to carry the casket out to the cemetery. They had to go up a little steep hill in reaching the body's last resting place. So in going around this little steep hill, one of the fellows slipped. That let down his part of the load. The other man slipped and the coffin dropped down, the lid flew off. The woman was jolted, so she raised up and she spoke a word or two. Of course, they were scared when she came back to life. They assisted her and carried her back home, and people were frightened very much. But she recovered and got well and lived several years after that. Then she grew sick again and lingered along and died again. So they had the same friends to come, and they had another casket and they had the funeral services. They called on these same brethren to act as pallbearers, and they started out. Of course, the bereaved husband walked along behind the casket with the minister. They got to this same little hill in the turn of the walk and the husband says, "Now, brethren, now be mighty, mighty careful." He says, "You remember what a terrible accident happened here three or four years ago right at this same place."

The Big Turnip

I remember having heard my mother tell about the man who'd travel along telling about his life and things he'd seen. A fellow had planted a turnip patch, and sowed a field of turnips, and there wasn't a seed to come up except one and that was right in the middle of the patch. Well, he thought he'd save that, and he hoed it and fertilized it and he kept the weeds clean from the field. That one turnip kept growing, and growing, and growing, and finally it just covered the whole patch. It was high as a house and it was a wonderful turnip. The tops came up and turned down.

Then they passed the story on to someone else. This person said he was going along and he saw some people working. They had the frame work up, and he climbed up on the framework and looked down and there was a big kettle, -very big kettle.

"Well, how big was it?"

"Oh, it was so big that the fellow accidently dropped his hammer and it took three days to hit the bottom, - you heard it hit three days after that."

"Well, what was he going to do with such a kettle as that?"

"Why, he had to have a kettle that big to cook that big turnip in you was telling about a while ago."

Is That Your Paw?

The flu epidemic of 1918 was a fearful time, because in a small town often there was hardly enough people who were well enough themselves to wait on the sick and bury the dead. From that, this story, they said, originated. The undertakers were busy, ministers were busy, doctors were busy, and nurses were busy, and everybody was busy. A woman lost her husband. They had some small children. Finally they got an undertaker to come out, and they made arrangements about the funeral. Of course, they were going and coming at the churches. It was hard to even get an hour to conduct a funeral. But, finally, they went out to the funeral with the proper arrangements. The minister began his discourse. He talked about what a good father the deceased had been, what a good provider he was, how well he was thought of among his fellow men and the people he dealt with and the people he'd worked with. He spoke of how good he had been to his family and his church and so on. He spoke very complimentary about this unfortunate man. This woman seated up next to the casket (or pretty close to it) bent over and spoke to her little son and says, "You look over there, honey, and see if that really is your paw."

We'll Take a Mortgage on the Hogs

An interesting story happened over at Old Fort, North Carolina. Alec Burnett, a mountaineer, lived up there on Mill Creek. He was a waggish kind of fellow, and he had a habit of drinking. I knew him very well. He had fun wherever he went. He had been down at Old Fort and bought a cow from some fellow down about Greenlee by the name of Tooten Williams, I believe. He'd gotten ahold of some booze somewhere along the line. He had a little pistol. It occurred to him that it would be fun to run the cow through Old Fort and fire off the pistol. He did it, and they hailed him before the magistrate and fined him 10 dollars and the cost.

"Well," he said, "I don't have a cent of money."
"Well, can we secure this," the magistrate said, "in something?"
"The cow's not mine."
"Well, haven't you got something else?"
"Well, I've got some hogs."
"Well," he said, "we'll take that. How many?"
"Well," he said, "five, five or six; we'll just say five."
"Well," he said, "all right, we'll take a mortgage on the hogs and you can pay it when you can. If you can't pay it or don't pay it, we'll come up and get the hogs."

So they wrote out the mortgage to secure the amount that he owed. He gave a mortgage on five bay hogs on lands of Nate Woody on the head of Mill Creek,— five hogs of brown noses and short tails, and so on. They gave a description and kept the mortgage. In the fullness of time he defaulted in the payment of the mortgage. A fellow asked him about it and he said, "You'll just have to gather up the hogs. I can't pay." So one morning the officer, the deputy, came up to Mill Creek at his home to get the hogs and he said, "They're up the hollow here." He says, "All right, we'll have to go up and get them." They started on up there and he passed around the chimney corner and he picked up a mattock. He put it on his shoulder and he walked on up a little higher. He went to go around a turn in Mill Creek, a little walkway making a turn around the hill, and he says, "You'll have to be pretty quiet. Them hogs are pretty wild."

He says, "They are not all that wild, are they?"

"Oh," he said, "yes, they're pretty wild. I guess you know'd they was groundhogs, didn't you?"

In addition to that he had also put in that old mortgage an old Army rifle, the kind used in the War Between the States.

"Well," he said, "what about the gun?"

"Well," he says, "the gun, I left that in Seven Pines. I set it down agin a tree and run, and you can have it if you want to go after it."

Who is your Pa?

We were going down the road, and we came to this house. There was a little boy standing down by the road just crying and crying.

We stopped, and we heard the biggest racket you ever heard up in the house.

"What's the matter, son?"

"Why, Ma and Pa are up there fightin'."

"Who is your Pa, son?"

"Well, that's what they're a fightin' over."

The Arkansas Traveler

'This is as I remember Arkansas Traveler [a minstrel type story to accompany the tune]. My boy, visualize a farmer, a countryman, sitting on his porch playing an old fiddle, while a stranger is on his horse at the gate asking questions (the farmer playing only the low part of the tune) [in between exchanges].

"Hello, stranger."

"Hello, yourself."

"I get to stay the night?"

"You get to go on."

"What'd you move out here for?"
"I moved out here to get handy to wood and water."
"What kind a wood do you burn?"
"Buckeye and sycamore."
"How far do you have to carry your water?"
"Oh, three miles and a half. Sometimes I have to swim the river to get that."
"What makes your corn so little and yallar?"
"Why, I planted the little and yallar kind."
"Why'nt you cover your house?"
"While it's raining I can't, and when the sun's shining it's as dry as any man's house."
"How long have you lived out here, Stranger?"
"Well, you see that mountain up there?"
"Yeah."
"Well, that was a hole in the ground when I moved out here."
"Where does this road go?"
"Don't go anywhere less'n it goes at night when I'm asleep. It's always there when I get up in the morning."
"Say, Stranger, how far is it to Little Rock?"
"Well, I don't know. Uh, there's a hell of a big'un down here in Molly Spring Branch."
"Why'nt you play the other part of that tune?"
"That's all the part there is to it."
"Let me stay all night and I'll teach you the other part of that tune."
"All right, throw your bridle rein over the gate post there and come in."
'The stranger comes in and takes the fiddle, and he's really a good fiddler, and he starts out playing the Arkansas Traveler. The old farmer gets excited and he says, "That beats anything I've ever seen. Come here, Old Woman. Boy, take that man's horse out there and put him in the crib and prop open the door to the fodder stack. Beats anything I've ever heard. Put some pumkins in the trough. Stranger, I wish you'd teach me the other part of that tune. Say, Old Woman, wish you'd knock the iron wedge in the head, and we'll have brains for supper. Say, skim that rat out o' the molasses and put some down for this stranger.
"Stranger, won't you play that tune for me one time more? Well, I just wish you would."
"Well, I'm pretty tired. I've come a long ways."
"Well, if you'll play that tune for me one time more, you may sleep with Sal!"

A LUNSFORD SAMPLER

The following ballads, hymns and songs are taken from Lunsford's "Memory Collection," with notations by Dr. John Forbes formerly of the Berea College Department of Music, now librarian at Baker University, Baldwin City, Kansas. Recognizing that songs in the oral tradition can never be fully captured on paper, no particular attempt was made to record all of the nuances of Lunsford's style, which often varied from verse to verse. These are the basic tunes and verses, sometimes taken from more than one recording. The keys and chords are merely suggestions for those who wish to learn the songs. Lower case letters denote minor chords. Chords are not given for some of the older ballads and hymns and those which Lunsford sang without instrumental accompaniment. This sampling includes ballads in the Child Collection, British broadsides and American ballads, hymns and spirituals, a variety of folk songs, a few popular songs in the oral tradition and fiddle tunes. Most of the songs and tunes were among Lunsford's favorites, but some were chosen for their unusual qualities or because they are not in most collections.

MERRIE GOLDEN TREE
(The Golden Vanity)

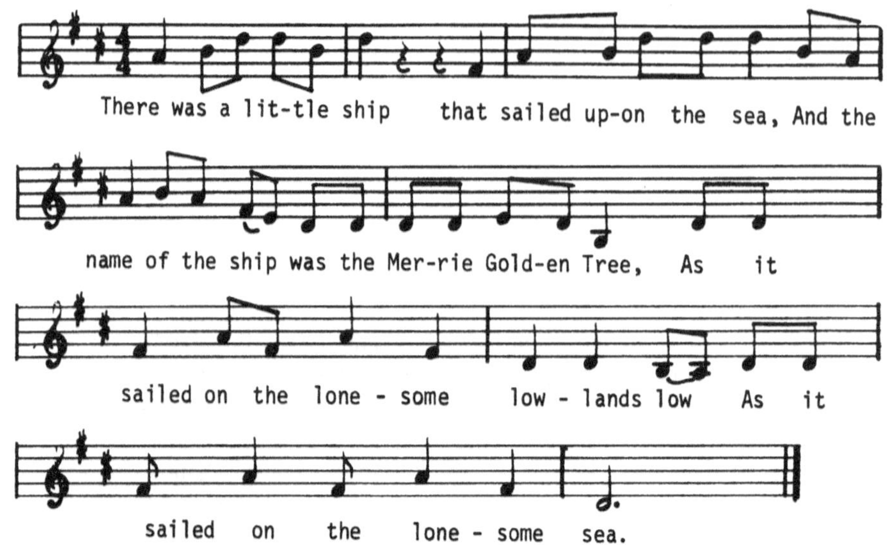

2. There was another ship that sailed upon the sea,
And the name that they gave it was the Merrie Turkalee,
As it sailed on the lonesome lowlands low,
As it sailed on the lonesome sea.

3. There was a little boy that ran amongst the men
Who said, "Captain, Captain, what will you give me then,
If I sink it in the lonesome lowlands low,
If I sink it in the lonesome sea?"

4. "Well, there will be money, and there will be a fee.
Besides, my loving daughter I will marry unto thee,
If you sink it in the lonesome lowlands low,
If you sink it in the lonesome sea."

5. So he smoothed his breast and off swam he,
And he swam til he came to the Merrie Turkalee,
As it sailed on the lonesome lowlands low,
As it sailed on the lonesome sea.

6. And he had a little auger all fitted for the use
And he bored nine holes in its old hull at once
And he sank it on the lonesome lowlands low,
And he sank it on the lonesome sea.

THE OLD MAN LIVED UNDER A HILL
(The Farmer's Curst Wife)

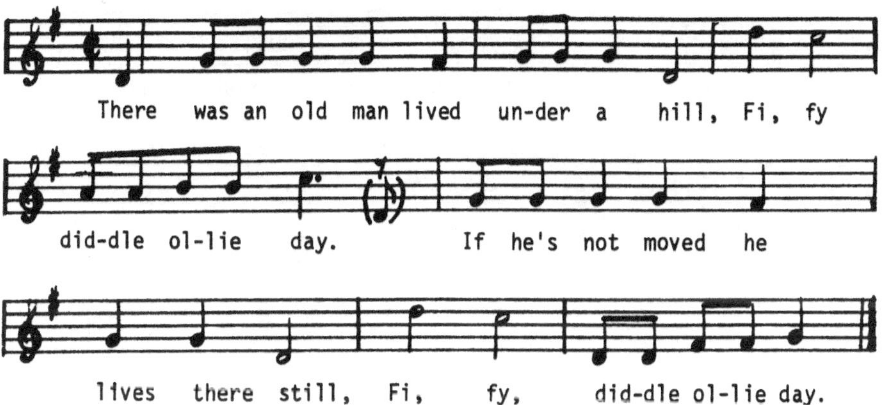

2. He geared up his horses and he went to the plow.
   Fi, fy, diddle ollie day.
   The way he got along, I don't know how.
   Fi, fy, diddle ollie day.

3. The Old Black Man came creepin' up the hill.
   Sayin' "One of your family I'm goin' to steal."

4. "I don't want your eldest son.
   But I want your old lady for the sins she's done."

5. He picked her up all on his back.
   He looked like a peddler with his pack.

6. He took her, then, on down to hell.
   He built up a fire to scorch her well.

7. He tried to bind her all with chains.
   She picked up a little devil, dashed out his brains.

8. Three little devils went scalin' round the walls.
   Sayin' "Take her away, Daddy, she's a-goin' to
   kill us all!"

LITTLE MARGET
(Sweet William and Lady Margaret)

2. She throwed back her ivory comb,
   Throwed back her long yellow hair.
   Said,"I'll go out and bid him farewell,
   And never more go there."

3. It was all lately in the night,
   When they were fast asleep.
   Little Marget appeared all dressed in white,
   A-standin' at their bed feet.

4. "How do you like that snow-white pillow?
   How do you like that sheet?
   How do you like that fair young lady
   That lies in your arms asleep?"

5. "Oh, well do I like my snow-white pillow.
   Oh, well do I like my sheet.
   Much better do I like that fair young lady
   That stands at my bed feet."

6. He called on his serving man to go
   And saddle the dappled roan.
   He went to her father's house and knocked.
   He knocked at the door alone.

7. "Is Little Marget in the house,
Or is she in the hall?"
"Little Marget's in her cold black coffin
With her face turned to the wall."

8. "Unfold, unfold those snow-white robes,
Be they ever so fine,
And let me kiss them cold corpy lips,
For I know they'll never kiss mine."

9. Oh, once he kissed her little white hand,
And twice he kissed her cheeks.
Three times he kissed her cold corpy lips,
And he fell in her arms asleep.

MERRIE GOLDEN TREE
(The Golden Vanity)

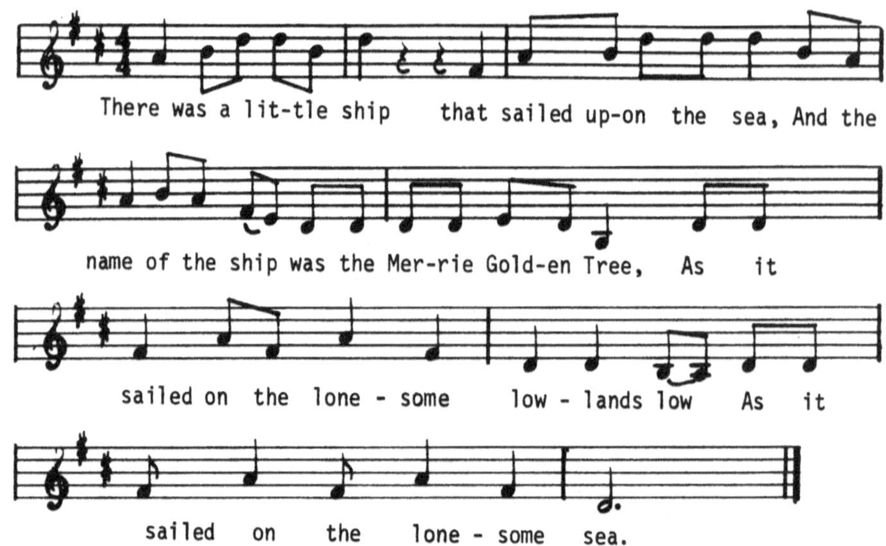

2. There was another ship that sailed upon the sea,
   And the name that they gave it was the Merrie Turkalee,
   As it sailed on the lonesome lowlands low,
   As it sailed on the lonesome sea.

3. There was a little boy that ran amongst the men
   Who said, "Captain, Captain, what will you give me then,
   If I sink it in the lonesome lowlands low,
   If I sink it in the lonesome sea?"

4. "Well, there will be money, and there will be a fee.
   Besides, my loving daughter I will marry unto thee,
   If you sink it in the lonesome lowlands low,
   If you sink it in the lonesome sea."

5. So he smoothed his breast and off swam he,
   And he swam til he came to the Merrie Turkalee,
   As it sailed on the lonesome lowlands low,
   As it sailed on the lonesome sea.

6. And he had a little auger all fitted for the use
   And he bored nine holes in its old hull at once
   And he sank it on the lonesome lowlands low,
   And he sank it on the lonesome sea.

7. Then he smoothed his breast and back swam he,
And he swam til he came to the Merrie Golden Tree
As it sailed on the lonesome lowlands low,
As it sailed on the lonesome sea.

8. And he said, "Captain, Captain, let me on board,
Or you'll not be as good as you told me you would,
If I'd sink it in the lonesome lowlands low,
If I'd sink it in the lonesome sea."

9. "Well, there'll be no money and there'll be no fee,
Nor my loving daughter will I marry unto thee,
Though you sank it in the lonesome lowlands low,
Though you sank it in the lonesome sea."

10. "'Twere not for the love that I have for your men,
I would do unto you as I did unto them.
I would sink you in the lonesome lowlands low,
I would sink you in the lonesome sea."

11. So he smote his breast and down sank he,
And he bid farewell to the Merrie Golden Tree
As it sailed on the lonesome lowlands low,
As it sailed on the lonesome sea.

THE DEATH OF QUEEN JANE

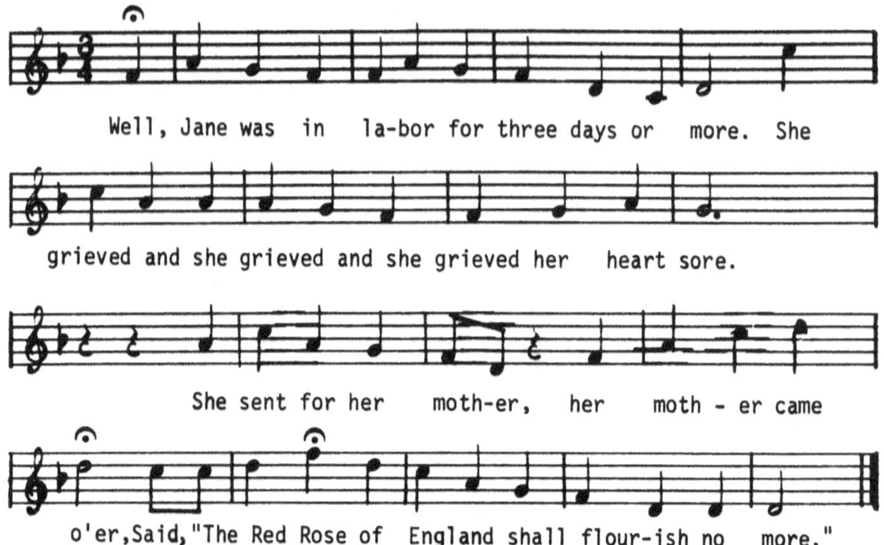

2. Well, Jane was in labor for three days or four.
   She grieved and she grieved and she grieved her heart sore.
   She sent for her father, her father came o'er,
   Said, "The Red Rose of England shall flourish no more."

3. Well, Jane was in labor for four days or more.
   She grieved and she grieved and she grieved her heart sore.
   She sent for Prince Henry, Prince Henry came o'er,
   Said, "The Red Rose of England shall flourish no more."

BLACK JACK DAVY
(The Gypsy Laddie)

2. "How old are you my pretty little miss?
How old are you my honey?"
She smiled so sweet with a tee hee hee,
"I"ll be sixteen next Sunday.
I'll be sixteen next Sunday."

3. "Oh will you come and go with me?
Come go with me my honey.
We'll go away to the deep blue sea.
You'll never want for money.
You'll never want for money."

4. Oh, she put on her Sunday shoes
All made of Spanish leather.
And he put on his old cork boots
And they both rode off together,
And they both rode off together.

5. The landlord come a-ridin' in
Inquiring for his lady.
Oh one of his maids then said to him,
"She's gone with Black Jack Davy.
She's gone with Black Jack Davy."

6. "Then bridle and saddle my old gray mare,
And hand me down my derby.
And I'll ride east and I'll ride west
'Til I overtake my lady.
'Til I overtake my lady."

7. Oh he rode east and he rode west.
He rode to the deep blue sea.
And there he found with tears in his eyes,
Oh there he found his lady.
Oh there he found his lady.

8. "Will you forsake your house and home,
Your husband and your baby?
Will you forsake all else on earth
And go with the Black Jack Davy?"
And go with the Black Jack Davy?"

9. "Last night as I slept on a long feather bed
Between my husband and baby.
I'll sleep tonight on the cold, cold ground,
Beside my Black Jack Davy,
Beside my Black Jack Davy."

OLD MAN IN THE NORTH COUNTRY
(The Two Sisters)

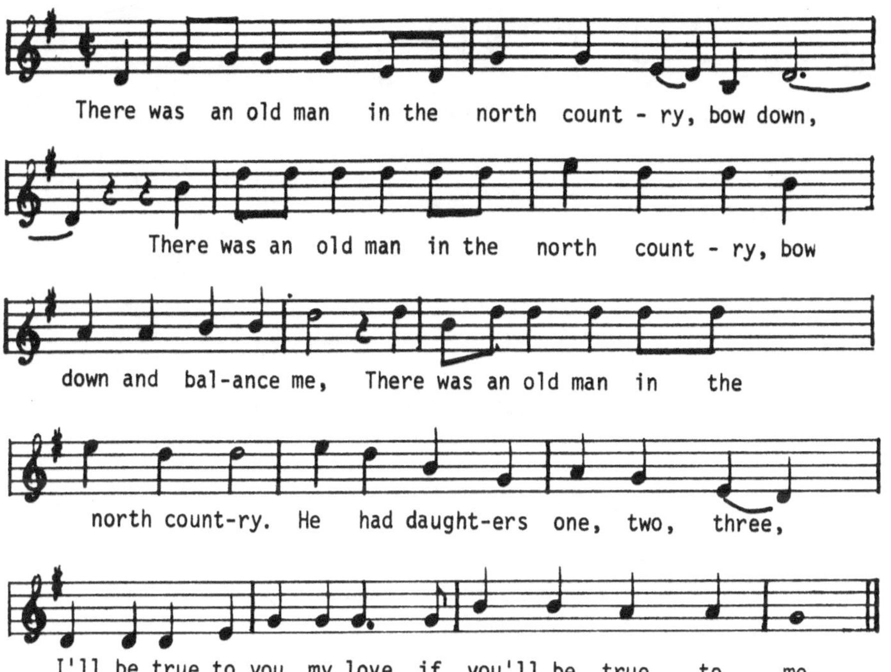

2. He brought the youngest a silken hat.
   Bow Down.
   He brought the youngest a silken hat.
   Bow Down and balance me.
   He brought the youngest a silken hat.
   The eldest daughter couldn't stand that.
   I'll be true to you my love,
   If you'll be true to me.

3. They walked down by the water's brim.
   The eldest pushed the youngest in.

4. She floated down to the miller's dam.
   The miller pulled her to dry land.

5. From her hand he took five rings,
   And then he pushed her in again.

6. They hung the miller on the gallows high.
   The eldest daughter hung close by.

THE PRETTY FAIR MISS
(Soldier's Return)

2. "Oh, I have a lover on yonder ocean.
He has been gone for seven long years.
If he should be gone for seven years longer,
No man on earth could marry me."

3. "Perhaps he's in the ocean drownded,
Or maybe he's in some battlefield slain.
Or if he's taken some pretty girl and married,
His fair young face you may not see again."

4. "If he is in the ocean drownded,
Or if he is in some battlefield slain,
Or if he's taken some pretty girl and married,
I love the girl that married him."

5. He pulled his hands both out of his pocket,
And his rings of love by many did fall.
He showed her the rings she'd placed on him.
Prostrate before him she did fall.

6. He picked her up all in his arms,
And kisses he gave her, one-two-three.
"If I had stayed away seven years longer,
No girl on earth could marry me."

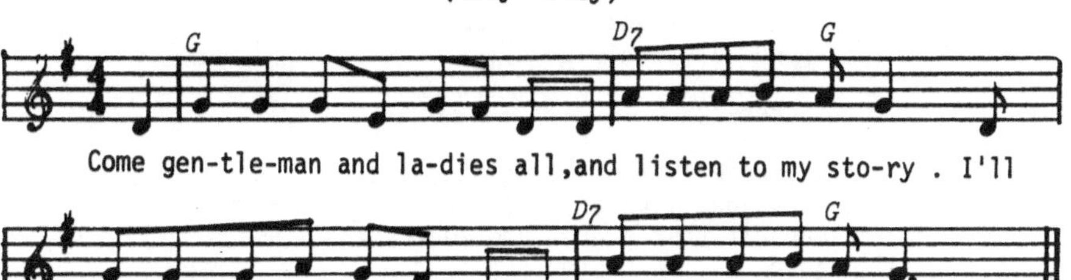

tell you of a plan I laid to ruin Miss Ka-ty Mo-rey.

Tum-ble di I dye ding dye a, Tum-ble di I dye ding dye a.

2. I went up to her father's house
Just like a clever fellow.
I told Miss Kate the grapes and plums
Were gettin' ripe and mellow.

(Chorus)

3. I told her that my sister Nan
Was down in yonder valley,
And wanted her to come down there
And spend a half an hour.

(Chorus)

4. She squeezed my hand most sweet and pleased.
Said, "One thing I do fear, sir.
My father's down in yonder field,
And he will see and hear, sir."

(Chorus)

5. "So, you go up in yonder's tree,
And see where he is, sir.
In yonder's grove we will go,
And there we'll sport and play, sir."

(Chorus)

6. The way I heaved to climb a tree
Not being the least offended,
And there she stood and gazed at me,
To see how I ascended.

(Chorus)

7. "It's your ugly looks I do disdain,
You look just like an owl, sir.
You can eat your grapes and suck their stems,
I'm goin' to the house, sir."

(Chorus)

8. Away she heeled across the field,
And left me half distracted.
I ripped, I tore, I cussed, I swore,
To see how Kate had acted.

(Chorus)

YOUNG MAN AND MAID

3. When his parents came to know this,
   To break it up they both did strive,
   Saying, "Son, oh son, why be so foolish?
   She is too poor to be your bride."

4. He fell on his knees before them.
   "Oh, cruel parents, pity me.
   How can you keep me from my heart's desire,
   When she is all the world to me?"

5. When the young lady came to know this,
   She walked through fields and meadows brown.
   She walked till she came to some deep, low waters,
   In a lonesome grave where she sat down.

6. She pulled out a silver dagger,
   And pierced it through her tender breast.
   Saying, "Here I lay my youthful body,
   Down in this lonesome grave to rest."

7. Her true love being on the waters near her,
   He chance did hear her dying groans.
   He ran, he ran like one distracted,
   Saying, "I am lost, I'm left alone."

8. He picked up the bloody dagger,
   And rolled her over in his arms.
   Saying, "Darlin', Darlin', What can save you?
   For you must die in all your charms."

9. She turned her dark blue eyes upon him,
   Saying, "Alas, true love, you've come too late.
   Prepare to meet me up in heaven,
   Where all our joys will be complete."

10. He picked up this bloody dagger,
    And pierced it through his tender breast
    Saying, "Here I'll lay my youthful body,
    Down in this lonesome grave to rest."

11. Oh cruel parents, oh take warning.
    Never try to part sweethearts.
    As you may know and to be sure,
    They'll destroy their lives for each other's hearts.

THE DISHONEST MILLER

There was an old man, he made his will and all he had was a

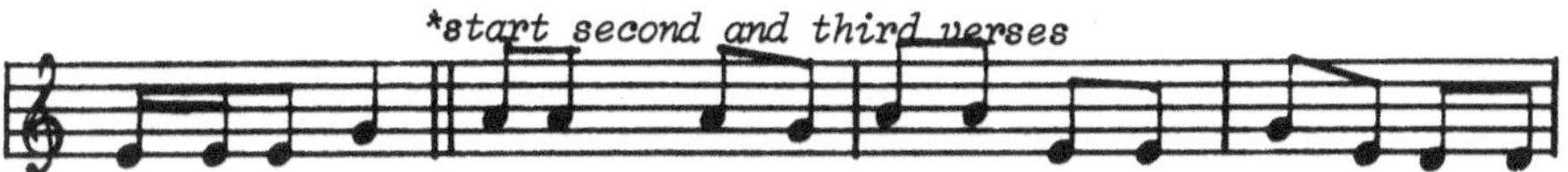

lit-tle old mill. He called up his eld-est son,said"Son,oh son, my

race is run.If you the mil-ler I should make,Tell me the toll you in-

tend for to take? "Dad,you know you've called me Heck.

Out of a bush-el I'll take a peck. If I the mil - ler

you should make, that is the toll I in - tend for to take."

Sing fod-a-lik-ka day. Sing fod - a - lik-ka day.

2. He then called up his second son.
Said, "Son, oh son, my race is run.
If you the miller I should make,
Tell me the toll you intend for to take?"
"Dad, you know you've called me Alf.
From each bushel I'll take half.
If I the miller you should make,
That is the toll I intend for to take.
Sing fod-a-likka-day,
Sing fod-a-likka-day.

3. He then called up his youngest son.
Said, "Son, oh son, my race is run.
If you the miller I should make,
Tell me the toll you intend for to take?"
"Dad, you know I'm a darlin' boy.
Taking toll is all my joy.
It pleases you both to call me Jack.
I'll steal the corn and swear to the sack.
Sing fod-a-likka-day,
Sing fod-a-likka-day.

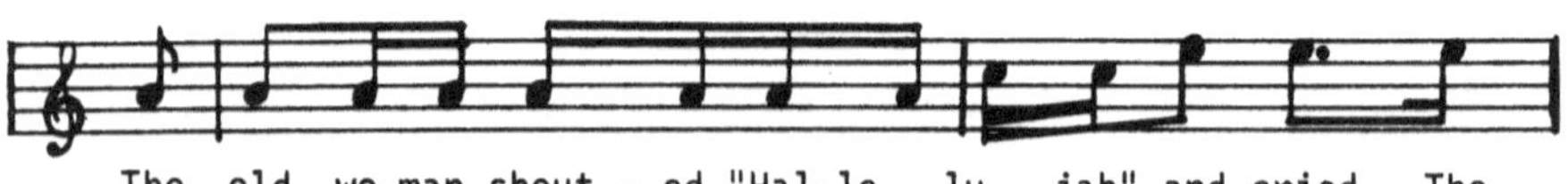

The old wo-man shout - ed "Hal-le - lu - jah" and cried. The

old man closed his eyes and died. Sing fod-a-lik -ka day.

Sing fod-a - lik-ka day.

DARBY'S RAM

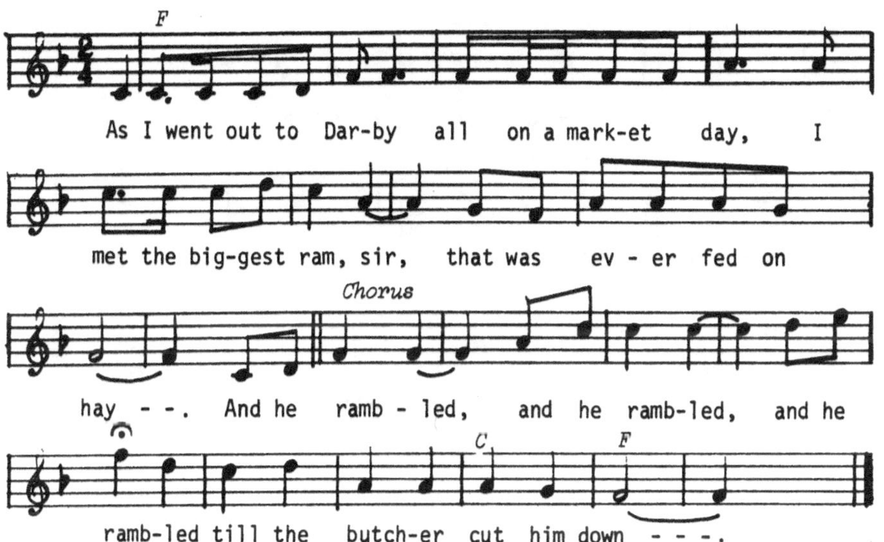

2. He had four feet to walk, sir.
He had four feet to stand,
And every one of them four feet
They covered an acre of land.

(Chorus)

3. The wool on that ram's back, sir,
It reached up to the sky.
The eagles built their nests there,
For I heard the young ones cry.

(Chorus)

4. The old ram had horns, sir,
That reached up to the moon.
A man climbed up in January,
And he didn't get back till June.

(Chorus)

5. The butcher that killed this ram, sir,
Was drowned in the blood.
The little boy that held the bowl
Was washed away in the flood.

(Chorus)

AWAKE, O AWAKE

2. "Oh go away, you'll wake my father.
He lies on yonder bed of rest,
And in his hand he carries a weapon,
To kill the boy that I love best."

3. "Oh go away, you'll wake my mother,
And that would be sad news to hear.
Oh go away and court some other,
And pour your true love in her ear."

4. "Oh I wish I were some little swallow,
Or some lonesome turtle dove.
I'd fly o'er hill and lonesome hollow,
And light on some low banks of love."

5. Oh he picked up a bloody dagger,
And pierced it through his snow-white breast.
Saying "Fare you well, I'm going to leave you.
I'll die for the one that I love best."

6. Then she picked up the bloody dagger,
She pierced it through her snow-white breast.
Saying "Fare you well, father; fare you well, mother,
I'll die for the one that I love best."

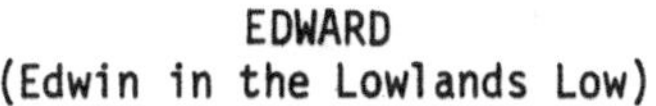

EDWARD
(Edwin in the Lowlands Low)

2. She rose by day in the morning.
To seek her love did go.
For she did love him dearly,
Who plowed the lowlands low.

3. "Oh father where is that stranger
Came here last night to dwell?"
"He's dead and buried," cried the father,
"And you no tales must tell."

4. "Oh father, cruel father,
You'll die a public show,
For the murdering of Young Edward,
Who plowed the lowlands low."

5. She went unto some counselors,
To let the deed be known.
Her father was arrested,
The trial to come on.

6. The jury found him guilty,
And he was hung also,
For the murdering of young Edward,
Who plowed the lowlands low.

7. The seashells in the ocean
Are waving to-and-fro.
Reminds me of young Edward,
Where ever I may go.

8. The fishes in the ocean,
They flutter o'er his breast.
And while his body is in motion,
I hope his soul's at rest.

MR. GARFIELD

(Spoken)
I was going down the street the other day, close to the depot, and I heard the report of a pistol. I said, "What does this mean?" A friend of mine looked up, and he gave me something like this:

> *(Sung)*
> Oh, they tell me Mr. Garfield is shot,
> And he's feeling mighty low, mighty low.
> Oh, they tell me Mr. Garfield is shot.

This excited me, and I went up there where there was a lot of people gathered around. I saw something had happened, so I went on in the house. There was Mr. Garfield lying there on the bed. About that time the doctor came in and set his saddle packets down on the bed, and he said, "Mr. Garfield, how are you feeling?" Mr. Garfield looked up kind of sad-like and gave him something sort of like this:

> Oh, I'm shot down very low down low.
> Oh, I'm shot down very low.

The doctor said, "Why, this'll never do. We'd better send for a preacher." The preacher came pretty quick. When he came in he walked over to the bedside where Mr. Garfield was, said, "Mr. Garfield, if you should die now, where do you think you'd spend eternity?" Mr. Garfield looked up kind of sad-like and gave him something like this:

Oh, I'll make my home in hell, law, law.
Oh, I'll make my home in hell.

The preacher said, "This'll never do. Better get your heart right. We'd better pray." So he got down and made a long prayer, got up, wiped the sweat off his face, said, "Brother Garfield, now where do you think you'll spend eternity?" He looked up at him and said:

Oh, I'll make my home in heaven, law, law.
I'll make my home in heaven.

There were a lot of people there that day, and they all stayed for dinner. I thought I'd stay with the rest of them. There was a town dude there, and they asked him what he'd have, and he gave them something like this:

Go pass around yo' ham and yo' eggs, law, law.
Go pass around yo' ham and yo' eggs.

There was a country fellow there and they asked him what he'd have, and he said, "Just give me something I'm usen to." And he leaned back and gave them something like this:

Go bring on yo' bacon and yo' beans, law, law.
Go bring on yo' bacon and yo' beans.

Mrs. Garfield came in and said, "Now Mr. Garfield, if the worst should come to the worst and you shouldn't get well, would you want me to get married again?" He looked up kind of sad-like and gave her something like this:

Don't you never let a chance go by, law, law.
Don't you never let a chance go by.

Well, I had to go home, and I didn't get back for a day or two. I was a-goin' up the street and I saw Mrs. Garfield all dressed in black. She had a bunch of roses in her hand. I said, "Mrs. Garfield, what're you going to do with those roses?" She looked up kind of sad-like, and she gave me something like this:

Goin' to place 'em on my husband's grave, law, law.
Goin' to place 'em on my husband's grave.

I said, "Mrs. Garfield, where'd you bury him at?" She looked up sort of sad-like and said:

> I buried him on that long flowery branch, law, law.
> I buried him on that long flowery branch.

I went on down the street, and I saw the sheriff coming up one side, and a man was going down the other side. Sheriff said, "Hands up over there!" The man stopped. The sheriff walked over and stuck a forty-four in his face and said, "Is this Charles Guiteau?" He said, "Yes, I passes for him." Sheriff looked him right in the eye and gave him something sort of like this:

> You're the very man I want, Guiteau.
> You're the very man I want.

He took him down to the jail. Finally I got in and spoke to Guiteau. He was in the jail looking kind of sad-like. I asked him how he was feeling. He looked up at me and gave me something sort of like this:

> I'll hang on the tenth of June, law, law.
> I'll hang on the tenth of June.

CZOLGOSZ

2. Czolgosz, you done me wrong.
You shot me in the side when I's walking along.
In Buffalo, In Buffalo.

3. Sent for the doctor, the doctor come.
He come in a trot when he ought to've run.
In Buffalo, In Buffalo.

4. Pistol fire, McKinley fall.
Doctor said, "McKinley, can't find the ball."
In Buffalo, In Buffalo.

5. Forty-four boxes all trimmed in braid.
Sixteen wheel drivers a-climbin' up the grade.
In Buffalo, In Buffalo.

6. McKinley in the sleeper, all trimmed in lace.
Please carry him to the baggage where I can't see his face.
In Buffalo, In Buffalo.

7. The engine whistled down the line,
A-blowing every station that McKinley was a-dyin'.
In Buffalo, In Buffalo.

8. Rubber-tire your buggies; decorate your hacks,
Take him to the graveyard where you can't bring him back.
In Buffalo, In Buffalo.

9. Seventeen boxes all trimmed in black,
Took McKinley to the graveyard but they didn't bring him back.
In Buffalo, In Buffalo.

10. All around the mountain in brick and cement.
There lays the rounder that killed our president.
In Buffalo, In Buffalo.

11. Mrs. McKinley took a trip away out west
Where she couldn't hear the people talk about McKinley's death.
In Buffalo, In Buffalo.

12. McKinley had a wife all dressed in red.
She's going back to Buffalo where McKinley fell dead.
In Buffalo, In Buffalo.

13. Seventeen boxes all trimmed in white,
Took Roosevelt to the White House but didn't bring him back.
In Buffalo, In Buffalo.

ON A BRIGHT AND SUMMER'S MORNING

2. I went upon the mountain,
Beyond yon high hill.
Sixteen or twenty
Ten thousand I did--
Ten thousand I did kill.

3. The money that I got for
The Venison and skin,
I hauled up to my daddy's barn,
And it wouldn't half go--
And it wouldn't half go in.

4. The boys and girls were skatin'
On a bright and summer's day.
The ice fell through, they all got wet.
The rest they run a--
The rest they run away.

5. I went upon the mountain
Beyond the hill so high.
The moon came around with lightenin' speed,
I'll take a ride says--
I'll take a ride says I

6. The moon went 'round the mountain.
It took a sudden whirl.
My foot slipped and I fell off,
And I landed in this--
And I landed in this world.

7. The man who made this song and tune
His name was Benjamin Young.
If you can tell a bigger lie
I'll say you oughta be--
I'll say you oughta be hung.

JESSE JAMES

2. Robert Ford, he caught his eye and he shot him on the sly,
   And the people, they said, he was brave.
   But he ate of Jesse's bread
   And he slept in Jesse's bed,
   Yet he laid poor Jesse in his grave.

3. All the people in the West, when they heard of Jesse's death,
They wondered how he came to die.
It was Ford's pistol ball
Brought him tumbling from the wall
And he laid poor Jesse in his grave.

(Chorus)

4. Oh Jesse was a man and a friend to the poor.
Little did he suffer man's pains.
But with his brother Frank
He robbed the Chicago Bank
And he stopped the Glendale train.

5. Oh, Jesse leaves a wife, she'll mourn all her life,
And the children they were brave.
But that dirty little coward,
He shot Mr. Howard
And he laid poor Jesse in his grave.

6. Oh, Jesse goes to rest with his hand upon his breast,
And the devil will be on his knee.
He was born one day
In the county of Clay
And he came from a great, great race.

(Chorus)

(The placement of the choruses is derived from the recording used.)

DRINKING OF THE WINE

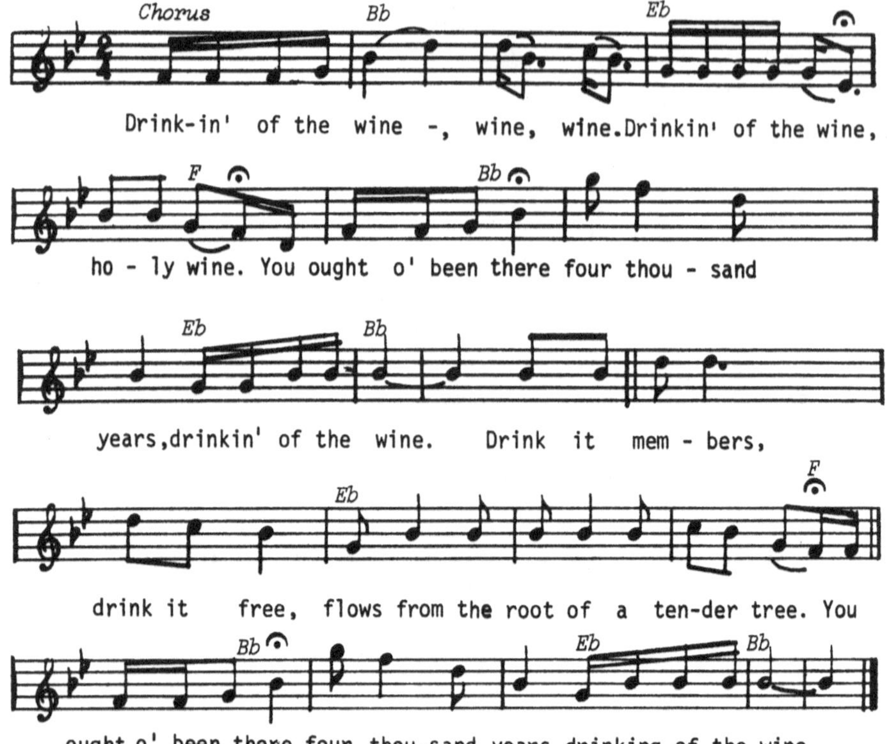

(Chorus)

2. If my sister calls for me,
   Tell her to meet me at Galilee.
   You ought o' been there four thousand years,
   Drinkin' of the wine.

   (Chorus)

3. If my mother calls for me,
   Tell her death has silenced me.
   You ought o' been here four thousand years,
   Drinkin' of the wine.

   (Chorus)

I SHALL NOT BE MOVED

2. If you get there before I do,
   Tell my friends I'm comin' too.
   Just like a tree that's planted by the water,
   I shall not be moved.

   (Chorus)

3. I went down in the valley to pray.
   My soul got happy and I stayed all day.
   Just like a tree that's planted by the water,
   I shall not be moved.

   (Chorus)

4. I'm a-goin' up to the mountain top.
The Lord's a-goin' to preach and the church's goin' to rock.
Just like a tree that's planted by the water,
I shall not be moved.

(Chorus)

HIDE THOU ME

2. Ever' little round gets higher, higher,
Hide thou me, hide thou me.
Ever' little round gets higher, higher,
Hide thou me, hide thou me.
Ever' little round gets higher, higher,
Let Thy bosom be my pillow.
Hide me, Oh, Rock of Ages, safe in thee.

THE SAME TRAIN

2. This train don't carry no liars,
This train, my Lord.
This train don't carry no liars,
This train, my Lord.
This train don't carry no liars,
Whiskey drinkers nor home-brew buyers,
This train, my Lord, Lord, Lord, Lord, Lord.

(Chorus)

GO WASH IN THAT BEAUTIFUL POOL

Verse and Chorus have the same melody. Begin and end with Chorus.

1. My father passed over the river,
   Is now in the kingdom above.
   He's safe above where the angels all dwell.
   Go wash in that beautiful pool.

   (Chorus)

2. My mother passed over the river,
   Is now in the kingdom above.
   She's safe above where the angels all dwell.
   Go wash in that beautiful pool.

   (Chorus)

JESUS LOVES ME

Though I forget Him and wander away,
He loves me, wherever I stray.
Back to his loving arms I flee,
When I remember that Jesus loves me.

(Chorus)

SWING LOW, CHARIOT

2. My mother's gone, swing low.
   She's gone to glory, swing low.
   The angels took her, swing low.
   Swing low, chariot, swing low.

   (Chorus)

3. I got a letter, swing low.
   It was sent from heaven, swing low.
   The angels sealed it, swing low.
   Swing low, chariot, swing low.

   (Chorus)

ROW US OVER THE TIDE

2. "We are so hungry, so lonely, and cold.
No home, no place to abide.
Momma, poppa, and Nellie have gone.
Row us over the tide.

(Chorus)

3. "Momma told Little Charlie one day,
Christ would care for her child.
And when she was far away,
He'd row us over the tide."

(Chorus)

4. The two little children were gone one day
Down by the fair river's side.
Jesus, so full of compassion and love,
Had rowed them over the tide.

MY HOME'S ACROSS THE SMOKY MOUNTAINS

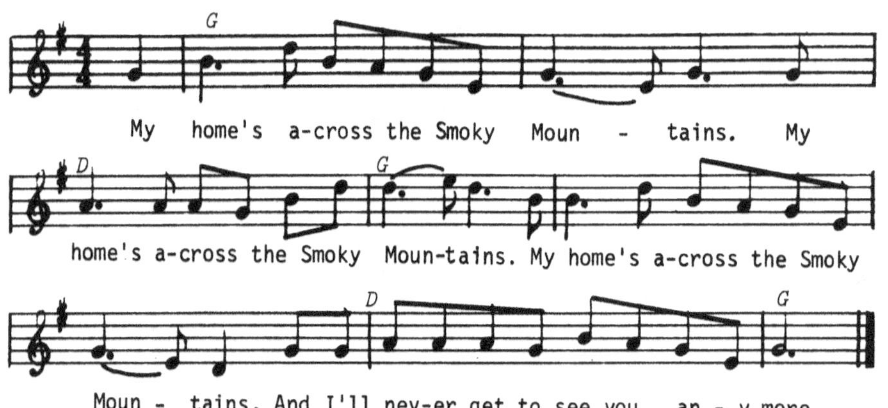

2. Goodbye my little Sugar Darlin'.
Goodbye my little Sugar Darlin'.
Goodbye my little Sugar Darlin'.
I'll never get to see you anymore.

3. Rock my baby, feed it candy.
Cause I'll never get to see it anymore.

4. I'm leavin' on a Monday morning.
And I'll never get to see you anymore.

5. My home's across the Smoky Mountains.
And I'll never get to see you anymore.

ITALY

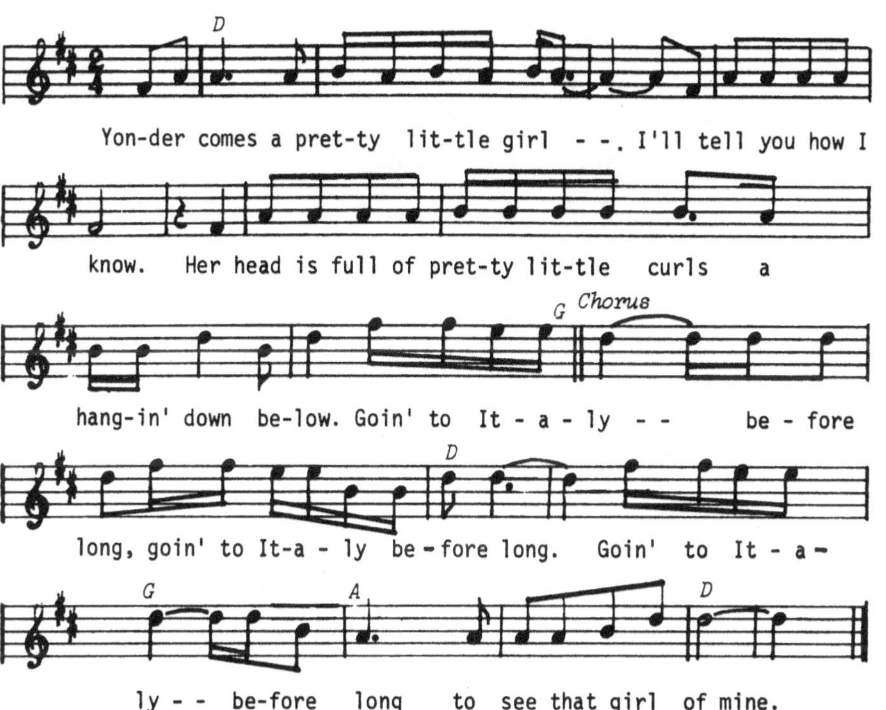

2. Apple like a cherry,
   Cherry like a rose.
   How I love my pretty little girl,
   God in heaven knows.

   (Chorus)

3. I asked that gal to marry me.
   I said I loved her well.
   She said before she married me,
   She'd sooner be in hell.

   (Chorus)

4. If ever I'm out late at night,
And late a-coming in.
I'll kiver up that bed of coals
And pull that latch-string in.

(Chorus)

5. I's skeered We's goin' to freeze to death,
During that last cold spell.
Had nothing but a load of green pine poles,
That wouldn't burn in hell.

(Chorus)

CINDY

2. She led me to the parlor,
She cooled me with her fan.
She swore that I was the prettiest thing
In the shape of mortal man.

(Chorus)

3. I wish I was an apple
A-hangin' in a tree.
Every time my sweetheart passed
She'd take a bite of me.

(Chorus)

4. She told me that she loved me,
She called me sugar-plum.
She throwed her arms around me.
I saw my time had come.

(Chorus)

5. Cindy got religion;
She shouted all around.
She got so full of glory,
She broke the preacher down.

(Chorus)

6. Cindy got religion,
She got it once before.
But when she heard this old banjo,
She's the first one on the floor.

(Chorus)

7. I wish I had a needle and thread
As fine as I could sew,
And a thimble from Baltimore
To make that needle go.

(Chorus)

8. I wish I had a needle and thread,
As fine as I could sew.
I'd sew the girls to my coattail
And down the road I'd go.

(Chorus)

THE WEEPING WILLOW

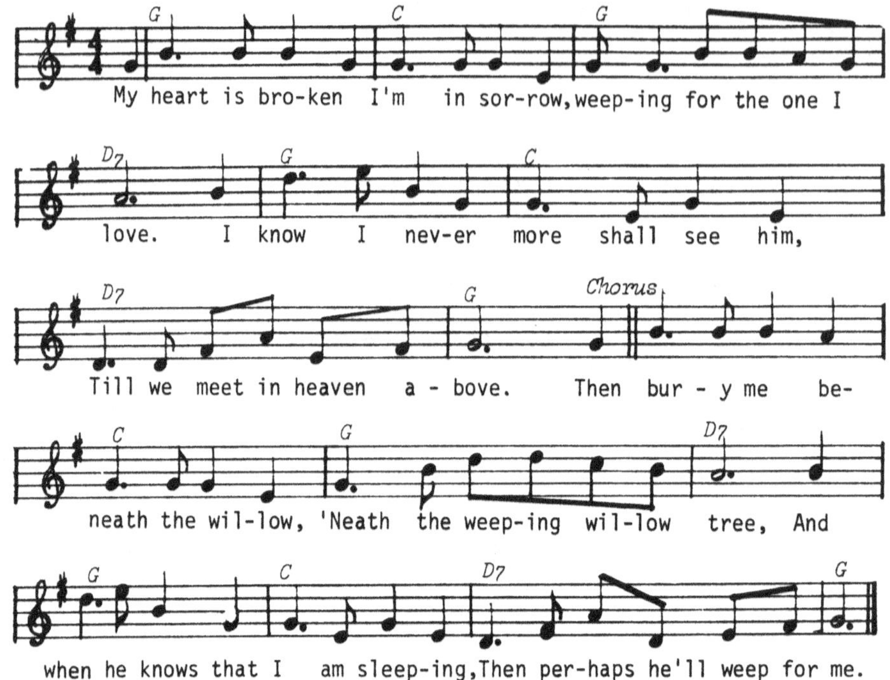

2. They told me that he did not love me.
   How could I believe it true?
   Until an angel whispered softly,
   "He will prove untrue to you."

   (Chorus)

3. Tomorrow was our wedding day,
   But God only knows where he's gone.
   He went his way to love another,
   And just left me here alone.

   (Chorus)

4. Place on my grave a snow-white lily,
   For to prove my love for him
   And tell him I died to save him,
   Though his love I did not win.

   (Chorus)

LULA WALL

2. Oh, one evenin' just at dark
When I met her at the park,
She was sittin' by the fountain all alone.
Then to her I tipped my hat.
Soon we both began to chat.
She's that aggravatin' beauty, Lula Wall.

(Chorus)

3. If she only would be mine
I would build a house so fine,
And all around it build a fence so tall.
Then no one except myself
Should ever gaze upon her face.
She's that aggravatin' beauty, Lula Wall.

(Chorus)

RED APPLE JUICE

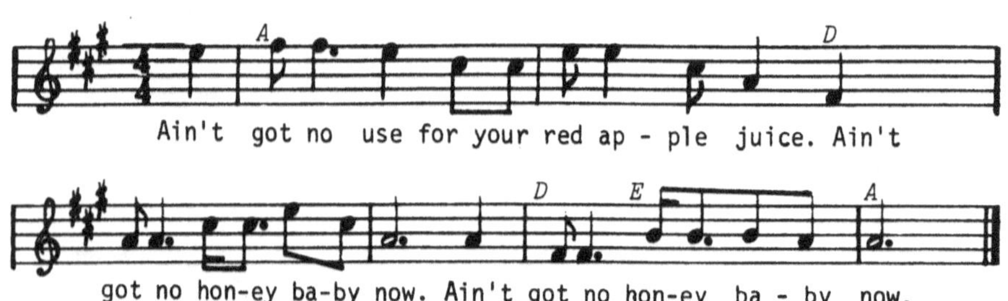

2. Ain't got no use for your red rocking chair,
Ain't got no honey baby there.
Ain't got no honey baby there.

3. Done all I could do to try to live with you,
Send you back to your mama some old day.
Send you back to your mama some old day.

4. It's who'll rock the cradle, who'll sing a song?
Who'll be your honey when I'm gone?
Who'll be your honey when I'm gone?

5. Ain't got no use for your red apple juice.
Ain't got no honey baby now.
Ain't got no honey baby now.

SWANNANOA TUNNEL

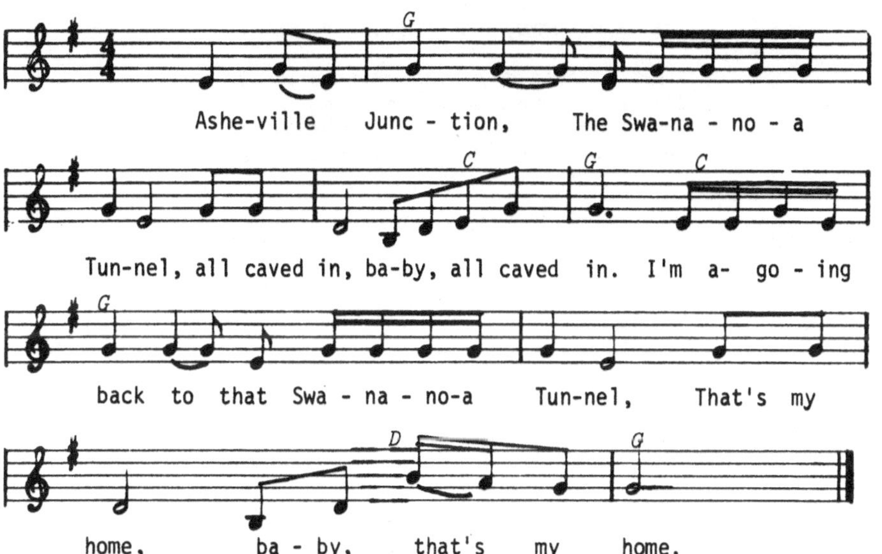

2. When you hear that watchdog a-howlin',
Somebody 'round, baby, somebody 'round.
When you hear that hoot owl a-squallin',
Somebody dyin', baby, somebody dyin'.

3. When you hear my pistol firing,
Somebody dead, baby, somebody dead
Riley Gardner killed my partner,
Couldn't kill me, baby, couldn't kill me.

4. Last December, I remember,
The wind blowed cold, baby, the wind blowed cold.
The hammer fallin' from my shoulder,
All day long, baby, all day long.

5. Ain't no hammer in this mountain
Outrings mine, baby, outrings mine.
This old hammer, it rings like silver,
It shines like gold, baby, shines like gold.

6. Take-a this hammer and throw it in the river,
It rings right on, baby, it shines right on.
I'm a-goin' back to the Sannanoa Tunnel,
That's my home, baby, that's my home.

7. Some of these days, it won't be long,
I'm goin' home, baby, I'm goin' home.
Some of these days I'll see that woman,
That's no dream, baby, that's no dream.

REUBEN

The wind is from the east, and the snow is from the north, and I'm

five hundred miles from my home.

2. She's standin' in the door,
Thinks she can hear that whistle blow.
She can hear the whistle blow five hundred miles.

3. If that train side-tracks,
I'll ride that freight train back.
I'll catch old Number Nine as she rolls by.

4. Oh my shoe's a-gettin' tore,
And my foot's a-gettin' sore.
I'll never leave my home anymore.

5. Oh them women up in town,
Say they'll chain Reuben down.
They'll chain Reuben down so low.

OLD STEPSTONE

2. I stood on my door step at evening and morn,
The wind shispered by with a moan.
Fields may be whitening, but I will be gone,
To roam o'er this wide world alone.

(Chorus)

3. I stood on my door step when school time was o'er,
And I wished for the time to go by.
Now it has passed, and I stand here tonight
To bid this old stepstone goodbye.

(Chorus)

FREE LITTLE BIRD

2. Oh, who will shoe them little feet,
And who will glove them little hands?
Who will kiss them red rosy cheeks
When I'm in some far distant land?

3. My Papa will shoe these little feet,
And my Mama will glove these little hands,
But you may kiss these red rosy cheeks,
When we're in some far distant land.

4. Take me home, little birdie, take me home.
Take me home by the light of the moon.
While the moon is shining bright and the stars are getting light,
Take me home to my Mama, take me home.

5. Oh, it's very good drinking of the ale,
And it's very good drinking of the wine.
But it's better by far, sittin' by that blue-eyed boy.
That's stole this tender heart of mine.

6. Oh, the willow tree may fade,
And the willow tree may twine,
But I never will prove false to the one I love best,
That's stole away this tender heart of mine.

MY DEAR OLD INNOCENT BOY

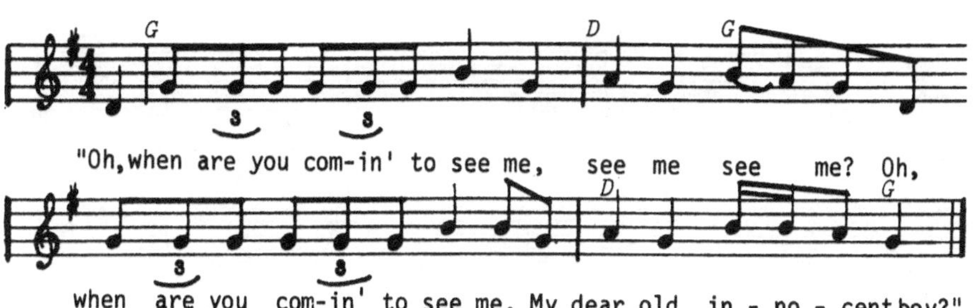

2. "I expect to come next Sunday . . .
If the weather's good."

3. "Oh, how long you think you'll court me . . .
My dear old innocent boy?"

4. "I guess I'll court you all night . . .
If the weather's good."

5. "Oh, when do you think we'll marry . . .
My dear old innocent boy?"

6. "I expect we'll marry in a week . . .
If the weather's good."

7. "Oh, what're we goin' to ride to the wedding . . .
My dear old innocent boy?"

8. "I expect I'll bring my log sled . . .
If the weather's good."

9. "Why don't you bring your buggy . . .
My dear old innocent boy?"

10. "Well, the ox won't work to the buggy . . .
For I never saw him try."

11. "Oh, who'll you bring to the wedding . . .
My dear old innocent boy?"

12. "I expect to bring my children . . .
If the weather's good."

13. "Well, I didn't know you had any children . . .
My dear old innocent boy."

14. "Oh yes, I have six children . . .
Jim, Joe, John, Sally, and the babies."

MOLE IN THE GROUND

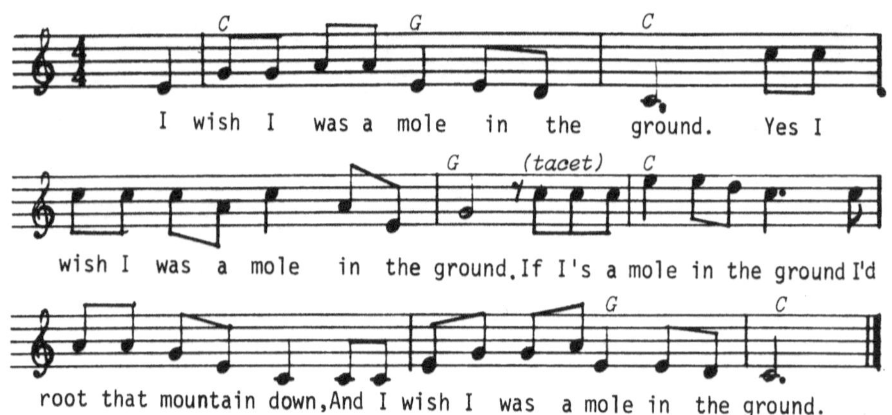

2. Oh, Tempe wants a nine-dollar shawl.
Yes, Tempe wants a nine-dollar shawl.
When I come o'er the hill with a forty-dollar bill,
Tis, baby where you been so long?

3. Oh, where have you been so long?
Yes, where have you been so long?
I've been in the Bend with the rough and rowdy men,
It's baby where you been so long?

4. Oh, I don't like a railroad man,
No, I don't like a railroad man.
A railroad man will kill you when he can,
And he'll drink up your blood like wine.

5. I wish I was a lizard in the spring.
Yes, I wish I was a lizard in the spring.
If I's a lizard in the spring I could hear my darlin' sing,
I wish I was a lizard in the spring.

JENNIE JENKINS

2. Will you wear red, oh my dear, oh my dear?
   Will you wear red, Jennie Jenkins?
   I won't wear red; it's the color of my head.
   I'll buy me a tally fallyizer.

   (Chorus)

3. Will you wear black, oh my dear, oh my dear?
   Will you wear black, Jennie Jenkins?
   I won't wear black; it's the color of my back.
   I'll buy me a tally fallyizer.

   (Chorus)

4. Will you wear blue, oh my dear, oh my dear?
Will you wear blue, Jennie Jenkins?
I won't wear blue; it's the color of my shoe.
I'll buy me a tally fallyizer.

(Chorus)

5. Will you wear brown, oh my dear, oh my dear?
Will you wear brown, Jennie Jenkins?
Yes, I'll wear brown; I'll go uptown.
I'll buy me a tally fallyizer.

(Chorus)

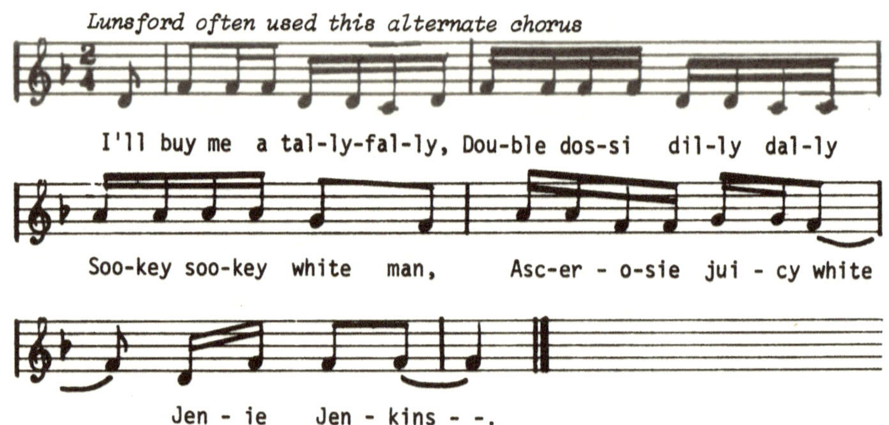

LITTLE TURTLE DOVE

2. I'm not gonna marry in the fall.
   I'll marry in the spring.
   I'm gonna marry a pretty little girl,
   Who wears a silver ring, ring,
   Who wears a silver ring.

3. I'm not gonna marry in the spring of the year.
   I'll marry in the fall.
   I'm gonna marry a pretty little girl,
   Who wears a dollar shawl, shawl,
   Who wears a dollar shawl.

4. The hog is in the pen
   And corn to feed him on.
   All I want is a pretty little girl
   To feed him when I'm gone, gone,
   To feed him when I'm gone.

5. I went upon the mountain
   To give my horn a blow.
   And every girl in the county said,
   "Yonder comes my beau, beau,
   Yonder comes my beau."

LAUREL LONESOME

CLUCK, OLD HEN

Transcribed by Joan Moser from recordings made by Artus Moser. Used by permission.

NEWT'S DREAM

SALLY GOODIN

WALKING IN THE PARLOR

RYE STRAW

TURKEY BUZZARD

BILLY IN THE LOWGROUND

Transcribed by Joan Moser from recordings made by Artus Moser. Used by permission.

www.ingramcontent.com/pod-product-compliance
Lightning Source LLC
LaVergne TN
LVHW090806070826
844660LV00022B/1099